REA's Test Prep Books Are The Best!

(a sample of the <u>hundreds of letters</u> REA receives each year)

" I am writing to congratulate you on preparing an exceptional study guide. In five years of teaching this course, I have never encountered a more thorough, comprehensive, concise, and realistic preparation for this examination. "

Teacher, Davie, FL

" I used your book to prepare for the test and found that the advice and the sample tests were highly relevant... Without using any other material, I earned very high scores and will be going to the graduate school of my choice. "

Student, New Orleans, LA

" I used your *CLEP Introductory Sociology* book and rank it 99% — thank you! "

Student, Jerusalem, Israel

" Your *GMAT* book greatly helped me on the test. Thank you. "

Student, Oxford, OH

" I recently got the *French SAT II* Exam book from REA. I congratulate you on first-rate French practice tests. "

Instructor, Los Angeles, CA

" Your *AP English Literature and Composition* book is most impressive. "

Student, Montgomery, AL

" The REA *LSAT* Test Preparation guide is a winner! "

Instructor, Spartanburg, SC

(more on next page)

REA's Test Prep Books Are The Best!
(a sample of the <u>hundreds of letters</u> REA receives each year)

(more on previous page)

The Best Test Preparation for the

ELM

California State University
Entry Level Mathematics Exam

ELM EDITORIAL BOARD

Archibald Sia, Ph.D.
Associate Professor of Elementary Education
California State University, Northridge
Northridge, California

Hugo Sun, Ph.D.
Professor of Mathematics
California State University, Fresno
Fresno, California

Robert S. Wilson, Ph.D.
Instructor of Mathematics
Sonoma State University
Rohnert Park, California

 Research & Education Association
61 Ethel Road West • Piscataway, New Jersey 08854

The Best Test Preparation for the
California State University
Entry Level Mathematics (ELM) Examination

Printed in the United States of America

Library of Congress Control Number 2003111679

International Standard Book Number 0-7386-0016-4

Research & Education Association
61 Ethel Road West
Piscataway, New Jersey 08854

 REA supports the effort to conserve and
protect environmental resources by
printing on recycled papers.

Contents

ELM
Entry Level Mathematics

Passing the ELM Examination

PASSING THE ELM EXAMINATION

ABOUT THE ELM EXAMINATION

Developed in conjunction with Educational Testing Service, the California State University Entry Level Mathematics Examination is required of incoming first-year students at Cal State unless they are granted an exemption based on any one of the following factors:

• A score of 3 or above on the College Board Advanced Placement Calculus AB, Calculus BC, or Statistics examinations

• A score of 550 or above on the Mathematics section of the SAT I: Reasoning Test

• A score of 23 or above on the Mathematics section of the ACT Assessment

• A score of 550 or above on the SAT II: Math Subject Test Level IC

• A score of 550 or above on the SAT II: Math Subject Test Level IIC

• The completion and transfer to Cal State of a college course that satisfies the requirement in Quantitative Reasoning, provided such a course was completed with a grade of "C" or better.

If you are not exempt based on these requirements, you must take the ELM before your freshman year, *prior* to enrollment. If you do not take the ELM prior to the time of enrollment, you will *not* be allowed to enroll.

Once you take the ELM, your score is used to place you into an appropriate freshman mathematics class. Higher scores afford greater choice regarding your freshman mathematics class. Lower scores result in placement into remedial mathematics. While being placed into remedial mathematics does not affect your admission to a CSU campus, and while students are not surcharged for being placed in this course, it is not considered college-level, and you will not receive credit for the course. Therefore, it is in your best interest to pass the test with the highest score possible, ensuring your placement into a higher-level course.

The ELM contains 50 multiple-choice questions, which you must answer in 90 minutes. The exam is divided into three different categories:

Numbers and Data, which accounts for approximately 35% of the questions, Algebra, which accounts for approximately 35% of the questions, and Geometry, which accounts for approximately 30% of the questions. Of the 50 multiple-choice questions, five are field-test questions that are not scored. You will not know which questions are being field-tested, so treat every question as though it counts.

REGISTRATION AND TEST DAY

To register for the exam, contact the Cal State campus where you intend to enroll. On the day of the test, you *must* bring the following to the test center:

• Your validated admission ticket

• Your Social Security number

• Acceptable identification: an ID that includes a photograph, your name, and your signature (e.g., photo driver's license, school ID with photo, valid passport with current photo and signature, or a letter signed by you and your high school principal or guidance counselor detailing your name and physical description)

• Check or money order payable to ETS for test fees (see registration bulletin)

• Several No. 2 pencils with erasers

You *may* want to bring:

• A watch (without an audible alarm)

• A bag or backpack (must be kept under your chair)

Important Note: Calculators are NOT allowed. The questions on the ELM do not require the use of calculators. The problems emphasize problem solving.

HOW TO DO YOUR BEST ON THE ELM

By reviewing and studying this book, you can achieve a top score on the ELM. The ELM assesses the mathematical skills that you have developed during your high school career. Most of the knowledge tested by the ELM is covered in your high school mathematics classes. You may find that some of the questions are more advanced than the material covered in your high school classes; this is because not everyone takes the same level of math during high school. At the same time, you may find that some of the math presented is at a more basic level than that of your high school math classes; this is because the ability to perform advanced math problems is tied directly to your understanding of basic arithmetical concepts.

The purpose of our book is to properly prepare you for the ELM. We do this by providing three full-length model exams that accurately reflect the ELM in both types of questions asked and degree of difficulty. REA's practice exams mirror the most recently administered ELM exams and include every question type you can expect to encounter on the ELM. Following each exam is an answer key, complete with detailed explanations and solutions designed specifically to clarify the material for the student. The explanations not only provide the correct answers, but also explain why the answer to a particular question is more acceptable than any other answer choice. By completing all three exams and studying the explanations that follow, you will systematically isolate your strengths and weaknesses. This knowledge will allow you to concentrate on the sections of the exam that prove to be most difficult.

ABOUT THE TEST EXPERTS

Our ELM Editorial Board, all California-based experts in mathematics or education, carefully crafted our tests and topical reviews to ensure fidelity to the actual exam. Our authors and editors researched the mechanics of the ELM exam to create precise depictions of the exam and appropriately challenge the student. Our experts are highly regarded in the educational community, having studied at the doctoral level and taught in their respective fields at Cal State. They have in-depth knowledge of the subjects presented in the book, and provide accurate questions that appeal to the student's interest. Each question is clearly explained in order to help the student achieve a top score on the ELM.

ABOUT THE REVIEW SECTIONS

Our ELM Test Preparation book offers six reviews that correspond to the subject areas you will find on the exam. These include Arithmetic, Elementary Algebra, Geometry, Intermediate Algebra, Word Problems, and Other Topics. Using our review will provide focus and structure, and will allow you to choose a particular subject or subtopic to study further. Each review provides a diagnostic quiz that will help you determine your strengths and weaknesses in the subject before you begin studying. The reviews are organized as follows:

Arithmetic Review
- Integers and Real Numbers
- Fractions
- Decimals
- Percentages
- Radicals
- Exponents and Scientific Notation

Elementary Algebra
- Operations with Polynomials
- Simplifying Algebraic Expressions
- Rational Expressions
- Equations and Linear Equations
- Two Linear Equations
- Quadratic Equations
- Inequalities
- Graphs

Geometry Review
- Points, Lines, and Angles
- Triangles
- Quadrilaterals
- Circles
- Solids
- Geometry Formulas

Intermediate Algebra
- Quadratic Equations
- Complex Numbers
- Linear Equations and Rational Expressions
- Absolute Value Equations
- Equations of Higher Degree
- Elementary Functions
- Fractional Exponents
- Sequences and Series

Other Topics
- The Fundamental Counting Principle
- Probability
- Statistics
- Data Interpretation

Word Problems
- Algebraic Word Problems
- Rate
- Work
- Mixture
- Interest
- Discount
- Profit
- Ratios and Proportions
- Geometry-based Word Problems
- Graphs

PARTICIPATE IN STUDY GROUPS

As a final word on how to prepare for this exam, you may want to study with others. This will allow you to share knowledge and obtain feedback from other members of your study group. You may find that study groups actually make preparing for an exam more enjoyable.

SCORING THE EXAM

To pass the ELM exam, you must earn a total scaled score of 50 or higher on the exam. When you receive your actual ELM test score, it will be an even-numbered scaled score ranging from 0 to 80. It is based on all 45 scored test questions (5 are field test questions). If you score above 50, you will be eligible for placement in baccalaureate-level mathematics classes. If you score less than 50, you will be placed in remedial mathematics.

You also will receive three subscores. A subscore is figured for each of the three content areas covered by the ELM (Numbers and Data, Algebra, and Geometry). They provide guidance as to what areas students need to work on if placed in a remedial course. The subscores will be represented graphically as score ranges on the 0-80 scale. They are based on subsets of 12 to 18 questions. The subscores are represented as ranges because they are less reliable than the total scaled score. These scores are useful to school officials in identifying where students' strengths and weaknesses in mathematics may lie and for tailoring programs accordingly for placement.

Determining your score on our sample tests is very easy. Simply go to the answer key and mark your correct and incorrect answers. Circle those numbers that correspond with field-test questions. Then, count the number of questions (minus field-test questions) that you answered correctly. You'll need to get 26 to 29 correct to pass, ETS officials say, so the same goes for our model tests. Why is the passing threshold expressed as a range? Quite simply because of variations among different forms of the ELM exam itself.

ELM TEST-TAKING STRATEGIES
How to Beat the Clock

On test day, you'll want to budget your time efficiently. Here's how:

1. Memorize the test directions. Don't waste valuable seconds reading directions on the day of the exam. Your time should be spent instead *answering* the questions.

2. Bring a watch to the exam and pace yourself. (Make sure you don't wear a calculator watch, as it most likely will be confiscated.) Work carefully and quickly. Do not spend too much time on any one question. If, after a few minutes, you cannot answer a particular question, make a note of it and continue. You can go back to it after you have completed easier questions first.

3. As you work on the test, be sure that your answers correspond with the proper numbers and letters on the answer sheet.

ELM STUDY SCHEDULE

It is important for you to discover the time and place for studying that works best for you. Some students set aside a certain number of hours every morning to study, while others may choose to study at night before going to sleep. Other students may study during the day, while waiting in line, or they may find another convenient time to do their studying. Only you will be able to know when and where your studying is most effective. Keep in mind that the most important factor is consistency. Use your time wisely. Work out a study routine and stick to it!

You may want to follow a schedule similar to the one below. The following schedule consists of a nine-week program. You can always condense the schedule, if necessary, by combining two weeks into one.

Week 1	Take the diagnostic quiz for each review (Arithmetic, Elementary Algebra, Geometry, Intermediate Algebra, and Word Problems). Rank your score on each quiz. On whichever quiz you scored the lowest, plan to study that review first. Make a list of the reviews in the order in which you plan to study them. Then read the introduction of this book for study hints and to learn more about the ELM.
Week 2	Study the subject which corresponds to the quiz on which you scored the lowest. Make sure you complete all the drills in the review and work out the example problems on your own to learn the processes involved in each type of problem.
Week 3	Study your next-to-lowest scoring area this week. Again, be sure to complete all the drills in the review and work out the example problems on our own to learn the processes involved in each type of problem.
Week 4	Study your third weakest area during Week 4. Completing all the drills and example problems will increase your ability to perform well on these types of problems.

Week 5	Study your second-to-strongest area this week. Since you probably did fairly well in this area, you may feel much more confident in this area than you have in other areas you studied in previous weeks. This may tempt you not to be as thorough in your studying habits this week, but taking the drills and studying the examples will only increase your chances of answering questions in this area correctly during the actual ELM test
Week 6	Study your strongest subject this week. Temptation to merely skim or even skip this chapter might be strong, but if you study thoroughly, you are bound to learn something new about this subject. Perhaps you will discover an easier way to approach a problem or a tip which will save you precious minutes during the actual test.
Week 7	Take ELM Practice Test 1 and grade yourself. Read the detailed explanations of answers. Try to find a pattern in those questions you answered incorrectly. Did you consistently answer questions incorrectly on the Pythagorean Theorem, for example? Perhaps you should review this subject to refresh your memory.
Week 8	Take ELM Practice Test 2 and grade yourself. Read the detailed explanations of answers. Did you improve in any of the areas from the last test? If there are areas which continue to trouble you, retake some of the drill questions or ask a teacher to explain some of those concepts to you.
Week 9	Take ELM Practice Test 3 and grade yourself. This should be your best score yet. Any subjects in which you still feel weak should be restudied. Feel free to take one or more of the tests again if you want to improve your test-taking skills or your ability to complete the test within the given 75-minute time frame.

ABOUT RESEARCH & EDUCATION ASSOCIATION

Research & Education Association (REA) is an organization of educators, scientists, and engineers specializing in various academic fields. Founded in 1959 with the purpose of disseminating the most recently developed scientific information to groups in industry, government, high schools, and universities, REA has since become a successful and highly respected publisher of study aids, test preps, handbooks, and reference works.

REA's Test Preparation series includes study guides for all academic levels in almost all disciplines. Research & Education Association publishes test preps for students who have not yet completed high school, as well as high school students preparing to enter college. Students from countries around the world seeking to attend college in the United States will find the assistance they need in REA's publications. For college students seeking advanced degrees, REA publishes test preps for many major graduate school admission examinations in a wide variety of disciplines, including engineering, law, and medicine. Students at every level, in every field, with every ambition can find what they are looking for among REA's publications.

Unlike most test preparation books—which present only a few practice tests that bear little resemblance to the actual exams—REA's series presents tests that accurately depict the official exams in both degree of difficulty and types of questions. REA's practice tests are always based upon the most recently administered exams, and include every type of question that can be expected on the actual exams.

REA's publications and educational materials are highly regarded and continually receive an unprecedented amount of praise from professionals, instructors, librarians, parents, and students. Our authors are as diverse as the fields represented in the books we publish. They are well-known in their respective disciplines and serve on the faculties of prestigious high schools, colleges, and universities throughout the United States and Canada.

ACKNOWLEDGMENTS

In addition to our authors, we would like to thank Dr. Max Fogiel, President, for his overall guidance, which brought this publication to completion; Larry B. Kling, Quality Control Manager, for supervising revisions; David Bordeau, Editorial Assistant, for coordinating revisions; Milt Cohen, mathematics instructor, Los Angeles Unified School District; Diane Goldschmidt, Melanie Seickel, Alicia Shapiro, and Ann Thayer-Cohen for their significant editorial contributions; and Michael C. Cote, Barbara Jacinto, and Network Typesetting, Inc., for typesetting the manuscript.

ELM

Entry Level Mathematics

Chapter 1
Arithmetic
Review

ARITHMETIC DIAGNOSTIC TEST

16 Questions

(Answer sheets appear at the back of the book.)

> **DIRECTIONS:** Each question has five multiple-choice answers. Select the single best answer.

1. $10^3 + 10^5 =$

   (A) 10^8 (B) 10^{15}

   (C) 20^8 (D) 2^{15}

   (E) 101,000

2. Evaluate the following: $48 - 24 \div 3 + 5 \times 2$.

   (A) 6 (B) 12

   (C) 18 (D) 26

   (E) 50

   $48 - 8 + 10$

   $40 + 10$

3. Divide $3\frac{1}{5}$ by $1\frac{1}{3}$.

   $\frac{16}{5} \div \frac{3}{4} = \frac{12}{5} = 2$

   (A) $2\frac{2}{5}$ (B) $3\frac{1}{15}$

   (C) $3\frac{3}{5}$ (D) $4\frac{4}{15}$

   (E) 8

4. Simplify $6\sqrt{7} + 4\sqrt{7} - \sqrt{5} + 5\sqrt{7}$.

   same radicals, add

   (A) $10\sqrt{7}$ (B) $15\sqrt{7} - \sqrt{5}$

   $15\sqrt{7} - \sqrt{5}$

3

(C) $15\sqrt{21} - \sqrt{5}$ (D) $15\sqrt{16}$

(E) 60

5. Find the sum of $5^3/_4$, $2^{11}/_{16}$, $7^1/_8$.

(A) $14^8/_{17}$ (B) $14^{15}/_{16}$

(C) $15^1/_2$ (D) $15^{15}/_{28}$

(E) $15^9/_{16}$

6. Simplify $7.5 \times 1^7/_9 \div 1.333...$

(A) $^1/_{18}$ (B) $5^5/_8$

(C) $6^2/_3$ (D) 10

(E) $17^7/_9$

7. Simplify $9.223 \div 4.01$.

(A) .023   (B) 2.3

(C) 23   (D) 230

(E) .23

8. Change the fraction $^7/_8$ to a decimal.

(A) .666   (B) .75

(C) .777   (D) .875

(E) 1.142

9. Which is the smallest number?

(A) $5 \times 10^{-3} / (3 \times 10^{-3})$ (B) $.3 / .2$

(C) $.3 / (3 \times 10^{-3})$ (D) $(5 \times 10^{-2}) / .1$

(E) $.3 / (3 \times 10^{-1})$

10. Simplify $\sqrt{36}$.

    (A) 3 (B) 6

    (C) 12 (D) 18

    (E) 72

11. Evaluate $\dfrac{-4+(-2)[-1+(-2)]}{-2}$.

    (A) -7 (B) -2

    (C) -1 (D) 4

    (E) 9

12. 46.863 rounded to the nearest hundredth is

    (A) 100. (B) 46.8.

    (C) 46.9. (D) 46.86.

    (E) 46.87.

13. $7.04 \times 2.5 =$

    (A) 17.6 (B) 176

    (C) 9.25 (D) 1.76

    (E) 17.51

14. $451 + 21 + 689 =$

    (A) 1,051 (B) 1,081

    (C) 1,161 (D) 1,261

    (E) 1,281

5

15. $\sqrt{.04} =$

    (A) .0016   (B) .08

    (C) .02   (D) .2

    (E) .16

16. Find 10% of 250.

    (A) 25   (B) 125

    (C) 175   (D) 225

    (E) 275

$$\begin{array}{r} 250 \\ \times\ .1 \\ \hline 25.0 \end{array}$$

ARITHMETIC DIAGNOSTIC TEST

ANSWER KEY

1. (E)	5. (E)	9. (D)	13. (A)
2. (E)	6. (D)	10. (B)	14. (C)
3. (A)	7. (B)	11. (C)	15. (D)
4. (B)	8. (D)	12. (D)	16. (A)

DETERMINE YOUR STRENGTHS AND WEAKNESSES

ARITHMETIC

Question Type	Question #	See Pages . . .
Integers	2, 11, 14	14–25
Fractions	3, 5, 6	25–36
Decimals and Fraction-Decimal Conversions	6, 7, 8, 9, 12, 13, 15	37–45
Percentages	16	46–53
Square Root	4, 10, 15	53–58
Exponents and Scientific Notation	1, 9	59–65

DETAILED EXPLANATIONS OF ANSWERS

ARITHMETIC DIAGNOSTIC TEST

1. **(E)**

    $10^3 = 1,000$ and $10^5 = 100,000$

    $10^3 + 10^5 = 101,000$

2. **(E)** When evaluating an expression without grouping symbols to indicate what operation should be done first, always do all multiplication and division first as they appear from left to right, then do any addition and subtraction, again as they appear from left to right. Therefore,

    $48 - 24 \div 3 + 5 \times 2 =$

    $48 - 8 + 10 =$

    $40 + 10 = 50$

3. **(A)** In order to divide $3^1/_5$ by $1^1/_3$, we must first change both mixed numbers into improper fractions.

    $$\frac{16}{5} \div \frac{4}{5} = \frac{16}{5} \times \frac{3}{4}$$

    $$= \frac{4}{5} \times \frac{3}{1} = \frac{12}{5}$$

Since the result is an improper fraction, we must convert it back into a mixed number.

$$\frac{12}{5} = \frac{10}{5} + \frac{2}{5} = 2 + \frac{2}{5}$$

Therefore, the correct answer is $2^2/_5$.

4. **(B)** To combine radicals, the radicands (the value under the radical sign) must be equal. The distributive property allows you to add and subtract radicals.

$$\left(6\sqrt{7} + 4\sqrt{7}\right) - \sqrt{5} + 5\sqrt{7}$$

$$(6+4)\sqrt{7} - \sqrt{5} + 5\sqrt{7}$$

$$10\sqrt{7} - \sqrt{5} + 5\sqrt{7}$$

$$(10+5)\sqrt{7} - \sqrt{5}$$

$$15\sqrt{7} - \sqrt{5}$$

5. **(E)** Since the lowest common denominator for $^3/_4$, $^{11}/_{16}$, and $^1/_8$ is 16, we change each fraction into equivalent fractions having a common denominator of 16.

$$5\frac{3}{4} = 5\frac{12}{16}$$

$$2\frac{11}{16} = 2\frac{11}{16}$$

$$7\frac{1}{8} = 7\frac{2}{16}$$

Adding the whole numbers 5, 2, and 7 yields

$$5 + 2 + 7 = 14.$$

Adding the numerators 12, 11, and 2 yields

$$12 + 11 + 2 = 25.$$

Writing this sum over the common denominator gives $^{25}/_{16}$, which changes to the proper fraction $1^9/_{16}$.

Adding this with the sum of the whole numbers

$$14 + 1\frac{9}{16} = 15\frac{9}{16}.$$

The correct answer is therefore $15^9/_{16}$.

6.   **(D)**   First, change all the numbers to the same form. All are easily converted to fractions and simplified:

$$7.5 \times 1\frac{7}{9} \div 1.333... = 7\frac{1}{2} \times \frac{16}{9} \div 1\frac{1}{3}$$

$$= \frac{15}{2} \times \frac{16}{9} \div \frac{4}{3}$$

$$= \frac{15}{2} \times \frac{16}{9} \times \frac{3}{4}$$

$$= 10$$

7.   **(B)**   To divide, make the divisor a whole number by moving the decimal point. Make sure that the decimal point of the dividend is moved the same number of places.

$$
\begin{array}{r}
2.3 \\
4.01.\,\overline{)\,9.22.3} \\
\underline{802} \\
1203 \\
\underline{1203}
\end{array}
$$

8.   **(D)**   To change a fraction to a decimal, divide the numerator (7) by the denominator (8)

$$7 \div 8$$

Add a decimal point after the 7 and necessary zeros.

$$
\begin{array}{r}
.875 \\
8\,\overline{)\,7.000} \\
\underline{-64} \\
60 \\
\underline{-56} \\
40 \\
\underline{-40} \\
0
\end{array}
$$

9.　**(D)**　To find the smallest number we will calculate each one.

(A)　$\dfrac{5\times 10^3}{3\times 10^{-3}} = \dfrac{5}{3} = 1.6$

(B)　$\dfrac{.3}{.2} = 1.5$

(C)　$\dfrac{.3}{3\times 10^{-3}} = \dfrac{.3\times 10^3}{3} = \dfrac{.3\times 10^2}{3} = 100$

(D)　$\dfrac{5\times 10^{-2}}{.1} = \dfrac{5\times 10^{-2}}{10^{-1}} = 5\times 10^{-1} = .5$

(E)　$\dfrac{.3}{3\times 10^{-1}} = \dfrac{.3\times 10}{3} = \dfrac{3}{3} = 1$

10.　**(B)**　Remember

$$36 = 6 \times 6$$

Therefore, the square root of 36 equals 6.

11.　**(C)**　When evaluating a problem, calculate what is inside the parentheses first. Continue doing the multiplication and division process before the addition and subtraction.

$$\dfrac{-4+(-2)[-1+(-2)]}{-2} = \dfrac{-4-2[-1-2]}{-2}$$

$$= \dfrac{-4-2[-3]}{-2}$$

$$= \dfrac{-4-2[-3]}{-2}$$

$$= \dfrac{-4+6}{-2}$$

$$= \dfrac{2}{-2} = -1$$

12. **(D)** The term "rounding off" means to drop everything or ignore all numbers to the right of the place requested. If the number following it is equal to or greater than 5, add 1 to the number and the following numbers are dropped. The hundredth place is the second number to the *right* of the decimal. Since 3 in the thousandth's place is less than 5, drop it. Therefore, the answer is 46.86.

13. **(A)**

$$
\begin{array}{r}
7.04 \quad \text{(2 decimal places)} \\
\times\ 2.5 \quad \text{(1 decimal place)} \\
\hline
3520 \\
1408 \\
\hline
17.600
\end{array}
$$

Remember to put the decimal point in the correct place (3 decimal places).

14. **(C)**

$$
\begin{array}{r}
451 \\
21 \\
689 \\
\hline
1161
\end{array}
$$

Remember to add digits in correct places (tens and hundreds).

15. **(D)** Remember $2 \times 2 = 4$. Then figure out where to put the decimal point.

.2	×	.2	=	.04
1	+	1	=	2
decimal		decimal		decimal
place		place		places

16. **(A)** Change 10% to a decimal.

$$10\% = \frac{10}{100} = 0.10$$

$$10\% \text{ of } 250 = 0.10 \times 250 = 25$$

ARITHMETIC REVIEW

1. INTEGERS AND REAL NUMBERS

Most of the numbers used in algebra belong to a set called the **real numbers** or **reals.** This set can be represented graphically by the real number line.

Given the number line below, we arbitrarily fix a point and label it with the number 0. In a similar manner, we can label any point on the line with one of the real numbers, depending on its position relative to 0. Numbers to the right of 0 are positive, while those to the left are negative. Value increases from left to right, so that if a is to the right of b, it is said to be greater than b.

If we now divide the number line into equal segments, we can label the points on this line with real numbers. For example, the point 2 lengths to the left of 0 is -2, while the point 3 lengths to the right of 0 is $+3$ (the + sign is usually assumed, so $+3$ is written simply as 3). The number line now looks like this:

These boundary points represent the subset of the reals known as the **integers**. The set of integers is made up of both the positive and negative whole numbers: $\{..., -4, -3, -2, -1, 0, 1, 2, 3, 4, ...\}$. Some subsets of integers are:

Natural Numbers or Positive Numbers—the set of integers starting with 1 and increasing:

$$\mathcal{N} = \{1, 2, 3, 4, ...\}.$$

Whole Numbers—the set of integers starting with 0 and increasing:

$$\mathcal{W} = \{0, 1, 2, 3, ...\}.$$

Negative Numbers—the set of integers starting with –1 and decreasing:

$$Z = \{-1, -2, -3, \ldots\}.$$

Prime Numbers—the set of positive integers greater than 1 that are divisible only by 1 and themselves:

$$\{2, 3, 5, 7, 11, \ldots\}.$$

Even Integers—the set of integers divisible by 2:

$$\{\ldots, -4, -2, 0, 2, 4, 6, \ldots\}.$$

Odd Integers—the set of integers not divisible by 2:

$$\{\ldots, -3, -1, 1, 3, 5, 7, \ldots\}.$$

PROBLEM

Classify each of the following numbers into as many different sets as possible. Example: real, integer …

(1) 0	(2) 9	(3) $\sqrt{6}$
(4) $1/2$	(5) $2/3$	(6) 1.5

Solution

(1) 0 is a real number and an integer.

(2) 9 is a real, natural number, and an integer.

(3) $\sqrt{6}$ is a real number.

(4) $1/2$ is a real number.

(5) $2/3$ is a real number.

(6) 1.5 is a real number and a decimal.

Absolute Value

The **absolute value** of a number is represented by two vertical lines around the number, and is equal to the given number, regardless of sign.

The absolute value of a real number A is defined as follows:

$$|A| = \begin{cases} A \text{ if } A \geq 0 \\ -A \text{ if } A < 0 \end{cases}$$

EXAMPLE

$$|5| = 5, \quad |-8| = -(-8) = 8$$

Absolute values follow the given rules:

(A) $\quad |-A| = |A|$

(B) $\quad |A| \geq 0$, equality holding only if $A = 0$

(C) $\quad \left|\dfrac{A}{B}\right| = \dfrac{|A|}{|B|}, B \neq 0$

(D) $\quad |AB| = |A| \times |B|$

(E) $\quad |A|^2 = A^2$

Absolute value can also be expressed on the real number line as the distance of the point represented by the real number from the point labeled 0.

3 unit lengths

So $|-3| = 3$ because -3 is 3 units to the left of 0.

PROBLEM

Classify each of the following statements as true or false. If it is false, explain why.

(1) $\quad |-120| > 1$ T

(2) $\quad |4 - 12| = |4| - |12|$ F

(3) $\quad |4 - 9| = 9 - 4$ T

(4) $\quad |12 - 3| = 12 - 3$ T

(5) $\quad |-12a| = 12|a|$ T

everything positive

Solution

(1) True

(2) False, $\quad |4 - 12| = |4| - |12|$

$$|-8| = 4 - 12$$

$$8 \neq -8$$

In general, $|a + b| \neq |a| + |b|$

(3) True

(4) True

(5) True

PROBLEM

Find the absolute value for each of the following:

(1) $|0|$ 0 (2) $|-\pi|$ π

(3) $|4|$ 4 (4) $|a|$, where a is a real number

Solution

(1) $|0|=0$

(2) $|-\pi|=\pi$

(3) $|4|=4$

(4) for $a>0$, $|a|=a$

for $a=0$, $|a|=0$

for $a<0$, $|a|=-a$

i.e., $|a|=\begin{cases} a \text{ if } a>0 \\ 0 \text{ if } a=0 \\ -a \text{ if } a<0 \end{cases}$

Positive and Negative Numbers

(A) **To add two numbers with like signs**, add their absolute values and write the sum with the common sign. So,

$$6+2=8, (-6)+(-2)=-8$$

(B) **To add two numbers with unlike signs,** find the difference between their absolute values, and write the result with the sign of the number with the greater absolute value. So,

$$(-4)+6=2, 15+(-19)=-4$$

(C) **To subtract a number b from another number a,** change the sign of b and add to a. Examples:

$$10-(3)=10+(-3)=7 \tag{1}$$

$$2 - (-6) = 2 + 6 = 8 \qquad (2)$$

$$(-5) - (-2) = -5 + 2 = -3 \qquad (3)$$

(D) **To multiply (or divide) two numbers having like signs**, multiply (or divide) their absolute values and write the result with a positive sign. Examples:

$$(5)(3) = 15 \qquad (1)$$

$$-6 / -3 = 2 \qquad (2)$$

(E) **To multiply (or divide) two numbers having unlike signs**, multiply (or divide) their absolute values and write the result with a negative sign. Examples:

$$(-2)(8) = -16 \qquad (1)$$

$$9 / -3 = -3 \qquad (2)$$

According to the law of signs for real numbers, the square of a positive or negative number is always positive. This means that it is impossible to take the square root of a negative number in the real number system.

Properties of Real Numbers

Commutative Law

$a + b = b + a$ for addition

$ab = ba$ for multiplication

Associative Law

$(a + b) + c = a + (b + c)$ for addition

$(ab)c = a(bc)$ for multiplication

Distributive Law

$a(b + c) = ab + ac$

Identity Law

$a + 0 = a$ for addition

$b \times 1 = b$ for multiplication

Inverse Law

$$a + (-a) = 0 \qquad \text{for addition}$$

$$b \times 1/b = 1 \text{ (if } b \neq 0) \qquad \text{for multiplication}$$

The number $1/b$ is the **multiplicative inverse** or the **reciprocal** of b. It follows that b is the reciprocal of $1/b$.

Order of Operations

To simplify an expression containing parentheses, multiplication, powers, addition, etc, use the rules for the **order of operations**, as follows:

1. parentheses or absolute value

2. powers

3. multiplication or division

4. addition or subtraction

PROBLEM

Calculate the value of each of the following expressions:

(1) $||2 - 5| + 6 - 14|$

(2) $|-5| \times |4| + \dfrac{|-12|}{4}$

Solution

(1) $||-zx3| + 6 - 14| \quad = \quad |3 + 6 - 14|$

$$= |9 - 14|$$

$$= |-5|$$

$$= 5$$

(2) $(5 \times 4) + 12/4 = 20 + 3$

$$= 23$$

Drill 1: Integers and Real Numbers

Addition

1. Simplify $4 + (-7) + 2 + (-5)$.

    (A) -6　　　　　　　　　　(B) -4

    (C) 0　　　　　　　　　　(D) 6

    (E) 18

2. Simplify $144 + (-317) + 213$.

    (A) -357　　　　　　　　　(B) -40

    (C) 40　　　　　　　　　　(D) 357

    (E) 674

3. Simplify $|4 + (-3)| + |-2|$.

    (A) -2　　　　　　　　　　(B) -1

    (C) 1　　　　　　　　　　(D) 3

    (E) 9

4. What integer makes the equation $-13 + 12 + 7 + ? = 10$ a true statement?

    (A) -22　　　　　　　　　(B) -10

    (C) 4　　　　　　　　　　(D) 6

    (E) 10

5. Simplify $4 + 17 + (-29) + 13 + (-22) + (-3)$.

    (A) -44　　　　　　　　　(B) -20

    (C) 23　　　　　　　　　　(D) 34

    (E) 78

Subtraction

6. Simplify $319 - 428$.

(A) – 111 (B) – 109

(C) – 99 (D) 109

(E) 747

7. Simplify 91,203 – 37,904 + 1,073.

(A) 54,372 (B) 64,701

(C) 128,034 (D) 129,107

(E) 130,180

8. Simplify |43 – 62| – |– 17 – 3|.

(A) – 39 (B) – 19

(C) – 1 (D) 1

(E) 39

9. Simplify – (– 4 – 7) + (– 2).

(A) – 22 (B) – 13

(C) – 9 (D) 7

(E) 9

10. In the Great Smoky Mountains National Park, Mt. Le Conte rises from 1,292 feet above sea level to 6,593 feet above sea level. How tall is Mt. Le Conte?

(A) 4,009 ft (B) 5,301 ft

(C) 5,699 ft (D) 6,464 ft

(E) 7,885 ft

Multiplication

11. Simplify (– 3) × (– 18) × (– 1).

(A) – 108 (B) – 54

(C) – 48 (D) 48

(E) 54

12. Simplify $|-42| \times |7|$.

    (A) -294 (B) -49

    (C) -35 (D) 284

    (E) 294

13. Simplify $(-6) \times 5 \times (-10) \times (-4) \times 0 \times 2$.

    (A) $-2,400$ (B) -240

    (C) 0 (D) 280

    (E) $2,700$

14. Simplify $-|(-6) \times 8|$.

    (A) -48 (B) -42

    (C) 2 (D) 42

    (E) 48

15. A city in Georgia had a record low temperature of $-3°F$ one winter. During the same year, a city in Michigan experienced a record low that was nine times the record low set in Georgia. What was the record low in Michigan that year?

    (A) $-31°F$ (B) $-27°F$

    (C) $-21°F$ (D) $-12°F$

    (E) $-6°F$

Division

16. Simplify $-24 / 8$.

    (A) -4 (B) -3

    (C) -2 (D) 3

    (E) 4

17. Simplify $(-180) / (-12)$.

    (A) -30 (B) -15

    (C) 1.5 (D) 15

    (E) 216

18. Simplify $|-76|/|-4|$.

    (A) -21 (B) -19

    (C) 13 (D) 19

    (E) 21.5

19. Simplify $|216/(-6)|$.

    (A) -36 (B) -12

    (C) 36 (D) 38

    (E) 43

20. At the end of the year, a small firm has $2,996 in its account for bonuses. If the entire amount is equally divided among the 14 employees, how much does each one receive?

    (A) $107   (B) $114

    (C) $170   (D) $210

    (E) $214

Order of Operations

21. Simplify $\dfrac{4+8\times2}{5-1}$.

    (A) 4 (B) 5

    (C) 6 (D) 8

    (E) 12

22. $96 \div 3 \div 4 \div 2 =$

    (A) 65 (B) 64

    (C) 16 (D) 8

    (E) 4

23. $3 + 4 \times 2 - 6 \div 3 =$

    (A) -1 (B) $^5/_3$

    (C) $^8/_3$ (D) 9

    (E) 12

24. $[(4 + 8) \times 3] \div 9 =$

(A) 4

(B) 8

(C) 12

(D) 24

(E) 36

25. $18 + 3 \times 4 \div 3 =$

(A) 3

(B) 5

(C) 10

(D) 22

(E) 28

26. $(29 - 17 + 4) \div 4 + |-2| =$

(A) $2^2/_3$

(B) 4

(C) $4^2/_3$

(D) 6

(E) 15

27. $(-3) \times 5 - 20 \div 4 =$

(A) -75

(B) -20

(C) -10

(D) $-8^3/_4$

(E) 20

28. $\dfrac{11 \times 2 + 2}{16 - 2 \times 2} =$

(A) $^{11}/_{16}$

(B) 1

(C) 2

(D) $3^2/_3$

(E) 4

29. $|-8 - 4| \div 3 \times 6 + (-4) =$

(A) 20

(B) 26

(C) 32

(D) 62

(E) 212

30. $32 \div 2 + 4 - 15 \div 3 =$

(A) 0

(B) 7

(C) 15

(D) 23

(E) 63

2. FRACTIONS

The fraction, a/b, where the **numerator** is a and the **denominator** is b, implies that a is being divided by b. The denominator of a fraction can never be zero since a number divided by zero is not defined. If the numerator is less than the denominator, the fraction is called a **proper fraction**. If the numerator is greater than the denominator, the fraction is called an **improper fraction**. A **mixed number** is the sum of a whole number and a fraction, i.e., $4^3/_8 = 4 + {}^3/_8$.

Operations with Fractions

(A) **To change a mixed number to an improper fraction**, multiply the whole number by the denominator of the fraction and add the numerator. This product becomes the numerator of the result and the denominator remains the same, e.g.,

$$5\frac{2}{3} = \frac{(5 \times 3) + 2}{3} = \frac{15 + 2}{3} = \frac{17}{3}$$

To change an improper fraction to a mixed number, divide the numerator by the denominator. The remainder becomes the numerator of the fractional part of the mixed number, and the denominator remains the same, e.g.,

$$\frac{35}{4} = 35 \div 4 = 8\frac{3}{4}$$

To check your work, change your result back to an improper fraction to see if it matches the original fraction.

(B) **To find the sum of two fractions having a common denominator,** add together the numerators of the given fractions and put this sum over the common denominator.

$$\frac{11}{3} + \frac{5}{3} = \frac{11 + 5}{3} = \frac{16}{3}$$

Similarly for subtraction,

$$\frac{11}{3} - \frac{5}{3} = \frac{11-5}{3} = \frac{6}{3} = 2$$

(C) **To find the sum of the two fractions having different denominators,** it is necessary to find the **lowest common denominator (LCD)** of the different denominators using a process called **factoring.**

To **factor** a number means to find two or more numbers that when multiplied together have a product equal to the original number. These two numbers are then said to be **factors** of the original number. For example, the factors of 6 are

(1) 1 and 6 since $1 \times 6 = 6$.

(2) 2 and 3 since $2 \times 3 = 6$.

Every number is the product of itself and 1. A **prime factor** is a number that does not have any factors besides itself and 1. This is important when finding the LCD of two fractions having different denominators.

To find the LCD of $^{11}/_6$ and $^5/_{16}$, we must first find the prime factors of each of the two denominators.

$6 = 2 \times 3$

$16 = 2 \times 2 \times 2 \times 2$

$LCD = 2 \times 2 \times 2 \times 2 \times 3 = 48$

Note that we do not need to repeat the 2 that appears in both the factors of 6 and 16.

Once we have determined the LCD of the denominators, each of the fractions must be converted into equivalent fractions having the LCD as a denominator.

Rewrite $^{11}/_6$ and $^5/_{16}$ to have 48 as their denominators.

$6 \times ? = 48$ $\qquad\qquad\qquad\qquad$ $16 \times ? = 48$

$6 \times 8 = 48$ $\qquad\qquad\qquad\qquad$ $16 \times 3 = 48$

If the numerator and denominator of each fraction is multiplied (or divided) by the same number, the value of the fraction will not change. This is because a fraction b/b, b being any number, is equal to the multiplicative identity, 1.

Therefore,

$$\frac{11}{6} \times \frac{8}{8} = \frac{88}{48} \qquad \frac{5}{16} \times \frac{3}{3} = \frac{15}{48}$$

We may now find

$$\frac{11}{6} + \frac{5}{16} = \frac{88}{48} + \frac{15}{48} = \frac{103}{48}$$

Similarly for subtraction,

$$\frac{11}{6} - \frac{5}{16} = \frac{88}{48} - \frac{15}{48} = \frac{73}{48}$$

(D) **To find the product of two or more fractions**, multiply the numerators of the given fractions to find the numerator of the product and multiply the denominators of the given fractions to find the denominator of the product, e.g.,

$$\frac{2}{3} \times \frac{1}{5} \times \frac{4}{7} = \frac{2 \times 1 \times 4}{3 \times 5 \times 7} = \frac{8}{105}$$

(E) **To find the quotient of two fractions**, invert the divisor and multiply, e.g.,

$$\frac{8}{9} \div \frac{1}{3} = \frac{8}{9} \times \frac{3}{1} = \frac{24}{9} = \frac{8}{3}$$

(F) **To simplify a fraction** is to convert it into a form in which the numerator and denominator have no common factor other than 1, e.g.,

$$\frac{12}{18} = \frac{12 \div 6}{18 \div 6} = \frac{2}{3}$$

(G) **A compound fraction** is a fraction whose numerator and/or denominator is made up of fractions. To simplify the fraction, find the LCD of all the fractions. Multiply both the numerator and denominator by this number and simplify.

PROBLEM

If $a = 4$ and $b = 7$, find the value of $\dfrac{a + \dfrac{a}{b}}{a - \dfrac{a}{b}}$.

Solution

By substitution,

$$\frac{a + \dfrac{a}{b}}{a - \dfrac{a}{b}} = \frac{4 + \dfrac{4}{7}}{4 - \dfrac{4}{7}}$$

In order to combine the terms, we must find the LCD of 1 and 7. Since both are prime factors, the LCD $= 1 \times 7 = 7$.

Multiplying both the numerator and denominator by 7, we get

$$\frac{7\left(4 + \dfrac{4}{7}\right)}{7\left(4 - \dfrac{4}{7}\right)} = \frac{28 + 4}{28 - 4} = \frac{32}{24}$$

By dividing both the numerator and denominator by 8, $^{32}/_{24}$ can be reduced to $^4/_3$.

Drill 2: Fractions

Fractions

DIRECTIONS: Add and write the answer in its *simplest* form.

1. $^5/_{12} + ^3/_{12} =$

   (A) $^5/_{24}$ (B) $^1/_3$

   (C) $^9/_{12}$ $\dfrac{8}{12} = \dfrac{2}{3}$ (D) $^2/_3$

   (E) $1^1/_3$

2. $^5/_8 + ^7/_8 + ^3/_8 =$

   (A) $^{15}/_{24}$ $^{15}/_8 = 1\,^7/_8$ (B) $^3/_4$

   (C) $^5/_6$ (D) $^7/_8$

   (E) $1^7/_8$

3. $131^2/_{15} + 28^3/_{15} =$ 131

   (A) $159^1/_6$ $\dfrac{+\,28}{159}$ (B) $159^1/_5$

   (C) $159^1/_3$ (D) $159^1/_2$

   (E) $159^3/_5$

4. $3^5/_{18} + 2^1/_{18} + 8^7/_{18} =$

   (A) $13^{13}/_{18}$ (B) $13^3/_4$

   (C) $13^7/_9$ (D) $14^1/_6$

   (E) $14^2/_9$

5. $17^9/_{20} + 4^3/_{20} + 8^{11}/_{20} =$

   (A) $29^{23}/_{60}$ (B) $30^{23}/_{20}$

   (C) $30^3/_{20}$ (D) $30^1/_5$

   (E) $30^3/_5$

Subtracting Fractions with the Same Denominator

DIRECTIONS: Subtract and write the answer in its *simplest* form.

6. $4^7/_8 - 3^1/_8 =$

   (A) $1^1/_4$ (B) $1^1/_2$

   (C) $1^3/_4$ (D) $1^7/_8$

   (E) 2

7. $132^5/_{12} - 37^3/_{12} =$

   (A) $94^1/_6$ (B) $95^1/_{12}$

   (C) $95^1/_6$ (D) $105^1/_6$

   (E) $169^2/_3$

8. $19^1/_3 - 2^2/_3 =$

   (A) $16^2/_3$ (B) $16^5/_6$

   (C) $17^1/_3$ (D) $17^2/_3$

   (E) $17^5/_6$

9. $8/_{21} - 5/_{21} =$

   (A) $1/_{21}$ (B) $1/_7$

   (C) $3/_{21}$ (D) $2/_7$

   (E) $3/_7$

10. $82^7/_{10} - 38^9/_{10} =$

(A) $43^4/_5$

(B) $44^1/_5$

(C) $44^2/_5$

(D) $45^1/_5$

(E) $45^2/_{10}$

Finding the LCD

DIRECTIONS: Find the lowest common denominator of each group of fractions.

11. $^2/_3$, $^5/_9$, and $^1/_6$.

(A) 9

(B) 18

(C) 27

(D) 54

(E) 162

12. $^1/_2$, $^5/_6$, and $^3/_4$.

(A) 2

(B) 4

(C) 6

(D) 12

(E) 48

13. $^7/_{16}$, $^5/_6$, and $^2/_3$.

(A) 3

(B) 6

(C) 12

(D) 24

(E) 48

14. $^8/_{15}$, $^2/_5$, and $^{12}/_{25}$.

(A) 5

(B) 15

(C) 25

(D) 75

(E) 375

15. $^2/_3$, $^1/_5$, and $^5/_6$.

(A) 15

(B) 30

(C) 48

(D) 90

(E) 120

16. $^1/_3$, $^9/_{42}$, and $^4/_{21}$.

    (A) 21

    (B) 42

    (C) 126

    (D) 378

    (E) 4,000

17. $^4/_9$, $^2/_5$, and $^1/_3$.

    (A) 15

    (B) 17

    (C) 27

    (D) 45

    (E) 135

18. $^7/_{12}$, $^{11}/_{36}$, and $^1/_9$.

    (A) 12

    (B) 36

    (C) 108

    (D) 324

    (E) 432

19. $^3/_7$, $^5/_{21}$, and $^2/_3$.

    (A) 21

    (B) 42

    (C) 31

    (D) 63

    (E) 441

20. $^{13}/_{16}$, $^5/_8$, and $^1/_4$.

    (A) 4

    (B) 8

    (C) 16

    (D) 32

    (E) 64

Adding Fractions with Different Denominators

DIRECTIONS: Add and write the answer in its *simplest* form.

21. $^1/_3 + ^5/_{12} =$

    (A) $^2/_5$

    (B) $^1/_2$

    (C) $^6/_{12}$

    (D) $^3/_4$

    (E) $1^1/_3$

22. $3^5/_9 + 2^1/_3 =$

    (A) $5^1/_2$ (B) $5^2/_3$

    (C) $5^8/_9$ (D) $6^1/_9$

    (E) $6^2/_3$

23. $12^9/_{16} + 17^3/_4 + 8^1/_8 =$

    (A) $37^7/_{16}$ (B) $38^7/_{16}$

    (C) $38^1/_2$ (D) $38^2/_3$

    (E) $39^3/_{16}$

24. $28^4/_5 + 11^{16}/_{25} =$

    (A) $39^2/_3$ (B) $39^4/_5$

    (C) $40^9/_{25}$ (D) $40^2/_5$

    (E) $40^{11}/_{25}$

25. $2^1/_8 + 1^3/_{16} + 5/_{12} =$

    (A) $3^{35}/_{48}$ (B) $3^3/_4$

    (C) $3^{19}/_{24}$ (D) $3^{13}/_{16}$

    (E) $4^1/_{12}$

Subtracting Fractions with Different Denominators

DIRECTIONS: Subtract and write the answer in its *simplest* form.

26. $8^9/_{12} - 2^2/_3 =$

    (A) $6^1/_{12}$ (B) $6^1/_6$

    (C) $6^1/_3$ (D) $6^7/_{12}$

    (E) $6^2/_3$

27. $185^{11}/_{15} - 107^2/_5 =$

    (A) $77^2/_{15}$ (B) $78^1/_5$

    (C) $78^3/_{10}$ (D) $78^1/_3$

    (E) $78^9/_{15}$

28. $34^2/_3 - 16^5/_6 =$
    - (A) 16
    - (B) $16^1/_3$
    - (C) $17^1/_2$
    - (D) 17
    - (E) $17^5/_6$

29. $3^{11}/_{48} - 2^3/_{16} =$
    - (A) $^{47}/_{48}$
    - (B) $1^1/_{48}$
    - (C) $1^1/_{24}$
    - (D) $2^{18}/_{48}$
    - (E) $1^7/_{24}$

30. $81^4/_{21} - 32^1/_3 =$
    - (A) $47^3/_7$
    - (B) $48^6/_7$
    - (C) $49^1/_6$
    - (D) $49^5/_7$
    - (E) $49^{13}/_{21}$

Multiplication

DIRECTIONS: Multiply and reduce the answer to lowest terms.

31. $^2/_3 \times ^4/_5 =$
    - (A) $^6/_8$
    - (B) $^3/_4$
    - (C) $^8/_{15}$
    - (D) $^{10}/_{12}$
    - (E) $^6/_5$

32. $^7/_{10} \times ^4/_{21} =$
    - (A) $^2/_{15}$
    - (B) $^{11}/_{31}$
    - (C) $^{28}/_{210}$
    - (D) $^1/_6$
    - (E) $^4/_{15}$

33. $5^1/_3 \times ^3/_8 =$
    - (A) $^4/_{11}$
    - (B) 2
    - (C) $^8/_5$
    - (D) $5^1/_8$
    - (E) $5^{17}/_{24}$

34. $6^1/_2 \times 3 =$
   (A) $9^1/_2$ (B) $18^1/_2$
   (C) $19^1/_2$ (D) 20
   (E) $12^1/_2$

35. $3^1/_4 \times 2^1/_3 =$
   (A) $5^7/_{12}$ (B) $6^2/_7$
   (C) $6^5/_7$ (D) $7^7/_{12}$
   (E) $7^{11}/_{12}$

Division

DIRECTIONS: Divide and reduce the answer.

36. $^3/_{16} \div ^3/_4 =$
   (A) $^9/_{64}$ (B) $^1/_4$
   (C) $^6/_{16}$ (D) $^9/_{16}$
   (E) $^3/_4$

37. $^4/_9 \div ^2/_3 =$
   (A) $^1/_3$ (B) $^1/_2$
   (C) $^2/_3$ (D) $^7/_{11}$
   (E) $^8/_9$

38. $5^1/_4 \div ^7/_{10} =$
   (A) $2^4/_7$ (B) $3^{27}/_{40}$
   (C) $5^{19}/_{20}$ (D) $7^1/_2$
   (E) $8^1/_4$

39. $4^2/_3 \div ^7/_9 =$
   (A) $2^{24}/_{27}$ (B) $3^2/_9$
   (C) $4^{14}/_{27}$ (D) $5^{12}/_{27}$
   (E) 6

40. $3^2/_5 \div 1^7/_{10} =$ $^{17}/_5 \cdot ^{17}/_{10}$ $^{17}/_5 \cdot ^{10}/_{17}$

    (A) 2

    (B) $3^4/_7$

    (C) $4^7/_{25}$

    (D) $5^1/_{10}$

    (E) $5^2/_7$

Changing an Improper Fraction to a Mixed Number

DIRECTIONS: Write each improper fraction as a mixed number in *simplest* form.

41. $^{50}/_4$

    (A) $10^1/_4$

    (B) $11^1/_2$

    (C) $12^1/_4$

    (D) $12^1/_2$

    (E) 25

42. $^{17}/_5$ 3

    (A) $3^2/_5$

    (B) $3^3/_5$

    (C) $3^4/_5$

    (D) $4^1/_5$

    (E) $4^2/_5$

43. $^{42}/_3$

    (A) $10^2/_3$

    (B) 12

    (C) $13^1/_3$

    (D) 14

    (E) $21^1/_3$

44. $^{85}/_6$

    (A) $9^1/_6$

    (B) $10^5/_6$

    (C) $11^1/_2$

    (D) 12

    (E) $14^1/_{16}$

45. $^{151}/_7$

    (A) $19^6/_7$

    (B) $20^1/_7$

    (C) $21^4/_7$

    (D) $31^2/_7$

    (E) $31^4/_7$

Changing a Mixed Number to an Improper Fraction

DIRECTIONS: Change each mixed number to an improper fraction in *simplest* form.

46. $2^3/_5$ $13/5$

    (A) $^4/_5$ (B) $^6/_5$

    (C) $^{11}/_5$ (D) $^{13}/_5$

    (E) $^{17}/_5$

47. $4^3/_4$ $19/4$

    (A) $^7/_4$ (B) $^{13}/_4$

    (C) $^{16}/_3$ (D) $^{19}/_4$

    (E) $^{21}/_4$

48. $6^7/_6$

    (A) $^{13}/_6$ (B) $^{43}/_6$

    (C) $^{19}/_{36}$ (D) $^{42}/_{36}$

    (E) $^{48}/_6$

49. $12^3/_7$

    (A) $^{87}/_7$ (B) $^{39}/_7$

    (C) $^{34}/_3$ (D) $^{187}/_{21}$

    (E) $^{252}/_7$

50. $21^1/_2$

    (A) $^{11}/_2$ (B) $^{22}/_2$

    (C) $^{24}/_2$ (D) $^{42}/_2$

    (E) $^{43}/_2$

3. DECIMALS

When we divide the denominator of a fraction into its numerator, the result is a **decimal**. The decimal is based upon a fraction with a denominator of 10, 100, 1,000, ... and is written with a **decimal point**. Whole numbers are placed to the left of the decimal point where the first place to the left is the units place; the second to the left is the tens; the third to the left is the hundreds, etc. The fractions are placed on the right where the first place to the right is the tenths; the second to the right is the hundredths, etc.

EXAMPLES

$$12\frac{3}{10} = 12.3 \qquad 4\frac{17}{100} = 4.17 \qquad \frac{3}{100} = .03$$

Since a **rational number** is of the form a/b, $b \neq 0$, then all rational numbers can be expressed as decimals by dividing b into a. The result is either a **terminating decimal**, meaning that b divides a with a remainder of 0 after a certain point; or **repeating decimal**, meaning that b continues to divide a so that the decimal has a repeating pattern of integers.

EXAMPLES

(A) $^1/_2 = .5$

(B) $^1/_3 = .333...$

(C) $^{11}/_{16} = .6875$

(D) $^2/_7 = .285714285714...$

(A) and (C) are terminating decimals; (B) and (D) are repeating decimals. This explanation allows us to define **irrational numbers** as numbers whose decimal form is non-terminating and non-repeating, e.g.,

$$\sqrt{2} = 1.414...$$
$$\sqrt{3} = 1.732...$$

PROBLEM

Express $- \, ^{10}/_{20}$ as a decimal.

Solution

$$- \, ^{10}/_{20} = - \, ^{50}/_{100} = - .5$$

PROBLEM

Write $^2/_7$ as a repeating decimal.

Solution

To write a fraction as a repeating decimal divide the numerator by the denominator until a pattern of repeated digits appears.

$2 \div 7 = .285714285714...$

Identify the entire portion of the decimal which is repeated. The repeating decimal can then be written in the shortened form:

$^2/_7 = .\overline{285714}$

Operations with Decimals

(A) **To add numbers containing decimals,** write the numbers in a column with the decimal points in line, one beneath the other. Add the numbers, placing the decimal point in the sum so that it is in line. It is important not to mix the digits in the tenths place with the digits in the hundredths place, etc.

EXAMPLES

$2.558 + 6.391$ $57.51 + 6.2$

$$\begin{array}{r} 2.558 \\ + 6.391 \\ \hline 8.949 \end{array} \qquad \begin{array}{r} 57.51 \\ + \ \ 6.20 \\ \hline 63.71 \end{array}$$

Similarly with subtraction,

$78.54 - 21.33$ $7.11 - 4.2$

$$\begin{array}{r} 78.54 \\ - 21.33 \\ \hline 57.21 \end{array} \qquad \begin{array}{r} 7.11 \\ - 4.20 \\ \hline 2.91 \end{array}$$

Note that if two numbers differ according to the amount of digits to the right of the decimal point, zeros must be added.

$.63 - .214$ $15.224 - 3.6891$

$$\begin{array}{r} .630 \\ - .214 \\ \hline .416 \end{array} \qquad \begin{array}{r} 15.2240 \\ - \ 3.6891 \\ \hline 11.5349 \end{array}$$

(B) **To multiply numbers with decimals**, multiply as usual. To figure out the number of decimal places that belong in the product, count the total number of decimal places of the total numbers being multiplied.

EXAMPLES

$$
\begin{array}{r}
6.555 \\
\times\ \ 4.5 \\
\hline
32775 \\
26220 \\
\hline
294975 \\
29.4975
\end{array}
$$
(3 decimal places)
(1 decimal place)

(4 decimal places)

$$
\begin{array}{r}
5.32 \\
\times\ .04 \\
\hline
2128 \\
000 \\
\hline
2128 \\
.2128
\end{array}
$$
(2 decimal places)
(2 decimal places)

(4 decimal places)

(C) **To divide numbers with decimals**, you must first make the divisor a whole number by moving the decimal point the appropriate number of places to the right. The decimal point of the dividend should also be moved the same number of places. Place a decimal point in the quotient, directly in line with the decimal point in the dividend.

EXAMPLES

12.92 / 3.4

$$
\begin{array}{r}
3.8 \\
3.4.\,\overline{\smash{)}12.9.2} \\
-102 \\
\hline
272 \\
-272 \\
\hline
0
\end{array}
$$

40.376 / 7.21

$$
\begin{array}{r}
5.6 \\
7.21.\,\overline{\smash{)}40.37.6} \\
-3605 \\
\hline
4326 \\
-4326 \\
\hline
0
\end{array}
$$

If the question asks you to find the correct answer to two decimal places, divide until you have three decimal places and then round off. If the third decimal place is a 5 or larger, the number in the second decimal place is increased by 1 to the next higher number and the existing number does not change. If the third decimal place is less than 5, that number is simply dropped.

PROBLEM

Find the answer to the following to 2 decimal places:

(1) 44.3 / 3   (2) 56.99 / 6

Solution

(1)
```
            14.766
    3 │   44.300
        - 3
          14
        - 12
          23
        - 21
          20
        - 18
          20
        - 18
           2
```

(2)
```
             9.498
    6 │   56.990
        - 54
          29
        - 24
          59
        - 54
          50
        - 48
           2
```

14.766 can be rounded off to 14.77.

9.498 can be rounded off to 9.50.

(D) **When comparing two numbers with decimals to see which is the larger, first look at the tenths place.** The larger digit in this place represents the larger number. If the two digits are the same, however, take a look at the digits in the hundredths place, and so on.

EXAMPLES

.518 and .216

5 is larger than 2, therefore

.518 is larger than .216

.723 and .726

6 is larger than 3, therefore

.726 is larger than .723

Drill 3: Decimals

Addition

1.   1.032 + 0.987 + 3.07 =

$$\begin{array}{r} 1.032 \\ .987 \\ + 3.07 \\ \hline 5.089 \end{array}$$

   (A) 4.089

   (B) 5.089

   (C) 5.189

   (D) 6.189

   (E) 13.972

2.   132.03 + 97.1483 =

$$\begin{array}{r} 132.03 \\ 97.1483 \\ \hline 229.1783 \end{array}$$

   (A) 98.4686

   (B) 110.3513

(C) 209.1783   (D) 229.1486

(E) 229.1783

3.   7.1 + 0.62 + 4.03827 + 5.813 =

(A) 0.2315127   (B) 16.45433

(C) 17.57127   (D) 18.561

(E) 40.4543

4.   8 + 17.43 + 9.2 =

(A) 34.63   (B) 34.86

(C) 35.63   (D) 176.63

(E) 189.43

5.   1036.173 + 289.04 =

(A) 382.6573   (B) 392.6573

(C) 1065.077   (D) 1325.213

(E) 3926.573

Subtraction

6.   3.972 − 2.04 =

(A) 1.932   (B) 1.942

(C) 1.976   (D) 2.013

(E) 2.113

7.   16.047 − 13.06 =

(A) 2.887   (B) 2.987

(C) 3.041   (D) 3.141

(E) 4.741

8.   87.4 − 56.27 =

(A) 30.27   (B) 30.67

(C) 31.1   (D) 31.13

(E) 31.27

9. 1046.8 − 639.14 =

    (A) 303.84   (B) 313.74

    (C) 407.66   (D) 489.74

    (E) 535.54

10. 10,000 − 842.91 =

    (A) 157.09   (B) 942.91

    (C) 5236.09   (D) 9057.91

    (E) 9157.09

Multiplication

11. 1.03 × 2.6 =

    (A) 2.18   (B) 2.678

    (C) 2.78   (D) 3.38

    (E) 3.63

12. 93 × 4.2 =

    (A) 39.06   (B) 97.2

    (C) 223.2   (D) 390.6

    (E) 3,906

13. 0.04 × 0.23 =

    (A) 0.0092   (B) 0.092

    (C) 0.27   (D) 0.87

    (E) 0.920

14. 0.0186 × 0.03 =

    (A) 0.000348   (B) 0.000558

    (C) 0.0548   (D) 0.0848

    (E) 0.558

15. $51.2 \times 0.17 =$

    (A) 5.29   (B) 8.534

    (C) 8.704   (D) 36.352

    (E) 36.991

Division

16. $123.39 / 3 =$

    (A) 31.12   (B) 41.13

    (C) 401.13   (D) 411.3

    (E) 4,113

17. $1428.6 / 6 =$

    (A) 0.2381   (B) 2.381

    (C) 23.81   (D) 238.1

    (E) 2,381

18. $25.2 / 0.3 =$

    (A) 0.84   (B) 8.04

    (C) 8.4   (D) 84

    (E) 840

19. $14.95 / 6.5 =$

    (A) 2.3   (B) 20.3

    (C) 23   (D) 230

    (E) 2,300

20. $46.33 / 1.13 =$

    (A) 0.41   (B) 4.1

    (C) 41   (D) 410

    (E) 4,100

Comparing

21. Which is the **largest** number in this set — {0.8, 0.823, 0.089, 0.807, 0.852}?

    (A) 0.8   (B) 0.823

    (C) 0.089   (D) 0.807

    (E) 0.852

22. Which is the **smallest** number in this set — {32.98, 32.099, 32.047, 32.5, 32.304}?

    (A) 32.98   (B) 32.099

    (C) 32.047   (D) 32.5

    (E) 32.304

23. In which set below are the numbers arranged correctly from smallest to largest?

    (A) {0.98, 0.9, 0.993}   (B) {0.113, 0.3, 0.31}

    (C) {7.04, 7.26, 7.2}   (D) {0.006, 0.061, 0.06}

    (E) {12.84, 12.801, 12.6}

24. In which set below are the numbers arranged correctly from largest to smallest?

    (A) {1.018, 1.63, 1.368}   (B) {4.219, 4.29, 4.9}

    (C) {0.62, 0.6043, 0.643}   (D) {16.34, 16.304, 16.3}

    (E) {12.98, 12.601, 12.86}

25. Which is the **largest** number in this set — {0.87, 0.89, 0.889, 0.8, 0.987}?

    (A) 0.87   (B) 0.89

    (C) 0.889   (D) 0.8

    (E) 0.987

Changing a Fraction to a Decimal

26. What is $^1/_4$ written as a decimal?

    (A) 1.4

    (B) 0.14

    (C) 0.2

    (D) 0.25

    (E) 0.3

27. What is $^3/_5$ written as a decimal?

    (A) 0.3

    (B) 0.35

    (C) 0.6

    (D) 0.65

    (E) 0.8

28. What is $^7/_{20}$ written as a decimal?

    (A) 0.35

    (B) 0.4

    (C) 0.72

    (D) 0.75

    (E) 0.9

29. What is $^2/_3$ written as a decimal?

    (A) 0.23

    (B) 0.33

    (C) 0.5

    (D) 0.6

    (E) 0.$\overline{6}$

30. What is $^{11}/_{25}$ written as a decimal?

    (A) 0.1125

    (B) 0.25

    (C) 0.4

    (D) 0.44

    (E) 0.5

4. PERCENTAGES

A **percent** is a way of expressing the relationship between part and whole, where whole is defined as 100%. A percent can be defined by a fraction with a denominator of 100. Decimals can also represent a percent. For instance,

$$56\% = 0.56 = {}^{56}/_{100}$$

PROBLEM

Compute the value.

(1) 90% of 400

(2) 180% of 400

(3) 50% of 500

(4) 200% of 4

Solution

The symbol % means per hundred, therefore $5\% = {}^{5}/_{100}$.

(1) 90% of $400 = 90/100 \times 400 = 90 \times 4 = 360$

(2) 180% of $400 = 180/100 \times 400 = 180 \times 4 = 720$

(3) 50% of $500 = 50/100 \times 500 = 50 \times 5 = 250$

(4) 200% of $4 = 200/100 \times 4 = 2 \times 4 = 8$

$$\frac{700}{100} \times 4$$

PROBLEM

What percent of

(1)   100 is 99.5?

(2)   200 is 4?

Solution

(1) $99.5 = x \times 100$

$99.5 = 100x$

$.995 = x;$

but this is the value of x per hundred. Therefore,

$$x = 99.5\%$$

(2) $4 = x \times 200$

$4 = 200x$

$.02 = x.$

Again, this must be changed to percent, so

$$2\% = x$$

Equivalent Forms of a Number

Some problems may call for converting numbers into an equivalent or simplified form in order to make the solution more convenient.

1. Converting a fraction to a decimal:

   $$1/2 = 0.50$$

   Divide the numerator by the denominator:

   $$\begin{array}{r} .50 \\ 2\overline{\smash{\big)}\ 1.00} \\ \underline{-\ 10} \\ 00 \end{array}$$

2. Converting a number to a percent:

   $$0.50 = 50\%$$

   Multiply by 100:

   $$0.50 = (0.50 \times 100)\% = 50\%$$

3. Converting a percent to a decimal:

   $$30\% = 0.30$$

   Divide by 100:

   $$30\% = 30/100 = 0.30$$

4. Converting a decimal to a fraction:

   $$0.500 = 1/2$$

   Convert .500 to 500/1,000 and then simplify the fraction by dividing the numerator and denominator by common factors:

   $$\frac{2 \times 2 \times 5 \times 5 \times 5}{2 \times 2 \times 2 \times 5 \times 5 \times 5}$$

   and then cancel out the common numbers to get $1/2$.

PROBLEM

Express

(1) 1.65 as a percent.

(2) 0.7 as a fraction.

(3) $-{}^{10}/_{20}$ as a decimal.

(4) ${}^{4}/_{2}$ as an integer.

Solution

(1) $1.65 \times 100 = 165\%$

(2) $0.7 = {}^{7}/_{10}$

(3) $-{}^{10}/_{20} = -0.5$

(4) ${}^{4}/_{2} = 2$

Drill 4: Percentages

Finding Percents

1. Find 3% of 80.

(A) 0.24   (B) 2.4

(C) 24   (D) 240

(E) 2,400

2. Find 50% of 182.

(A) 9   (B) 90

(C) 91   (D) 910

(E) 9,100

3. Find 83% of 166.

(A) 0.137   (B) 1.377

(C) 13.778   (D) 137

(E) 137.78

4. Find 125% of 400.

(A) 425   (B) 500

(C) 525   (D) 600

(E) 825

5. Find 300% of 4.

  (A) 12   (B) 120

  (C) 1,200   (D) 12,000

  (E) 120,000

6. Forty-eight percent of the 1,200 students at Central High are males. How many male students are there at Central High?

  (A) 57   (B) 576

  (C) 580   (D) 600

  (E) 648

7. For 35% of the last 40 days, there has been measurable rainfall. How many days out of the last 40 days have had measurable rainfall?

  (A) 14   (B) 20

  (C) 25   (D) 35

  (E) 40

8. Of every 1,000 people who take a certain medicine, 0.2% develop severe side effects. How many people out of every 1,000 who take the medicine develop the side effects?

  (A) 0.2   (B) 2

  (C) 20   (D) 22

  (E) 200

9. Of 220 applicants for a job, 75% were offered an initial interview. How many people were offered an initial interview?

  (A) 75   (B) 110

  (C) 120   (D) 155

  (E) 165

10. Find 0.05% of 4,000.

   (A) 0.05
   (B) 0.5
   (C) 2
   (D) 20
   (E) 400

Changing Percents to Fractions

11. What is 25% written as a fraction?

   (A) $\frac{1}{25}$
   (B) $\frac{1}{5}$
   (C) $\frac{1}{4}$
   (D) $\frac{1}{3}$
   (E) $\frac{1}{2}$

12. What is $33\frac{1}{3}$% written as a fraction?

   (A) $\frac{1}{4}$
   (B) $\frac{1}{3}$
   (C) $\frac{1}{2}$
   (D) $\frac{2}{3}$
   (E) $\frac{5}{9}$

13. What is 200% written as a fraction?

   (A) $\frac{1}{2}$
   (B) $\frac{2}{1}$
   (C) $\frac{20}{1}$
   (D) $\frac{200}{1}$
   (E) $\frac{2,000}{1}$

14. What is 84% written as a fraction?

   (A) $\frac{1}{84}$
   (B) $\frac{4}{8}$
   (C) $\frac{17}{25}$
   (D) $\frac{21}{25}$
   (E) $\frac{44}{50}$

15. What is 2% written as a fraction?

   (A) $\frac{1}{50}$
   (B) $\frac{1}{25}$
   (C) $\frac{1}{10}$
   (D) $\frac{1}{4}$
   (E) $\frac{1}{2}$

Changing Fractions to Percents

16. What is $^2/_3$ written as a percent?

    (A) 23%　　　　　　　　(B) 32%

    (C) $33^1/_3$%　　　　　　(D) $57^1/_3$%

    (E) $66^2/_3$%

17. What is $^3/_5$ written as a percent?

    (A) 30%　　　　　　　　(B) 35%

    (C) 53%　　　　　　　　(D) 60%

    (E) 65%

18. What is $^{17}/_{20}$ written as a percent?

    (A) 17%　　　　　　　　(B) 70%

    (C) 75%　　　　　　　　(D) 80%

    (E) 85%

19. What is $^{45}/_{50}$ written as a percent?

    (A) 45%　　　　　　　　(B) 50%

    (C) 90%　　　　　　　　(D) 95%

    (E) 97%

20. What is $1^1/_4$ written as a percent?

    (A) 114%　　　　　　　　(B) 120%

    (C) 125%　　　　　　　　(D) 127%

    (E) 133%

Changing Percents to Decimals

21. What is 42% written as a decimal?

    (A) 0.42　　　　　　　　(B) 4.2

    (C) 42　　　　　　　　　(D) 420

    (E) 422

22. What is 0.3% written as a decimal?

    (A) 0.0003

    (B) 0.003

    (C) 0.03

    (D) 0.3

    (E) 3

23. What is 8% written as a decimal?

    (A) 0.0008

    (B) 0.008

    (C) 0.08

    (D) 0.80

    (E) 8

24. What is 175% written as a decimal?

    (A) 0.175

    (B) 1.75

    (C) 17.5

    (D) 175

    (E) 17,500

25. What is 34% written as a decimal?

    (A) 0.00034

    (B) 0.0034

    (C) 0.034

    (D) 0.34

    (E) 3.4

Changing Decimals to Percents

26. What is 0.43 written as a percent?

    (A) 0.0043%

    (B) 0.043%

    (C) 4.3%

    (D) 43%

    (E) 430%

27. What is 1 written as a percent?

    (A) 1%

    (B) 10%

    (C) 100%

    (D) 111%

    (E) 150%

28. What is 0.08 written as a percent?

   (A) 0.08%　　　　　　　　(B) 8%

   (C) 8.8%　　　　　　　　(D) 80%

   (E) 800%

29. What is 3.4 written as a percent?

   (A) 0.0034%　　　　　　　(B) 3.4%

   (C) 34%　　　　　　　　　(D) 304%　　3.4

   (E) 340%

30. What is 0.645 written as a percent?

   (A) 64.5%　　　　　　　(B) 65%

   (C) 69%　　　　　　　　(D) 70%

   (E) 645%

5. RADICALS

The **square root** of a number is a number that when multiplied by itself results in the original number. So, the square root of 81 is 9 since 9 × 9 = 81. However, − 9 is also a root of 81 since (− 9) (− 9) = 81. Every positive number will have two roots. Yet, the principal root is the positive one. Zero has only one square root, while negative numbers do not have real numbers as their roots.

A **radical sign** indicates that the root of a number or expression will be taken. The **radicand** is the number of which the root will be taken. The **index** tells how many times the root needs to be multiplied by itself to equal the radicand, e.g.,

(1)　　$\sqrt[3]{64}$;

　　　　3 is the index and 64 is the radicand. Since

　　　　$4 \times 4 \times 4 = 64,\ \sqrt[3]{64} = 4$

(2)　　$\sqrt[5]{32}$;

5 is the index and 32 is the radicand. Since

$$2 \times 2 \times 2 \times 2 \times 2 = 32, \sqrt[5]{32} = 2$$

Operations with Radicals

(A) **To multiply two or more radicals,** we utilize the law that states

$$\sqrt{a} \times \sqrt{b} = \sqrt{ab}.$$

Simply multiply the whole numbers as usual. Then, multiply the radicands and put the product under the radical sign and simplify, e.g.,

(1) $\sqrt{12} \times \sqrt{5} = \sqrt{60} = \sqrt{4 \times 15} = \sqrt{4}\sqrt{15} = 2\sqrt{15}$

(2) $3\sqrt{2} \times 4\sqrt{8} = 12\sqrt{16} = 48$

(3) $2\sqrt{10} \times 6\sqrt{5} = 12\sqrt{50} = 60\sqrt{2}$

(B) **To divide radicals,** simplify both the numerator and the denominator. By multiplying the radical in the denominator by itself, you can make the denominator a rational number. The numerator, however, must also be multiplied by this radical so that the value of the expression does not change. You must choose as many factors as necessary to rationalize the denominator, e.g.,

(1) $\dfrac{\sqrt{128}}{\sqrt{2}} = \dfrac{\sqrt{64} \times \sqrt{2}}{\sqrt{2}} = \dfrac{8\sqrt{2}}{\sqrt{2}} = 8$

(2) $\dfrac{\sqrt{10}}{\sqrt{3}} = \dfrac{\sqrt{10} \times \sqrt{3}}{\sqrt{3} \times \sqrt{3}} = \dfrac{\sqrt{30}}{3}$

(3) $\dfrac{\sqrt{8}}{2\sqrt{3}} = \dfrac{\sqrt{8} \times \sqrt{3}}{2\sqrt{3} \times \sqrt{3}} = \dfrac{\sqrt{24}}{2 \times 3} = \dfrac{2\sqrt{6}}{6} = \dfrac{\sqrt{6}}{3}$

(C) **To add two or more radicals,** the radicals must have the same index and the same radicand. Only where the radicals are simplified can these similarities be determined, e.g.,

(1) $6\sqrt{2} + 2\sqrt{2} = (6+2)\sqrt{2} = 8\sqrt{2}$

(2) $\sqrt{27} + 5\sqrt{3} = \sqrt{9}\sqrt{3} + 5\sqrt{3} = 3\sqrt{3} + 5\sqrt{3} = 8\sqrt{3}$

(3) $7\sqrt{3} + 8\sqrt{2} + 5\sqrt{3} = 12\sqrt{3} + 8\sqrt{2}$

Similarly to subtract,

(1) $12\sqrt{3} - 7\sqrt{3} = (12 - 7)\sqrt{3} = 5\sqrt{3}$

(2) $\sqrt{90} - \sqrt{20} = \sqrt{16}\sqrt{5} - \sqrt{4}\sqrt{5} = 4\sqrt{5} - 2\sqrt{5} = 2\sqrt{5}$

(3) $\sqrt{50} - \sqrt{3} = 5\sqrt{2} - \sqrt{3}$

Drill 5: Radicals

Multiplication

DIRECTIONS: Multiply and simplify each answer.

1. $\sqrt{6} \times \sqrt{5} =$

   (A) $\sqrt{11}$ $\sqrt{30}$ (B) $\sqrt{30}$ *square + mult.*

   (C) $2\sqrt{5}$ (D) $3\sqrt{10}$

   (E) $2\sqrt{3}$

2. $\sqrt{3} \times \sqrt{12} =$ $\sqrt{36}$

   (A) 3   (B) $\sqrt{15}$

   (C) $\sqrt{36}$ (D) 6

   (E) 8

3. $\sqrt{7} \times \sqrt{7} =$

   (A) 7   (B) 49

   (C) $\sqrt{14}$ (D) $2\sqrt{7}$

   (E) $2\sqrt{14}$

4. $3\sqrt{5} \times 2\sqrt{5} =$ $\sqrt{25}$ $6 \cdot 5$

   (A) $5\sqrt{5}$ (B) 25

   (C) 30   (D) $5\sqrt{25}$

   (E) $6\sqrt{5}$

5. $4\sqrt{6} \times \sqrt{2} =$

    (A) $4\sqrt{8}$

    (C) $5\sqrt{8}$

    (E) $8\sqrt{3}$

    (B) $8\sqrt{2}$

    (D) $4\sqrt{12}$

Division

DIRECTIONS: Divide and simplify each answer.

6. $\sqrt{10} \div \sqrt{2} =$

    (A) $\sqrt{8}$

    (C) $\sqrt{5}$

    (E) $2\sqrt{3}$

    (B) $2\sqrt{2}$

    (D) $2\sqrt{5}$

7. $\sqrt{30} \div \sqrt{15} =$

    (A) $\sqrt{2}$

    (C) $3\sqrt{5}$

    (E) $5\sqrt{3}$

    (B) $\sqrt{45}$

    (D) $\sqrt{15}$

8. $\sqrt{100} \div \sqrt{25} =$

    (A) $\sqrt{4}$

    (C) $5\sqrt{3}$

    (E) 4

    (B) $5\sqrt{5}$

    (D) 2

9. $\sqrt{48} \div \sqrt{8} =$

    (A) $4\sqrt{3}$

    (C) $\sqrt{6}$

    (E) 12

    (B) $3\sqrt{2}$

    (D) 6

10. $3\sqrt{12} \div \sqrt{3} =$

    (A) $3\sqrt{15}$

    (C) 9

    (E) $3\sqrt{36}$

    (B) 6

    (D) 12

Addition

DIRECTIONS: Simplify each radical and add.

11. $\sqrt{7} + 3\sqrt{7} =$

    (A) $3\sqrt{7}$

    (B) $4\sqrt{7}$

    (C) $3\sqrt{14}$

    (D) $4\sqrt{14}$

    (E) $3\sqrt{21}$

12. $\sqrt{5} + 6\sqrt{5} + 3\sqrt{5} =$

    (A) $9\sqrt{5}$

    (B) $9\sqrt{15}$

    (C) $5\sqrt{10}$

    (D) $10\sqrt{5}$

    (E) $18\sqrt{15}$

13. $3\sqrt{32} + 2\sqrt{2} =$

    (A) $5\sqrt{2}$

    (B) $\sqrt{34}$

    (C) $14\sqrt{2}$

    (D) $5\sqrt{34}$

    (E) $6\sqrt{64}$

14. $6\sqrt{15} + 8\sqrt{15} + 16\sqrt{15} =$

    (A) $15\sqrt{30}$

    (B) $30\sqrt{45}$

    (C) $30\sqrt{30}$

    (D) $15\sqrt{45}$

    (E) $30\sqrt{15}$

15. $6\sqrt{5} + 2\sqrt{45} =$

    (A) $12\sqrt{5}$

    (B) $8\sqrt{50}$

    (C) $40\sqrt{2}$

    (D) $12\sqrt{50}$

    (E) $8\sqrt{5}$

Subtraction

DIRECTIONS: Simplify each radical and subtract.

16. $8\sqrt{5} - 6\sqrt{5} =$ $2\sqrt{5}$

    (A) $2\sqrt{5}$

    (B) $3\sqrt{5}$

    (C) $4\sqrt{5}$

    (D) $14\sqrt{5}$

    (E) $48\sqrt{5}$

17. $16\sqrt{33} - 5\sqrt{33} =$ $11\sqrt{33}$

    (A) $3\sqrt{33}$

    (B) $33\sqrt{11}$

    (C) $11\sqrt{33}$

    (D) $11\sqrt{0}$

    (E) $\sqrt{33}$

18. $14\sqrt{2} - 19\sqrt{2} =$ $-5\sqrt{2}$

    (A) $5\sqrt{2}$

    (B) $-5\sqrt{2}$

    (C) $-33\sqrt{2}$

    (D) $33\sqrt{2}$

    (E) $-4\sqrt{2}$

19. $10\sqrt{2} - 3\sqrt{8} =$

    (A) $6\sqrt{6}$

    (B) $-2\sqrt{2}$

    (C) $7\sqrt{6}$

    (D) $4\sqrt{2}$

    (E) $-6\sqrt{6}$

20. $4\sqrt{3} - 2\sqrt{12} =$

    (A) $-2\sqrt{9}$

    (B) $-6\sqrt{15}$

    (C) 0

    (D) $6\sqrt{15}$

    (E) $2\sqrt{12}$

6. EXPONENTS AND SCIENTIFIC NOTATION

When a number is multiplied by itself a specific number of times, it is said to be **raised to a power**. The way this is written is

$$a^n = b$$

where a is the number or **base**, n is the **exponent** or **power** that indicates the number of times a is to be multiplied by itself, and b is the product of this multiplication.

In the expression 3^2, 3 is the base and 2 is the exponent. This means that 3 is multiplied by itself 2 times and the product is 9.

$$3^2 = 3 \times 3 = 9$$

An exponent can be either positive or negative. A negative exponent implies a fraction. Such that, if n is a positive integer

$$a^{-n} = \frac{1}{a^n}, a \neq 0. \text{ So, } 2^{-4} = \frac{1}{2^4} = \frac{1}{16}.$$

An exponent that is 0 gives a result of 1, assuming that the base is not equal to 0.

$$a^0 = 1, a \neq 0.$$

An exponent can also be a fraction. If m and n are positive integers,

$$a^{\frac{m}{n}} = \sqrt[n]{a^m}$$

The numerator remains the exponent of a, but the denominator tells what root to take. For example,

(1) $4^{\frac{3}{2}} = \sqrt[2]{4^3} = \sqrt{64} = 8$ (2) $3^{\frac{4}{2}} = \sqrt[2]{3^4} = \sqrt{81} = 9$

If a fractional exponent were negative, the same operation would take place, but the result would be a fraction. For example,

(1) $27^{-\frac{2}{3}} = \frac{1}{27^{2/3}} = \frac{1}{\sqrt[3]{27^2}} = \frac{1}{\sqrt[3]{729}} = \frac{1}{9}$

PROBLEM

Simplify the following expressions.

(1) -3^{-2}

(2) $(-3)^{-2}$

(3) $\dfrac{-3}{4^{-1}}$

Solution

(1) Here the exponent applies only to 3. Since

$$x^{-y} = \frac{1}{x^y}, \qquad -3^{-2} = -(3)^{-2} = -\frac{1}{3^2} = -\frac{1}{9}$$

(2) In this case the exponent applies to the negative base. Thus,

$$(3)^{-2} = \frac{1}{(-3)^2} = \frac{1}{(-3)(-3)} = \frac{1}{9}$$

(3) $\dfrac{-3}{4^{-1}} = \dfrac{-3}{\left(\dfrac{1}{4}\right)^1} = \dfrac{-3}{\dfrac{1^1}{4^1}} = \dfrac{-3}{\dfrac{1}{4}}$

Division by a fraction is equivalent to multiplication by that fraction's reciprocal, thus

$$\frac{-3}{\frac{1}{4}} = -3 \times \frac{4}{1} = -12 \quad \text{and} \quad \frac{-3}{4^{-1}} = -12$$

General Laws of Exponents

(A) $a^p a^q = a^{p+q}$

$$4^2 4^3 = 4^{2+3} = 1{,}024$$

(B) $(a^p)^q = a^{pq}$

$$(2^3)^2 = 2^6 = 64$$

(C) $\dfrac{a^p}{a^q} = a^{p-q}$

$$\frac{3^6}{3^2} = 3^4 = 81$$

(D) $(ab)^p = a^p b^p$

$$(3 \times 2)^2 = 3^2 \times 2^2 = (9)(4) = 36$$

(E) $\left(\dfrac{a}{b}\right)^p = \dfrac{a^p}{b^p}, \ b \neq 0$

$$\left(\frac{4}{5}\right)^2 = \frac{4^2}{5^2} = \frac{16}{25}$$

Scientific Notation

In **scientific notation** there is only one digit before the decimal point, and the remaining digits follow it. The base, a, is 10 and the exponent, n, is how many places the decimal point has been shifted. A negative exponent means the decimal point was shifted to the right and a positive exponent means the decimal point was shifted to the left.

EXAMPLES

$$5.23 \times 10^2 = 523$$
$$8.9 \times 10^{-4} = 0.00089$$

PROBLEM

Convert to scientific notation.

(1) 0.0042   (2) 25×10^3

Solution

(1)   0.004.2

Move the decimal point 3 places to the right.

$$4.2 \times 10^{-3}$$

(2) $25 \times 10^3 = 25 \times 1,000 = 2.5000.$

Move the decimal point 4 places to the left.

$$2.5 \times 10^4$$

Drill 6: Exponents and Scientific Notation

Multiplication

DIRECTIONS: Simplify.

→ add (handwritten)

1. $4^6 \times 4^2 =$

   (A) 4^4

   (B) 4^8 *(circled)*

   (C) 4^{12}

   (D) 16^8

   (E) 16^{12}

2. $2^2 \times 2^5 \times 2^3 =$

   (A) 2^{10} *(circled)*

   (B) 4^{10}

   (C) 8^{10}

   (D) 2^{30}

   (E) 8^{30}

3. $6^6 \times 6^2 \times 6^4 =$

   (A) 18^8

   (B) 18^{12}

   (C) 6^{12} *(circled)*

   (D) 6^{48}

   (E) 18^{48}

← invisible ! (handwritten)

4. $a^4b^2 \times a^3b =$

   a^7b^2 (handwritten)

   (A) ab

   (B) $2a^7b^2$

   (C) $2a^{12}b$

   (D) a^7b^3 *(circled)*

   (E) a^7b^2 *(circled)*

5. $m^8n^3 \times m^2n \times m^4n^2 =$

   (A) $3m^{16}n^6$

   (B) $m^{14}n^6$ *(circled)*

   (C) $3m^{14}n^5$

   (D) $3m^{14}n^5$

   (E) m^2

Division

DIRECTIONS: Simplify.

6. $6^5 \div 6^3 =$

   (A) 0

   (B) 1

   (C) 6

   (D) 12

   (E) 36

7. $11^8 \div 11^5 =$

   (A) 1^3

   (B) 11^3

   (C) 11^{13}

   (D) 11^{40}

   (E) 88^5

8. $x^{10}y^8 \div x^7 y^3 =$

   (A) $x^2 y^5$

   (B) $x^3 y^4$

   (C) $x^3 y^5$

   (D) $x^2 y^4$

   (E) $x^5 y^3$

9. $a^{14} \div a^9 =$

   (A) 1^5

   (B) a^5

   (C) $2a^5$

   (D) a^{23}

   (E) $2a^{23}$

10. $c^{17}d^{12}e^4 \div c^{12}d^8 e =$

   (A) $c^4 d^5 e^3$

   (B) $c^4 d^4 e^3$

   (C) $c^5 d^8 e^4$

   (D) $c^5 d^4 e^3$

   (E) $c^5 d^4 e^4$

Power to a Power

DIRECTIONS: Simplify.

11. $(3^6)^2 =$ multiply

3

    (A) 3^4 (B) 3^8

    (C) 3^{12} (D) 9^6

    (E) 9^8

12. $(4^3)^5 =$ 4^{15}

    (A) 4^2 (B) 2^{15}

    (C) 4^8 (D) 20^3

    (E) 4^{15}

13. $(a^4b^3)^2 =$ $a^8 b^6$

    (A) $(ab)^9$ (B) a^8b^6

    (C) $(ab)^{24}$ (D) a^6b^5

    (E) $2a^4b^3$

14. $(r^3p^6)^3 =$

    (A) r^9p^{18} (B) $(rp)^{12}$

    (C) r^6p^9 (D) $3r^3p^6$

    (E) $3r^9p^{18}$

15. $(m^6n^5q^3)^2 =$ 12

    (A) $2m^6n^5q^3$ (B) m^4n^3q

    (C) $m^8n^7q^5$ (D) $m^{12}n^{10}q^6$

    (E) $2m^{12}n^{10}q^6$

Scientific Notation

DIRECTIONS: Convert to scientific notation.

16. 0.0000415 4.15×10^{-5}

    (A) 4.15×10^5 (B) 4.15×10^{-4}

    (C) 4.15×10^{-7} (D) 4.15×10^{-5}

    (E) 4.15×10^{-6}

17. $12.1 \times \dfrac{1}{10^5}$ $\dfrac{12.1}{1}$ $\times \dfrac{2}{20^5}$

    (A) 1.21×10^{-5} (B) 1.21×10^6

    (C) 1.21×10^{-6} (D) 1.21×10^5

    (E) 1.21×10^{-4}

18. 50100.0

    (A) 5.01×10^{-1} (B) 5.01×10^3

    (C) 5.01×10^4 (D) 5.01×10^5

    (E) 5.01×10^6

19. 10.5

    (A) 1.05×10^1 (B) 1.05×10^2

    (C) 1.05×10^{-2} (D) 1.05×10^3

    (E) 1.05×10^{-1}

20. $\dfrac{1}{2,000}$ $\frac{1}{23}$

    (A) 2^3 (B) 2^{-3}

    (C) 5.0×10^{-3} (D) 5.0×10^{-4}

    (E) 2.0×10^{-3}

ARITHMETIC DRILLS

ANSWER KEY

Drill 1 – Integers and Real Numbers

1. (A)	9. (E)	17. (D)	25. (D)
2. (C)	10. (B)	18. (D)	26. (D)
3. (D)	11. (B)	19. (C)	27. (B)
4. (C)	12. (E)	20. (E)	28. (C)
5. (B)	13. (C)	21. (B)	29. (A)
6. (B)	14. (A)	22. (E)	30. (C)
7. (A)	15. (B)	23. (D)	
8. (C)	16. (B)	24. (A)	

Drill 2 – Fractions

1. (D)	14. (D)	27. (D)	40. (A)
2. (E)	15. (B)	28. (E)	41. (D)
3. (C)	16. (B)	29. (C)	42. (A)
4. (A)	17. (D)	30. (B)	43. (D)
5. (C)	18. (B)	31. (C)	44. (E)
6. (C)	19. (A)	32. (A)	45. (C)
7. (C)	20. (C)	33. (B)	46. (D)
8. (A)	21. (D)	34. (C)	47. (D)
9. (B)	22. (C)	35. (D)	48. (B)
10. (A)	23. (B)	36. (B)	49. (A)
11. (B)	24. (E)	37. (C)	50. (E)
12. (D)	25. (A)	38. (D)	
13. (E)	26. (A)	39. (E)	

Drill 3 – Decimals

1. (B)	9. (C)	17. (D)	25. (E)
2. (E)	10. (E)	18. (D)	26. (D)
3. (C)	11. (B)	19. (A)	27. (C)
4. (A)	12. (D)	20. (C)	28. (A)
5. (D)	13. (A)	21. (E)	29. (E)
6. (A)	14. (B)	22. (C)	30. (D)
7. (B)	15. (C)	23. (B)	
8. (D)	16. (B)	24. (D)	

Drill 4 – Percentages

1. (B)	9. (E)	17. (D)	25. (D)
2. (C)	10. (C)	18. (E)	26. (D)
3. (E)	11. (C)	19. (C)	27. (C)
4. (B)	12. (B)	20. (C)	28. (B)
5. (A)	13. (B)	21. (A)	29. (E)
6. (B)	14. (D)	22. (B)	30. (A)
7. (A)	15. (A)	23. (C)	
8. (B)	16. (E)	24. (B)	

Drill 5 – Radicals

1. (B)	6. (C)	11. (B)	16. (A)
2. (D)	7. (A)	12. (D)	17. (C)
3. (A)	8. (D)	13. (C)	18. (B)
4. (C)	9. (C)	14. (E)	19. (D)
5. (E)	10. (B)	15. (A)	20. (C)

Drill 6 – Exponents and Scientific Notation

1. (B)	6. (E)	11. (C)	16. (D)
2. (A)	7. (B)	12. (E)	17. (E)
3. (C)	8. (C)	13. (B)	18. (C)
4. (D)	9. (B)	14. (A)	19. (A)
5. (B)	10. (D)	15. (D)	20. (D)

ELM

Entry Level Mathematics

Chapter 2
Elementary Algebra
Review

ELEMENTARY ALGEBRA DIAGNOSTIC TEST

12 Questions

(Answer sheets appear at the back of the book.)

> **DIRECTIONS:** Each question has five multiple-choice answers. Select the single best answer.

1. Solve for the value of y:

    $3x + 2y = 12$

    $2x - 2y = 8$

    (A) 0

    (C) 3

    (E) 5

    (B) 2

    (D) 4

2. Simplify $(-4a^3x^4)^2$.

    (A) $-4a^5x^6$

    (C) $8a^6x^8$

    (E) $-16a^6x^8$

    (B) $8a^5x^6$

    (D) $16a^6x^8$

3. What is the factorization of $x^2 + ax - 2x - 2a$?

    (A) $(x+2)(x-a)$

    (C) $(x+2)(x+a)$

    (E) None of these

    (B) $(x-2)(x+a)$

    (D) $(x-2)(x-a)$

4. If $abc \neq 0$, then $\dfrac{3a^2bc^3 + 9a^3b^2c^4}{27ab^2c + 15a^2b^2c^3} =$

(A) $\dfrac{ab(c^2+3)}{c(9+5a)}$

(B) $\dfrac{a(c^2+3ab)}{b(9+5ac^2)}$

(C) $\dfrac{a(c^2+3ab)}{c(9+5ac^2)}$

(D) $\dfrac{c^2+3ab}{9+5ac^2}$

(E) $\dfrac{a}{c(9+5ac^2)}$

5. Find the sum of:

$$8x^2 - 4xy - y^2 - 4x^2 - 5xy - x^2 - 4xy + y^2 - 7y^2 + 2x^2$$

(A) $3x^2 - 9xy - 4y^2 - 2$

(B) $6x^2 - 13xy - 7y^2$

(C) $-18x^2y^2xy$

(D) $5x^2 - 13xy - 7y^2$

(E) $-13xy - 1$

6. $\dfrac{\dfrac{1}{x}-\dfrac{1}{y}}{\dfrac{1}{x^2}-\dfrac{1}{y^2}} =$

(A) $\dfrac{x^2y^2}{x^2+y^2}$

(B) $\dfrac{xy}{x+y}$

(C) $\dfrac{xy}{(x+y)^2}$

(D) $\dfrac{xy}{y^2-x^2}$

(E) $\left(\dfrac{xy}{x+y}\right)^2$

7. Find the roots of the following equation:

$$x^2 - 5x + 6 = 0$$

(A) 1 and 5   (B) 1 and 6

(C) 2 and 3   (D) 2 and 5

(E) 3 and 5

Handwritten: $(x-2)(x-3)=0$ $x = 2, 3$ $(x \quad 5)(x \quad 1)$ FOIL

8. Find the solution set of the following pair of equations:

$$\begin{cases} 3x + 4y = -6 \\ 5x + 6y = -8 \end{cases}$$

Handwritten: $8x + 16y = -24$

(A) $\{(1, 2)\}$ (B) $\{(1, 3)\}$

(C) $\{(2, 3)\}$ (D) $\{(2, -3)\}$

(E) $\{(3, -3)\}$

Handwritten: $25x + 20 = -30$ $15x + 18y = -24$ $20y = -60$ $(x \quad)(x \quad)$ $x^2 - 3x - 2x + 6$ $x^2 - 5x + 6$

9. Solve $3(x + 2) < 5x.$

(A) $x = 3$ (B) $x > 3$

(C) $x < 3$ (D) $x \geq 2$

(E) $x < -6$

Handwritten: $y = -3$ $5(x) - 18 = -8$ $+12 \quad +18$ $5x = 10$

10. Simplify $\dfrac{x^2 - y^2}{x^3 - x^2 y}.$

(A) $\dfrac{y}{x}$ (B) $\dfrac{x+y}{y}$

(C) $\dfrac{x-y}{x^2}$ (D) $\dfrac{x+y}{x^2}$

(E) $\dfrac{-y}{x^2 - x}$

11. Find the roots of $x^2 - 10x + 21 = 0$.

    (A) 10, 21

    (C) 3, 7

    (E) 0, 2.1

    (B) −3, −7

    (D) 1, 21

$x - 7 = 0$

$x - 3 = 0$

$x = 3, 7$

$(x - 3)(x - 7) = 0$

12. Which of the following is an equation of line ℓ?

    (A) $y = -3$

    (B) $x = 3$

    (C) $x = -3$

    (D) $y = 3$

    (E) $y = 3x$

$-7x - 3x$

ELEMENTARY ALGEBRA DIAGNOSTIC TEST

ANSWER KEY

1. (A)	4. (B)	7. (C)	10. (D)
2. (D)	5. (D)	8. (D)	11. (C)
3. (B)	6. (B)	9. (B)	12. (D)

DETERMINE YOUR STRENGTHS AND WEAKNESSES

ELEMENTARY ALGEBRA

Question Type	Question #	See Pages . . .
Operations with Polynomials	2, 5	81–88
Simplifying Algebraic Expressions	3, 6, 7, 10, 11	88–93
Rational Expressions	4, 6, 10	93–100
Linear Equations	1, 8	100–106
Two Linear Equations	1, 8	106–113
Quadratic Equations	7, 11	114–119
Inequalities	9	119–123
Graphs	12	123–127

DETAILED EXPLANATIONS OF ANSWERS

ELEMENTARY ALGEBRA DIAGNOSTIC TEST

1.   **(A)**
   Add like terms, and notice that the y column is eliminated.

$$3x + 2y = 12$$
$$\underline{2x - 2y = 8}$$
$$5x = 20$$
$$x = 4$$

Substitute the 4 for the x in the equation $3x + 2y = 12$.

$$3(4) + 2y = 12$$
$$12 + 2y = 12$$
$$2y = 0$$
$$y = 0$$

2.   **(D)**
   Rewrite each constant and variable separately.

$$(-4a^3x^4)^2 = (-4)^2 (a^3)^2 (x^4)^2$$

From the General Laws of Exponents

$$(a^p)^q = a^{pq}.$$

Therefore, the variables equal a^6x^8. Squaring a negative gives a positive number. Therefore, the correct answer is $16a^6x^8$.

3.   **(B)**
   First, group the expression and then find the monomial factor for each group as follows:

$$(x^2 + ax) + (-2x - 2a) = x(x + a) + (-2)(x + a).$$

Then, the final factorization is formed by using $(x + a)$ and $(x - 2)$. So,

$$x^2 + ax - 2x - 2a = (x - 2)(x + a).$$

4.   **(B)**

$$\frac{3a^2bc^3 + 9a^3b^2c}{27ab^2c + 15a^2b^2c^3} = \frac{3a^2bc(c^2 + 3ab)}{3ab^2c(9 + 5ac^2)}$$

$$= \frac{a(c^2 + 3ab)}{b(9 + 5ac^2)}$$

5.   **(D)**

Write each term under other like terms (like terms = expressions that contain exactly the same variables and the same exponents, but possibly different coefficients). In the terms y^2 and $-y^2$, the coefficient 1 is usually not written: ($y^2 = 1y^2$, $-y^2 = -1y^2$).

$$8x^2 - 4xy - y^2$$
$$-4x^2 - 5xy$$
$$x^2 - 4xy + y^2$$
$$\overline{+\ 2x^2 \qquad -7y^2}$$

To add the like terms, find the sum of the numerical coefficients and affix the common variable.

$$(8 - 4 - 1 + 2)x^2 + (-4 - 5 - 4)xy + (-1 + 1 - 7)y^2$$

$$= 5x^2 - 13xy - 7y^2$$

6.   **(B)**

$$\frac{\dfrac{1}{x} - \dfrac{1}{y}}{\dfrac{1}{x^2} - \dfrac{1}{y^2}} = \frac{\dfrac{y - x}{xy}}{\dfrac{y^2 - x^2}{x^2y^2}}$$

$$= \left(\frac{y-x}{xy}\right)\left(\frac{x^2y^2}{y^2-x^2}\right)$$

$$= (y-x)\left(\frac{xy}{(y+x)(y-x)}\right)$$

$$= \frac{xy}{x+y}$$

7. **(C)**

$$x^2 - 5x + 6 = 0$$

$$(x-2)(x-3) = 0$$

$$x = 2 \quad \text{or} \quad x = 3$$

8. **(D)**

$$\begin{cases} 3x + 4y = -6 & \quad (1) \\ 5x + 6y = -8 & \quad (2) \end{cases}$$

Multiply equation (1) by 3 and equation (2) by 2. Subtract equation (2) from equation (1):

$$9x + 12y = -18$$

$$-(10x + 12y = -16)$$

$$-x = -2$$

$$x = 2$$

Substitute $x = 2$ into (1):

$$3(2) + 4y = -6$$

$$4y = -12$$

$$y = -3$$

Therefore, the solution set is $\{(2, -3)\}$.

9. **(B)**

$$3(x + 2) < 5x$$

$$3x + 6 < 5x$$

Subtracting $3x$ from both sides.

$$6 < 2x$$

$$3 < x$$

Dividing both sides by 2.

10. **(D)**

$$\frac{x^2 - y^2}{x^3 - x^2y} = \frac{(x - y)(x + y)}{x^2(x - y)}$$

Factoring the numerator and denominator.

$$= \frac{x + y}{x^2}$$

11. **(C)**

$$x^2 - 10x + 21 = 0$$

$$(x - 3)(x - 7) = 0$$

$$x = 3 \quad \text{or} \quad x = 7$$

12. **(D)**
Look at some values of x and y.

x	y
0	3
−4	3
3	3

The value of x has no effect on y which is 3. This gives the equation $y = 3$.

ELEMENTARY ALGEBRA REVIEW

In algebra, letters or variables are used to represent numbers. A **variable** is defined as a placeholder, which can take on any of several values at a given time. A **constant**, on the other hand, is a symbol which takes on only one value at a given time. A **term** is a constant, a variable, or a combination of constants and variables. For example: 7.76, $3x$, xyz, $5z/x$, $(0.99)x^2$ are terms. If a term is a combination of constants and variables, the constant part of the term is referred to as the **coefficient** of the variable. If a variable is written without a coefficient, the coefficient is assumed to be 1.

EXAMPLES

$3x^2$

coefficient: 3

variable: x

y^3

coefficient: 1

variable: y

An **expression** is a collection of one or more terms. If the number of terms is greater than 1, the expression is said to be the sum of the terms.

EXAMPLES

9, $9xy$, $6x + x/3$, $8yz - 2x$

An algebraic expression consisting of only one term is called a **monomial;** of two terms is called a **binomial;** of three terms is called a **trinomial**. In general, an algebraic expression consisting of two or more terms is called a **polynomial**.

Review of Exponents with Variables

1. $a^p a^q = a^{p+q}$

    $x^2 x^3 = x^{2+3} = x^5$

2. $(a^p)^q = a^{pq}$

    $(y^4)^3 = y^{12}$

3. $\dfrac{a^p}{a^q} = a^{p-q}$

$\dfrac{z^5}{z^3} = z^{5-3} = z^2$

4. $(ab)^p = a^p b^p$

$(xy)^4 = x^4 y^4$

5. $\left(\dfrac{a}{b}\right)^p = \dfrac{a^p}{b^p}, \ b \neq 0$

$\left(\dfrac{y}{z}\right)^3 = \dfrac{y^3}{z^3}$

1. OPERATIONS WITH POLYNOMIALS

(A) **Addition of polynomials** is achieved by combining like terms, terms which differ only in their numerical coefficients. For example,

$$P(x) = (x^2 - 3x + 5) + (4x^2 + 6x - 3)$$

Note that the parentheses are used to distinguish the polynomials.

By using the commutative and associative laws, we can rewrite $P(x)$ as:

$$P(x) = (x^2 + 4x^2) + (6x - 3x) + (5 - 3)$$

Using the distributive law, $ab + ac = a(b + c)$, yields:

$$(1 + 4)x^2 + (6 - 3)x + (5 - 3) = 5x^2 + 3x + 2$$

(B) **Subtraction of two polynomials** is achieved by first changing the sign of all terms in the expression which is being subtracted and then adding this result to the other expression. For example,

$$(5x^2 + 4y^2 + 3z^2) - (4xy + 7y^2 - 3z^2 + 1)$$

$$= 5x^2 + 4y^2 + 3z^2 - 4xy - 7y^2 + 3z^2 - 1$$

$$= (5x^2) + (4y^2 - 7y^2) + (3z^2 + 3z^2) - 4xy - 1$$

$$= 5x^2 - 3y^2 + 6z^2 - 4xy - 1$$

(C) **Multiplication of two or more monomials** is achieved by using the laws of exponents, the rules of signs, and the commutative and associative laws of multiplication. Begin by multiplying the coefficients and then multiply the variables according to the laws of exponents. For example,

$$(y^2) (5) (6y^2) (yz) (2z^2)$$

$$= (1) (5) (6) (1) (2) (y^2) (y^2) (yz) (z^2)$$

$$= 60[(y^2) (y^2) (y)] [(z) (z^2)]$$

$$= 60(y^5) (z^3)$$

$$= 60y^5z^3$$

(D) **Multiplication of a polynomial by a monomial** is achieved by multiplying each term of the polynomial by the monomial and combining the results. For example,

$$(4x^2 + 3y) (6xz^2)$$

$$= (4x^2) (6xz^2) + (3y) (6xz^2)$$

$$= 24x^3z^2 + 18xyz^2$$

(E) **Multiplication of a polynomial by a polynomial** is achieved by multiplying each of the terms of one polynomial by each of the terms of the other polynomial and combining the results. For example,

$$(5y + z + 1) (y^2 + 2y)$$

$$[(5y) (y^2) + (5y) (2y)] + [(z) (y^2) + (z) (2y)] + [(1) (y^2) + (1) (2y)]$$

$$= (5y^3 + 10y^2) + (y^2z + 2yz) + (y^2 + 2y)$$

$$= (5y^3) + (10y^2 + y^2) + (y^2z) + (2yz) + (2y)$$

$$= 5y^3 + 11y^2 + y^2z + 2yz + 2y$$

(F) **Division of a monomial by a monomial** is achieved by first dividing the constant coefficients and the variable factors separately, and then multiplying these quotients. For example,

$$6xyz^2 \div 2y^2z$$

$$= (6/2) (x/1) (y/y^2) (z^2/z)$$

$$= 3xy^{-1}z$$

$$= 3xz/y$$

(G) **Division of a polynomial by a polynomial** is achieved by following the given procedure called long division.

Step 1: The terms of both the polynomials are arranged in order of ascending or descending powers of one variable.

Step 2: The first term of the dividend is divided by the first term of the divisor which gives the first term of the quotient.

Step 3: This first term of the quotient is multiplied by the entire divisor and the result is subtracted from the dividend.

Step 4: Using the remainder obtained from Step 3 as the new dividend, Steps 2 and 3 are repeated until the remainder is zero or the degree of the remainder is less than the degree of the divisor.

Step 5: The result is written as follows:

$$\frac{\text{dividend}}{\text{divisor}} = \text{quotient} + \frac{\text{remainder}}{\text{divisor}}$$

$$\text{divisor} \neq 0$$

e.g., $(2x^2 + x + 6) \div (x + 1)$

$$
\begin{array}{r}
2x - 1 \\
x + 1 \overline{\smash{\big)}\ 2x^2 + x + 6} \\
-(2x^2 + 2x) \\
\hline
-x + 6 \\
-(-x - 1) \\
\hline
7
\end{array}
$$

The result is

$$(2x^2 + x + 6) \div (x + 1) = 2x - 1 + \frac{7}{x+1}$$

Drill 1: Operations with Polynomials

Addition

1. $9a^2b + 3c + 2a^2b + 5c =$

    (A) $19a^2bc$

    (B) $11a^2b + 8c$

    (C) $11a^4b^2 + 8c^2$

    (D) $19a^4b^2c^2$

    (E) $12a^2b + 8c^2$

2. $14m^2n^3 + 6m^2n^3 + 3m^2n^3 =$ *23m⁶n⁹*

   (A) $20m^2n^3$ (B) $23m^6n^9$

   (C) $23m^2n^3$ (D) $32m^6n^9$

   (E) $23m^8n^{27}$

3. $3x + 2y + 16x + 3z + 6y =$ *19x + 8y + 3z*

   (A) $19x + 8y$ (B) $19x + 11yz$

   (C) $19x + 8y + 3z$ (D) $11xy + 19xz$

   (E) $30xyz$

4. $(4d^2 + 7e^3 + 12f) + (3d^2 + 6e^3 + 2f) =$ *7d² + 13e³ 14z²*

   (A) $23d^2e^3f$ (B) $33d^2e^2f$

   (C) $33d^4e^6f^2$ (D) $7d^2 + 13e^3 + 14f$

   (E) $23d^2 + 11e^3f$

5. $3ac^2 + 2b^2c + 7ac^2 + 2ac^2 + b^2c =$ *12a³c⁶ + 3b⁴c²*

   (A) $12ac^2 + 3b^2c$ (B) $14ab^2c^2$

   (C) $11ac^2 + 4ab^2c$ (D) $15ab^2c^2$

   (E) $15a^2b^4c^4$

Subtraction

6. $14m^2n - 6m^2n =$ *8m²n*

   (A) $20m^2n$ (B) $8m^2n$

   (C) $8m$ (D) 8

   (E) $8m^4n^2$

7. $3x^3y^2 - 4xz - 6x^3y^2 =$ *−3x³y²− 4xz*

   (A) $-7x^2y^2z$ (B) $3x^3y^2 - 10x^4y^2z$

   (C) $-3x^3y^2 - 4xz$ (D) $-x^2y^2z - 6x^3y^2$

   (E) $-7xyz$

8. $9g^2 + 6h - 2g^2 - 5h =$ $7g^2 - 1h$

(A) $15g^2h - 7g^2h$ (B) $7g^4h^2$

(C) $11g^2 + 7h$ (D) $11g^2 - 7h^2$

(E) $7g^2 + h$

9. $7b^3 - 4c^2 - 6b^3 + 3c^2 =$ $b^3 - c^2$

(A) $b^3 - c^2$ (B) $-11b^2 - 3c^2$

(C) $13b^3 - c$ (D) $7b - c$

(E) 0

10. $11q^2r - 4q^2r - 8q^2r =$ $-1q^2r$

(A) $22q^2r$ (B) q^2r

(C) $-2q^2r$ (D) $-q^2r$

(E) $2q^2r$

Multiplication

$15p^at^2$

11. $5p^2t \times 3p^2t =$

(A) $15p^2t$ (B) $15p^4t$

(C) $15p^4t^2$ (D) $8p^2t$

(E) $8p^4t^2$

12. $(2r + s)\,14r =$

(A) $28rs$ (B) $28r^2 + 14sr$

(C) $16r^2 + 14rs$ (D) $28r + 14sr$

(E) $17r^2s$

13. $(4m + p)(3m - 2p) =$

(A) $12m^2 + 5mp + 2p^2$ (B) $12m^2 - 2mp + 2p^2$

(C) $7m - p$ (D) $12m - 2p$

(E) $12m^2 - 5mp - 2p^2$

$-8mp + 3mp$

14. $(2a + b)(3a^2 + ab + b^2) =$

    (A) $6a^3 + 5a^2b + 3ab^2 + b^3$

    (B) $5a^3 + 3ab + b^3$

    (C) $6a^3 + 2a^2b + 2ab^2$

    (D) $3a^2 + 2a + ab + b + b^2$

    (E) $6a^3 + 3a^2b + 5ab^2 + b^3$

$6a^3 + 2a^2b + b^3 + 3a^2b + ab^2 + b^3$

$6a^3 + 5a^4b^2 + b^6$

15. $(6t^2 + 2t + 1)\, 3t =$ $18t^3 + 6t^2 + 3t$

    (A) $9t^2 + 5t + 3$ (B) $18t^2 + 6t + 3$

    (C) $9t^3 + 6t^2 + 3t$ (D) $18t^3 + 6t^2 + 3t$

    (E) $12t^3 + 6t^2 + 3t$

Division

$x-2\,\overline{)\,x^2 + x - 6}$

16. $(x^2 + x - 6) \div (x - 2) =$

    (A) $x - 3$ (B) $x + 2$

    (C) $x + 3$ (D) $x - 2$

    (E) $2x + 2$

17. $24b^4c^3 \div 6b^2c =$

    (A) $3b^2c^2$ (B) $4b^4c^3$

    (C) $4b^3c^2$ (D) $4b^2c^2$

    (E) $3b^4c^3$

18. $(3p^2 + pq - 2q^2) \div (p + q) =$

    (A) $3p + 2q$ (B) $2q - 3p$

    (C) $3p - q$ (D) $2q + 3p$

    (E) $3p - 2q$

19. $(y^3 - 2y^2 - y + 2) \div (y - 2) =$

    (A) $(y - 1)^2$ (B) $y^2 - 1$

    (C) $(y + 2)(y - 1)$ (D) $(y + 1)^2$

    (E) $(y + 1)(y - 2)$

20. $(m^2 + m - 14) \div (m + 4) =$

(A) $m - 2$

(B) $m - 3 + \dfrac{-2}{m + 4}$

(C) $m - 3 + \dfrac{4}{m + 4}$

(D) $m - 3$

(E) $m - 2 + \dfrac{-3}{m + 4}$

2. SIMPLIFYING ALGEBRAIC EXPRESSIONS

To factor a polynomial completely is to find the prime factors of the polynomial with respect to a specified set of numbers.

The following concepts are important while factoring or simplifying expressions.

1. The factors of an algebraic expression consist of two or more algebraic expressions which when multiplied together produce the given algebraic expression.

2. A **prime factor** is a polynomial with no factors other than itself and 1. The **least common multiple** (**LCM**) for a set of numbers is the smallest quantity divisible by every number of the set. For algebraic expressions the least common numerical coefficients for each of the given expressions will be a factor.

3. The **greatest common factor** (**GCF**) for a set of numbers is the largest factor that is common to all members of the set. For algebraic expressions, the greatest common factor is the polynomial of highest degree and the largest numerical coefficient which is a factor of all the given expressions.

Some important formulae useful for the factoring of polynomials are listed below.

(A) $ac + ad = a(c + d)$

Remember to factor out all common monomial factors first.

$3x^2 - 6x = 3x(x - 2)$

(B) $a^2 - b^2 = (a + b)(a - b)$

$a^3 + b^3 = (a + b)(a^2 - ab + b^2)$

$$a^3 - b^3 = (a - b)(a^2 + ab + b^2)$$

Look for easily recognizable patterns: the **difference of the squares,** the **sum of two cubes,** and the **difference of two cubes.**

$$w^2 - 16 = (w + 4)(w - 4)$$

$$a^3 - 125 = (a - 5)(a^2 + 5b + 25)$$

Here are the perfect square integers less than 300:

1, 4, 9, 16, 25, 36, 49, 64, 81, 100, 121, 144, 169, 196, 225, 256, and 289.

Here are the perfect cubes less than 600:

1, 8, 27, 64, 125, 216, 343, and 512.

If a perfect square is with a squared variable, look to factor by using the formula for the difference of the squares. If a perfect cube is with a cubed variable, look to factor by the difference of two cubes or the sum of two cubes.

(C) $a^2 + 2ab + b^2 = (a + b)^2 = (a + b)(a + b)$

$a^2 - 2ab + b^2 = (a - b)^2 = (a - b)(a - b)$

A **perfect square trinomial** is another special product formula.

$$z^2 + 6z + 9 = z^2 + 2(3)z + 3^2$$

$$= (z + 3)(z + 3) = (z + 3)^2$$

(D) $x^2 + (a + b)x + ab = (x + a)(x + b)$

To factor binomials with the lead coefficient of one just list the factors of the third term of the trinomial. Then pick the factorization in which the sum of factors is the coefficient of the middle term.

$$x^2 - 6x + 8$$

The factors of the third term are

8(1), 4(2), − 8(− 1), and − 4(− 2).

The sums of the factors are

9, 6, − 9, and − 6.

Therefore, the factorization of $x^2 - 6x + 8 =$

$(x - 4)(x - 2)$.

(E) $acx^2 + (ad + bc)x + bd = (ax + b)(cx + d)$

$5x^2 + 7x + 2 = (5x + 2)(x + 1)$

If the trinomial is of the form $ax^2 + bx + c$, the trinomial will factor into two binomials with integer coefficients if the value of $b^2 - 4ac$ is a perfect square. Using the example above $a = 5$, $b = 7$, and $c = 2$.

$7^2 - 4(5)(2) = 49 - 40 = 9$

which is a perfect square.

(F) $ac + bc + ad + bd = (a + b)(c + d)$

Sometimes **factoring by grouping** can be used although there is no factor common to all four terms.

$3x^3y - 4x^2y^2 - 6x^2y + 8xy^2$

$xy(3x^2 - 4xy - 6x + 8y)$

Factor out all common monomial factors.

$xy(x(3x - 4y) - 2(3x - 4y))$

Factor by grouping.

$xy(x - 2)(3x - 4y)$

(G) $(a + b)^3 = a^3 + 3a^2b + 3ab^2 + b^3 = (a + b)(a + b)(a + b)$

$(a - b)^3 = a^3 - 3a^2b + 3ab^2 - b^3 = (a - b)(a - b)(a - b)$

$a^2 + b^2 + c^2 + 2ab + 2ac + 2bc = (a + b + c)^2$

$a^4 - b^4 = (a - b)(a^3 + a^2b + ab^2 + b^3)$

$a^5 - b^5 = (a - b)(a^4 + a^3b + a^2b^2 + ab^3 + b^4)$

$a^6 - b^6 = (a - b)(a^5 + a^4b + a^3b^2 + a^2b^3 + ab^4 + b^5)$

$a^n - b^n = (a - b)(a^{n-1} + a^{n-2}b + a^{n-3}b^2 + \ldots + ab^{n-2} + b^{n-1})$

where n is any positive integer (1, 2, 3, 4, ...).

$a^n + b^n = (a + b)(a^{n-1} - a^{n-2}b + a^{n-3}b^2 - \ldots - ab^{n-2} + b^{n-1})$

where n is any positive odd integer (1, 3, 5, 7, ...).

The above lists some formulae that are common with higher degree polynomials. Become familiar with their appearance. Concentrate on the methods (A) through (F) since most expressions will be simplified using those formulae.

The procedure for factoring an algebraic expression completely is as follows:

Step 1: First find the greatest common factor if there is any. Then examine each factor remaining for greatest common factors.

Step 2: Continue factoring the factors obtained in Step 1 until all factors other than monomial factors are prime.

EXAMPLE

Factoring $4 - 16x^2$,

$$4 - 16x^2 = 4(1 - 4x^2) = 4(1 + 2x)(1 - 2x)$$

PROBLEM

Express each of the following as a single term.

(1) $3x^2 + 2x^2 - 4x^2$

(2) $5axy^2 - 7axy^2 - 3xy^2$

Solution

(1)   Factor x^2 in the expression.

$$3x^2 + 2x^2 - 4x^2 = (3 + 2 - 4)x^2 = 1x^2 = x^2$$

(2)   Factor xy^2 in the expression and then factor a.

$$5axy^2 - 7axy^2 - 3xy^2 = (5a - 7a - 3)xy^2$$
$$= [(5 - 7)a - 3]xy^2$$
$$= (-2a - 3)xy^2$$

Drill 2: Simplifying Algebraic Expressions

1. $16b^2 - 25z^2 =$

(A) $(4b - 5z)^2$ (B) $(4b + 5z)^2$

(C) $(4b - 5z)(4b + 5z)$ (D) $(16b - 25z)^2$

(E) $(5z - 4b)(5z + 4b)$

$x^2 + 2x - 4x - 8$

2. $x^2 - 2x - 8 =$ $(x - 4)(x + 2)$

   (A) $(x - 4)^2$

   (B) $(x - 6)(x - 2)$

   (C) $(x + 4)(x - 2)$

   (D) $(x - 4)(x + 2)$

   (E) $(x - 4)(x - 2)$

3. $2c^2 + 5cd - 3d^2 =$

   (A) $(c - 3d)(c + 2d)$

   (B) $(2c - d)(c + 3d)$

   (C) $(c - d)(2c + 3d)$

   (D) $(2c + d)(c + 3d)$

   (E) Not possible

$(2c + 3d)(2c$

4. $4t^3 - 20t =$

   (A) $4t(t^2 - 5)$

   (B) $4t^2(t - 20)$

   (C) $4t(t + 4)(t - 5)$

   (D) $2t(2t^2 - 10)$

   (E) Not possible

$4t(t^2 - 5)$

5. $x^2 + xy - 2y^2 =$

   $x^2 + xy - 2y$

   (A) $(x - 2y)(x + y)$

   (B) $(x - 2y)(x - y)$

   (C) $(x + 2y)(x + y)$

   (D) $(x + 2y)(x - y)$ $x^2 - yx + 2yx$

   (E) Not possible

$(x + 2y)(x - y)$

6. $5b^2 + 17bd + 6d^2 =$

   x^2

   (A) $(5b + d)(b + 6d)$

   (B) $(5b + 2d)(b + 3d)$

   (C) $(5b - 2d)(b - 3d)$

   (D) $(5b - 2d)(b + 3d)$

   (E) Not possible

$(5b + 2d)(b + 3d)$

$15b + 2b + 6d^2$

7. $x^2 + x + 1 =$

   (A) $(x + 1)^2$

   (B) $(x + 2)(x - 1)$ $-1x + 2x$

   (C) $(x - 2)(x + 1)$

   (D) $(x + 1)(x - 1)$ $-1x + 1x$

   (E) Not possible

$(x \quad)(x \quad)$

8. $3z^3 + 6z^2 =$

   (A) $3(z^3 + 2z^2)$

   (B) $3z^2(z + 2)$

$3z^3 + 6z^2$ $3z^2(z + 2z)$

(C) $3z(z^2 + 2z)$

(D) $z^2(3z + 6)$

(E) $3z^2(1 + 2z)$

9. $m^2p^2 + mpq - 6q^2 =$ *[handwritten: 3q⁶]*

   (A) $(mp - 2q)(mp + 3q)$

   (B) $mp(mp - 2q)(mp + 3q)$

   (C) $mpq(1 - 6q)$

   (D) $(mp + 2q)(mp + 3q)$

   (E) Not possible

[handwritten: m²p² + 3mpq - 2]

10. $2h^3 + 2h^2t - 4ht^2 =$ *[handwritten crossed out]*

   (A) $2(h^3 - t)(h + t)$

   (B) $2h(h - 2t)^2$

   (C) $4h(ht - t^2)$

   (D) $2h(h + t) - 4ht^2$

   (E) $2h(h + 2t)(h - t)$

[handwritten: 2h(h² + ht - t²)]

3. RATIONAL EXPRESSIONS

A **rational expression** is an algebraic fraction such as

$$\frac{x^2 + 3}{x - 4}.$$

Operations with rational expressions use the same principles as arithmetic fractions.

(A) **To simplify a rational expression** means to reduce it to its lowest terms. To do this factor both the numerator and the denominator and divide out all common factors. For example,

$$\frac{x^2 - 1}{x^2 + 2x + 1} = \frac{(x+1)(x-1)}{(x+1)(x+1)} = \frac{x-1}{x+1}$$

(B) **To multiply and divide rational expressions** use factoring. Remember, division is carried out by inverting the divisor and multiplying. For example,

$$\left(\frac{x^2 + 2x + 1}{x}\right)\left(\frac{x^2 - x}{x^2 - 1}\right)$$

$$\left(\frac{(x+1)(x+1)}{x}\right)\left(\frac{x(x-1)}{(x-1)(x+1)}\right) = x+1$$

$$\frac{3x^2 - x - 2}{6x^2 - 5x - 6} \div \frac{2x^2 + 5x + 3}{4x^2 - 9}$$

$$\left(\frac{3x^2 - x - 2}{6x^2 - 5x - 6}\right)\left(\frac{4x^2 - 9}{2x^2 + 5x + 3}\right)$$

$$\left(\frac{(3x+2)(x-1)}{(2x-3)(3x+2)}\right)\left(\frac{(2x-3)(2x+3)}{(2x+3)(x+1)}\right) = \frac{x-1}{x+1}$$

(C) **To add or subtract rational expressions**, a common denominator must be found. As in arithmetic fractions the Lowest Common Denominator (LCD) is used. For example,

$$\frac{x}{x+1} + \frac{2}{x^2 - 1}$$

Factor $x^2 - 1 = (x + 1)(x - 1)$. Therefore, the LCD is $(x + 1)(x - 1)$.

$$\frac{x(x-1)}{(x+1)(x-1)} + \frac{2}{(x+1)(x-1)} = \frac{x}{(x+1)(x-1)}$$

$$= \frac{(x-2)(x+1)}{(x+1)(x-1)}$$

$$= \frac{x-2}{x-1}$$

Note: By keeping the denominator in factored form it is easier to see if any further simplification can be done after the addition or subtraction.

PROBLEM

Simplify $\dfrac{\dfrac{1}{x-1} - \dfrac{1}{x-2}}{\dfrac{1}{x-2} + \dfrac{1}{x-3}}$.

Solution

Simplify the expression in the numerator by using the addition rule:

$$\frac{a}{b} + \frac{c}{d} = \frac{ad + bc}{bd}$$

Notice *bd* is the Lowest Common Denominator, LCD. We obtain

$$\frac{x-2-(x-1)}{(x-1)(x-2)} = \frac{-1}{(x-1)(x-2)}$$

in the numerator.

Repeat this procedure for the expression in the denominator:

$$\frac{x-3-(x-2)}{(x-2)(x-3)} = \frac{-1}{(x-2)(x-3)}$$

We now have

$$\frac{\dfrac{-1}{(x-1)(x-2)}}{\dfrac{-1}{(x-2)(x-3)}}$$

which is simplified by inverting the fraction in the denominator and multiplying it by the numerator and cancelling like terms.

$$\frac{-1}{(x-1)(x-2)} \times \frac{(x-2)(x-3)}{-1} = \frac{x-3}{x-1}$$

A form of simplification of rational expressions that is easy to simplify is

$$\frac{a-b}{b-a}.$$

To simplify factor (− 1) from the numerator.

$$\frac{(-1)(-a+b)}{b-a} = -1$$

Recognizing this form when working with rational expressions will be helpful in finding the simplest solution.

Drill 3: Rational Expressions

Simplification

1. $\dfrac{x+y}{x^2-y^2}$ =

   (A) $x^3 - y^3$

   (B) $\dfrac{1}{x-y}$

   (C) $x - y$

   (D) $\dfrac{1}{y-x}$

   (E) $\dfrac{1}{x^2-y^2}$

2. $\dfrac{-24x^3y^4}{18x^4y^3}$ = $\dfrac{-12}{9}$ = $-\dfrac{4}{3}\dfrac{y}{x}$

   (A) $\dfrac{-4x}{3y}$

   (B) $\dfrac{4y^7}{3x^7}$

   (C) $\dfrac{-4y}{3x}$ $\dfrac{10}{1}$

   (D) $\dfrac{6y}{x}$

   (E) $\dfrac{-4}{3x^7y^7}$

3. $\dfrac{4x^2+8x+3}{6+x-2x^2}$ =

   (A) $\dfrac{2x+1}{2-x}$

   (B) $2x^2 + 9x + 9$

   (C) $\dfrac{2x+3}{2-x}$

   (D) $\dfrac{2x+1}{3+2x}$

   (E) $\dfrac{(2x+3)^2}{2-x}$

4. $\dfrac{x^2-9}{x^2x-6} =$

(A) $\dfrac{x-3}{x+2}$

(B) $\dfrac{2x^2}{-x}$

(C) $\dfrac{x+3}{x-3}$

(D) $\dfrac{-3}{x}$

(E) $\dfrac{x+3}{x+2}$

5. $\dfrac{(5x+5y)(2x-y)}{y-2x} =$

(A) $-5(x+y)$

(B) $5(2x-y)$

(C) $-5(x-y)$

(D) $5(x+y)$

(E) $10xy$

Multiplication and Division

6. $(x+1)\left(\dfrac{1}{x^2+2x+1}\right) =$

(A) $\dfrac{1}{(x+1)^3}$

(B) $(x+1)^3$

(C) $\dfrac{1}{x^2+x}$

(D) $\dfrac{1}{x+1}$

(E) $(x+1)$

7. $\dfrac{x^2-16}{x^2-25} \div \dfrac{x+4}{x-5} =$

(A) $\dfrac{(x+4)^2}{(x-5)^2}$

(B) $\dfrac{x-4}{x+5}$

(C) $\dfrac{x+4}{x-5}$

(D) $\dfrac{x+5}{x-4}$

(E) $\dfrac{x-4}{x-5}$

8. $\dfrac{\dfrac{x-1}{x+2}}{\dfrac{x^2-x}{x^2+2x}} =$

(A) -1

(B) $2x$

(C) $\dfrac{(x-1)^2}{(x+2)^2}$

(D) $\dfrac{x^2+x-1}{x^2+2}$

(E) 1

9. $\left(\dfrac{2x^2}{y}\right)\left(\dfrac{y^2}{x^3}\right) =$

(A) $\dfrac{2x^5}{y^3}$

(B) $\dfrac{y}{2x}$

(C) $\dfrac{2y}{x}$

(D) $\dfrac{2x^2+y^2}{y+x^3}$

(E) $2x-y$

10. $\left(\dfrac{a+3}{a-5}\right)\left(\dfrac{2a-10}{3a+9}\right) =$

(A) $\dfrac{2}{3}$

(B) $\dfrac{(a+3)^2}{(a-5)^2}$

(C) $\dfrac{2a+3}{3a-5}$

(D) $\dfrac{2(a+3)}{3(a-5)}$

(E) $\dfrac{3}{2}$

Addition and Subtraction

11. $\dfrac{2}{x-3} + \dfrac{5}{x+2} =$

(A) $\dfrac{7}{(x-3)(x+2)}$ (B) $\dfrac{7}{2x-1}$

(C) $\dfrac{7x-11}{(x-3)(x+2)}$ (D) $\dfrac{7x+3}{(x-3)(x+2)}$

(E) $\dfrac{2(x+2)}{5(x-3)}$

12. $\dfrac{x+8}{x-3} - \dfrac{x-14}{3-x} =$

(A) -2 (B) $\dfrac{6}{(x-3)^3}$

(C) $\dfrac{x+8}{x-14}$ (D) 6

(E) 2

13. $\dfrac{3x}{x-1} - 2x - x^2 =$

(A) $\dfrac{-x^3 - x^2 + 5x}{x-1}$ (B) $\dfrac{-x^2 + x}{x-1}$

(C) $\dfrac{x^3 - x^2 + 5x}{x-1}$ (D) $\dfrac{3x}{x-1}$

(E) $\dfrac{x^2 + x}{x-1}$

14. $\dfrac{3}{x+2} + \dfrac{5}{x-4} =$

(A) $\dfrac{8x-2}{(x+2)(x-4)}$ (B) -4

(C) $\dfrac{8x-14}{(x+2)(x-4)}$ (D) $\dfrac{15(x-4)}{x+2}$

(E) $\dfrac{6x}{(x+2)(x-4)}$

15. $\dfrac{x+2}{x+5} - \dfrac{x-3}{x+7} =$

(A) $\dfrac{-1}{2}$ (B) $\dfrac{3x+31}{(x+5)(x+7)}$

(C) $\dfrac{2x^2+11x-1}{(x+5)(x+7)}$ (D) $\dfrac{7x+29}{(x+5)(x+7)}$

(E) $\dfrac{7x+29}{(x+2)(x-3)}$

4. EQUATIONS

An **equation** is defined as a statement that two separate expressions are equal.

A **solution** to the equation is a number that makes the equation true when it is substituted for the variable. For example, in the equation $3x = 18$, 6 is the solution since $3(6) = 18$. Depending on the equation, there can be more than one solution. The set of numbers that are permissible values for a variable is the **domain**. The numbers in the domain that satisfy the equation are in the **solution set** of the equation. Equations with the same solutions are said to be **equivalent equations**. An equation without a solution is said to have a solution set that is the **empty** or **null** set and is represented by ϕ.

Replacing an expression within an equation by an equivalent expression will result in a new equation with solutions equivalent to the original equation. Given the equation below

$$3x + y + x + 2y = 15$$

by combining like terms, we get,

$$3x + y + x + 2y = 4x + 3y$$

Since these two expressions are equivalent, we can substitute the simpler form into the equation to get

$$4x + 3y = 15.$$

Performing the same operation to both sides of an equation by the same expression will result in a new equation that is equivalent to the original equation.

1. **Addition or subtraction**

$$y + 6 = 10$$

We can add (− 6) to both sides.

$$y + 6 + (-6) = 10 + (-6)$$

$$y + 0 = 10 - 6$$

$$y = 4$$

2. **Multiplication or division**

$$3x = 6$$

$$3x/3 = 6/3$$

$$x = 2$$

$3x = 6$ is equivalent to $x = 2$.

3. **Raising to a power**

$$a = x^2 y$$

$$a^2 = (x^2 y)^2$$

$$a^2 = x^4 y^2$$

This can be applied to negative and fractional powers as well. For example,

$$x^2 = 3y^4$$

If we raise both members to the − 2 power, we get

$$(x^2)^{-2} = (3y^4)^{-2}$$

$$\frac{1}{(x^2)^2} = \frac{1}{(3y^4)^2}$$

$$\frac{1}{x^4} = \frac{1}{9y^8}$$

If we raise both members to the $\frac{1}{2}$ power, which is the same as taking the square root, we get:

$$(x^2)^{1/2} = (3y^4)^{1/2}$$

$$x = \sqrt{3}y^2$$

4.   The **reciprocal** of both members of an equation is equivalent to the original equation. Note: The reciprocal of 0 is undefined.

$$\frac{2x+y}{z} = \frac{5}{2} \qquad\qquad \frac{z}{2x+y} = \frac{2}{5}$$

PROBLEM

Solve, justifying each step. $3x - 8 = 7x + 8$

Solution

	$3x - 8 = 7x + 8$
Adding 8 to both sides,	$3x - 8 + 8 = 7x + 8 + 8$
Additive inverse property,	$3x + 0 = 7x + 16$
Additive identity property,	$3x = 7x + 16$
Adding $(-7x)$ to both sides,	$3x - 7x = 7x + 16 - 7x$
Commuting,	$-4x = 7x - 7x + 16$
Additive inverse property,	$-4x = 0 + 16$
Additive identity property,	$-4x = 16$
Dividing both sides by -4,	$x = {}^{16}/_{-4}$
	$x = -4$

Check: Replacing x by -4 in the original equation:

$$3x - 8 = 7x + 8$$

$$3(-4) - 8 = 7(-4) + 8$$

$$-12 - 8 = -28 + 8$$

$$-20 = -20$$

Linear Equations

A linear equation with one unknown is one that can be put into the form $ax + b = 0$, where a and b are constants, $a \neq 0$.

To solve a linear equation means to transform it into the form $x = -b/a$.

1. If the equation has unknowns on both sides of the equality, it is convenient to put similar terms on the same sides. For example,

    $$4x + 3 = 2x + 9$$

    $$4x + 3 - 2x = 2x + 9 - 2x$$

    $$(4x - 2x) + 3 = (2x - 2x) + 9$$

    $$2x + 3 = 0 + 9$$

    $$2x + 3 - 3 = 0 + 9 - 3$$

    $$2x = 6$$

    $$2x/2 = 6/2$$

    $$x = 3$$

2. If the equation appears in fractional form, it is necessary to transform it, using cross multiplication, and then repeating the same procedure as in 1, we obtain:

    $$\frac{3x + 4}{3} \qquad \frac{7x + 2}{5}$$

    By using cross multiplication we would obtain:

    $$3(7x + 2) = 5(3x + 4).$$

    This is equivalent to:

    $$21x + 6 = 15x + 20,$$

    which can be solved as in 1:

    $$21x + 6 = 15x + 20$$

    $$21x - 15x + 6 = 15x - 15x + 20$$

    $$6x + 6 - 6 = 20 - 6$$

    $$6x = 14$$

    $$x = 14/6$$

$$x = {}^7/_3$$

3. If there are radicals in the equation, it is necessary to square both sides and then apply 1:

$$\sqrt{3x+1} = 5$$

$$\left(\sqrt{3x+1}\right)^2 = 5^2$$

$$3x + 1 = 25$$

$$3x + 1 - 1 = 25 - 1$$

$$3x = 24$$

$$x = {}^{24}/_3$$

$$x = 8$$

PROBLEM

Solve the equation $2(x + 3) = (3x + 5) - (x - 5)$.

Solution

We transform the given equation to an equivalent equation where we can easily recognize the solution set.

$$2(x + 3) = 3x + 5 - (x - 5)$$

Distribute, $\qquad 2x + 6 = 3x + 5 - x + 5$

Combine terms, $\qquad 2x + 6 = 2x + 10$

Subtract $2x$ from both sides, $\qquad 6 = 10$

Since $6 = 10$ is not a true statement, there is no real number which will make the original equation true. The equation is inconsistent and the solution set is ϕ, the empty set.

PROBLEM

Solve the equation $2({}^2/_3y + 5) + 2(y + 5) = 130$.

Solution

The procedure for solving this equation is as follows:

$${}^4/_3y + 10 + 2y + 10 = 130, \qquad \text{Distributive property}$$

$${}^4/_3y + 2y + 20 = 130, \qquad \text{Combining like terms}$$

$$^4/_3y + 2y = 110, \quad \text{Subtracting 20 from both sides}$$

$$^4/_3y + {}^6/_3y = 110, \quad \text{Converting } 2y \text{ into a fraction with denominator 3}$$

$$^{10}/_3y = 110, \quad \text{Combining like terms}$$

$$y = 110 \times {}^3/_{10} = 33, \quad \text{Dividing by } {}^{10}/_3$$

Check: Replace y by 33 in the original equation,

$$2(^2/_3(33) + 5) + 2(33 + 5) = 130$$

$$2(22 + 5) + 2(38) = 130$$

$$2(27) + 76 = 130$$

$$54 + 76 = 130$$

$$130 = 130$$

Therefore, the solution to the given equation is $y = 33$.

Drill 4: Linear Equations

DIRECTIONS: Solve for x.

1. $4x - 2 = 10$

    (A) -1 (B) 2

    (C) 3   (D) 4

    (E) 6

2. $7z + 1 - z = 2z - 7$

    (A) -2 (B) 0

    (C) 1   (D) 2

    (E) 3

3. $^1/_3b + 3 = {}^1/_2b$

    (A) $^1/_2$ (B) 2

    (C) $3^3/_5$ (D) 6

    (E) 18

4. $0.4p + 1 = 0.7p - 2$

   (A) 0.1   (B) 2

   (C) 5   (D) 10

   (E) 12

5. $4(3x + 2) - 11 = 3(3x - 2)$

   (A) − 3   (B) −1

   (C) 2   (D) 3

   (E) 7

5. TWO LINEAR EQUATIONS

Equations of the form $ax + by = c$, where a, b, and c are constants and $a, b \neq 0$ are called **linear equations** with two unknown variables.

There are several ways to solve systems of linear equations in two variables:

Method 1: **Addition or subtraction** – if necessary, multiply the equations by numbers that will make the coefficients of one unknown in the resulting equations numerically equal. If the signs of equal coefficients are the same, subtract the equation, otherwise add.

The result is one equation with one unknown; we solve it and substitute the value into the other equations to find the unknown that we first eliminated.

Method 2: **Substitution** – find the value of one unknown in terms of the other, substitute this value in the other equation and solve.

Method 3: **Graph** – graph both equations. The point of intersection of the drawn lines is a simultaneous solution for the equations and its coordinates correspond to the answer that would be found analytically.

If the lines are parallel they have no simultaneous solution.

Dependent equations are equations that represent the same line; therefore, every point on the line of a dependent equation represents a solution. Since there is an infinite number of points on a line, there is an infinite number of simultaneous solutions, for example:

$$4 \begin{cases} 2x + y = 8 \\ 2 \end{cases} 4x + 2y = 16$$

The equations above are dependent, they represent the same line, all points that satisfy either of the equations are solutions of the system.

A system of linear equations is consistent if there is only one solution for the system.

A system of linear equations is inconsistent if it does not have any solutions.

Example of a consistent system. Find the point of intersection of the graphs of the equations as shown in the figure.

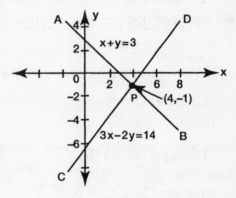

$$x + y = 3$$

$$3x - 2y = 14$$

To solve these linear equations, solve for y in terms of x. The equations will be in the form $y = mx + b$, where m is the slope and b is the intercept on the y-axis.

$x + y = 3$	
$y = 3 - x$	Subtract x from both sides.
$3x - 2y = 14$	Subtract $3x$ from both sides.
$-2y = 14 - 3x$	Divide by -2.
$y = -7 + {}^{3}/_{2}x$	

The graphs of the linear functions, $y = 3 - x$ and $y = -7 + {}^{3}/_{2}x$ can be determined by plotting only two points. For example, for $y = 3 - x$, let $x = 0$, then $y = 3$. Let $x = 1$, then $y = 2$. The two points on this first line are $(0, 3)$ and $(1, 2)$. For $y = -7 + {}^{3}/_{2}x$, let $x = 0$, then $y = -7$. Let $x = 1$, then $y = -5{}^{1}/_{2}$. The two points on this second line are $(0, -7)$ and $(1, -5{}^{1}/_{2})$.

To find the point of intersection P of

$$x + y = 3 \quad \text{and} \quad 3x - 2y = 14,$$

solve them algebraically. Multiply the first equation by 2. Add these two equations to eliminate the variable y.

$$2x + 2y = 6$$
$$3x - 2y = 14$$
$$\overline{}$$
$$5x = 20$$

Solve for x to obtain $x = 4$. Substitute this into $y = 3 - x$ to get $y = 3 - 4 = -1$. P is $(4, -1)$. AB is the graph of the first equation, and CD is the graph of the second equation. The point of intersection P of the two graphs is the only point on both lines. The coordinates of P satisfy both equations and represent the desired solution of the problem. From the graph, P seems to be the point $(4, -1)$. These coordinates satisfy both equations, and hence are the exact coordinates of the point of intersection of the two lines.

To show that $(4, -1)$ satisfies both equations, substitute this point into both equations.

$x + y = 3$	$3x - 2y = 14$
$4 + (-1) = 3$	$3(4) - 2(-1) = 14$
$4 - 1 = 3$	$12 + 2 = 14$
$3 = 3$	$14 = 14$

Example of an inconsistent system. Solve the equations $2x + 3y = 6$ and $4x + 6y = 7$ simultaneously.

We have two equations in two unknowns,

$$2x + 3y = 6 \quad (1)$$

and

$$4x + 6y = 7 \quad (2)$$

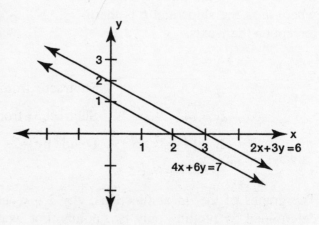

There are several methods to solve this problem. We have chosen to multiply each equation by a different number so that when the two equations are added, one of the variables drops out. Thus,

Multiplying equation (1) by 2: $\qquad 4x + 6y = 12 \qquad (3)$

Multiplying equation (2) by -1: $\quad -4x - 6y = -7 \qquad (4)$

Adding equations (3) and (4): $\qquad\qquad 0 = 5$

We obtain a peculiar result!

Actually, what we have shown in this case is that if there were a simultaneous solution to the given equations, then 0 would equal 5. But the conclusion is impossible; therefore, there can be no simultaneous solution to these two equations, hence no point satisfying both.

The straight lines which are the graphs of these equations must be parallel if they never intersect, but not identical, which can be seen from the graph of these equations (see the accompanying diagram).

Example of a dependent system. Solve the equations $2x + 3y = 6$ and $y = - (2x/3) + 2$ simultaneously.

We have two equations in two unknowns.

$$2x + 3y = 6 \tag{1}$$

and

$$y = - (2x/3) + 2 \tag{2}$$

There are several methods of solving for this problem. Since equation (2) already gives us an expression for y, we use the method of substitution. Substituting $- (2x/3) + 2$ for y in the first equation:

$$2x + 3(-2x/3 + 2) = 6$$

Distributing, $2x - 2x + 6 = 6$

$$6 = 6$$

Apparently we have gotten nowhere! The result $6 = 6$ is true, but indicates no solution. Actually, our work shows that no matter what real number x is, if y is determined by the second equation, then the first equation will always be satisfied.

The reason for this peculiarity may be seen if we take a closer look at the equation $y = - (2x/3) + 2$. It is equivalent to $3y = -2x + 6$, or $2x + 3y = 6$.

In other words, the two equations are equivalent. Any pair of values of x and y which satisfies one satisfies the other.

It is hardly necessary to verify that in this case the graphs of the given equations are identical lines, and that there are an infinite number of simultaneous solutions of these equations.

Two systems of linear equations are said to be equivalent if and only if they have the same solution set.

PROBLEM

Solve for x and y.

$$x + 2y = 8 \tag{1}$$

$$3x + 4y = 20 \tag{2}$$

Solution

Solve equation (1) for x in terms of y:

$$x = 8 - 2y \tag{3}$$

Substitute $(8 - 2y)$ for x in (2):

$$3(8 - 2y) + 4y = 20 \tag{4}$$

Solve (4) for y as follows:

Distribute: $24 - 6y + 4y = 20$

Combine like terms and then subtract 24 from both sides:

$$24 - 2y = 20$$

$$24 - 24 - 2y = 20 - 24$$

$$-2y = -4$$

Divide both sides by -2:

$$y = 2$$

Substitute 2 for y in equation (1):

$$x + 2(2) = 8$$

$$x = 4$$

Thus, our solution is $x = 4$, $y = 2$.

Check: Substitute $x = 4$, $y = 2$ in equations (1) and (2):

$$4 + 2(2) = 8$$

$$8 = 8$$

$$3(4) + 4(2) = 20$$

$$20 = 20$$

PROBLEM

Solve algebraically.

$$4x + 2y = -1 \tag{1}$$

$$5x - 3y = 7 \tag{2}$$

Solution

We arbitrarily choose to eliminate x first.

Multiply (1) by 5: $20x + 10y = -5$ (3)

Multiply (2) by 4: $20x - 12y = 28$ (4)

Subtract (3) – (4): $22y = -33$ (5)

Divide (5) by 22: $y = -\frac{33}{22} = -\frac{3}{2}$

To find x, substitute $y = -\frac{3}{2}$ in either of the original equations. If we use equation (1), we obtain $4x + 2(-\frac{3}{2}) = -1$, $4x - 3 = -1$, $4x = 2$, $x = \frac{1}{2}$.

The solution $(\frac{1}{2}, -\frac{3}{2})$ should be checked in both equations of the given system.

Replacing $(\frac{1}{2}, -\frac{3}{2})$ in equation (1):

$$4x + 2y = -1$$

$$4(\tfrac{1}{2}) + 2(-\tfrac{3}{2}) = -1$$

$$\tfrac{4}{2} - 3 = -1$$

$$2 - 3 = -1$$

$$-1 = -1$$

Replacing $(\frac{1}{2}, -\frac{3}{2})$ in equation (2):

$$5x - 3y = 7$$

$$5(\tfrac{1}{2}) - 3(-\tfrac{3}{2}) = 7$$

$$\tfrac{5}{2} + \tfrac{9}{2} = 7$$

$$\tfrac{14}{2} = 7$$

$$7 = 7$$

(Instead of eliminating x from the two given equations, we could have eliminated y by multiplying equation (1) by 3, multiplying equation (2) by 2, and then adding the two derived equations.)

Drill 5: Two Linear Equations

DIRECTIONS: Find the solution set for each pair of equations.

1. $\begin{pmatrix} 3x + 4y = -2 \\ x - 6y = -8 \end{pmatrix}$

    (A) $(2, -1)$ (B) $(1, -2)$

    (C) $(-2, -1)$ (D) $(1, 2)$

    (E) $(-2, 1)$

2. $\begin{pmatrix} -2x + y = -10 \\ -2x - 4y = 4 \end{pmatrix}$

    (A) $(6, -2)$ (B) $(-6, 2)$

    (C) $(-2, 6)$ (D) $(2, 6)$

    (E) $(-6, -2)$

3. $\begin{pmatrix} 6x + 5y = -4 \\ 3x - 3y = 9 \end{pmatrix}$

    (A) $(1, -2)$ (B) $(1, 2)$

    (C) $(2, -1)$ (D) $(-2, 1)$

    (E) $(-1, 2)$

4. $4x + 3y = 9$
    $2x - 2y = 8$

    (A) $(-3, 1)$ (B) $(1, -3)$

    (C) $(3, 1)$ (D) $(3, -1)$

    (E) $(-1, 3)$

5. $x + y = 7$
    $x = y - 3$

    (A) $(5, 2)$ (B) $(-5, 2)$

    (C) $(2, 5)$ (D) $(-2, 5)$

    (E) $(2, -5)$

6. $3 \left(5x + 6y = 4 \right)$
   $5 \left(3x - 2y = 1 \right)$

   $15x + 18y = 12$
   $15x - 10y = 5$
   $18 =$

   (A) $(3, 6)$ (B) $(\frac{1}{2}, \frac{1}{4})$

   (C) $(-3, 6)$ (D) $(2, 4)$

   (E) $(\frac{1}{3}, \frac{3}{2})$

7. $x - 2y = 7$
   $x + y = -2$

   (A) $(-2, 7)$ (B) $(3, -1)$

   (C) $(-7, 2)$ (D) $(1, -3)$

   (E) $(1, -2)$

8. $4x + 3y = 3$
   $-2x + 6y = 3$

   (A) $(\frac{1}{2}, \frac{2}{3})$ (B) $(-0.3, 0.6)$

   (C) $(\frac{2}{3}, -1)$ (D) $(-0.2, 0.5)$

   (E) $(0.3, 0.6)$

9. $4x - 2y = -14$
   $8x + y = 7$

   (A) $(0, 7)$ (B) $(2, -7)$

   (C) $(7, 0)$ (D) $(-7, 2)$

   (E) $(0, 2)$

10. $6x - 3y = 1$
    $-9x + 5y = -1$

    (A) $(1, -1)$ (B) $(\frac{2}{3}, 1)$

    (C) $(1, \frac{2}{3})$ (D) $(-1, 1)$

    (E) $(\frac{2}{3}, -1)$

$-6x + 5y = -4$
$6x - 6y = 18$
$11y = -22$
$x = 1 \quad y = -2$

$6x + 5(-2) = -4$
$6x + 10 = -4$
$ +10 \quad +10$
$6x = 6$
$6x = 6$

6. QUADRATIC EQUATIONS

A second degree equation in x of the type $ax^2 + bx + c = 0$, $a \neq 0$, a, b, and c are real numbers, is called a **quadratic equation.**

To solve a quadratic equation is to find values of x which satisfy $ax^2 + bx + c = 0$. These values of x are called **solutions**, or **roots**, of the equation.

A quadratic equation has a maximum of two roots. Methods of solving quadratic equations:

1. **Direct solution**: Given $x^2 - 9 = 0$.

    We can solve directly by isolating the variable x:

    $$x^2 = 9$$

    $$x = \pm 3$$

2. **Factoring**: Given a quadratic equation $ax^2 + bx + c = 0$, a, b, and $c \neq 0$, to factor means to express it as the product $a(x - r_1)(x - r_2) = 0$, where r_1 and r_2 are the two roots.

    Some helpful hints to remember are:

    (a) $r_1 + r_2 = -{}^b/_a$

    (b) $r_1 r_2 = {}^c/_a$

    Given $x^2 - 5x + 4 = 0$.

    Since $r_1 + r_2 = -{}^b/_a = -{}^{(-5)}/_1 = 5$, so the possible solutions are (3, 2), (4, 1), and (5, 0). Also $r_1 r_2 = {}^c/_a = {}^4/_1 = 4$; this equation is satisfied only by the second pair, so $r_1 = 4$, $r_2 = 1$ and the factored form is $(x - 4)(x - 1) = 0$.

    If the coefficient of x^2 is not 1, it is necessary to divide the equation by this coefficient and then factor.

    Given $2x^2 - 12x + 16 = 0$

    Dividing by 2, we obtain:

    $$x^2 - 6x + 8 = 0$$

    Since $r_1 + r_2 = -{}^b/_a = 6$, the possible solutions are (6, 0), (5, 1), (4, 2), and (3, 3). Also $r_1 r_2 = 8$, therefore, the only possible answer is (4, 2) and the expression $x^2 - 6x + 8 = 0$ can be factored as $(x - 4)(x - 2)$.

PROBLEM

Solve the equation $x^2 + 8x + 15 = 0$.

Solution

Since $(x + a)(x + b) = x^2 + bx + ax + ab = x^2 + (a + b)x + ab$, we may factor the given equation, $0 = x^2 + 8x + 15$, replacing $a + b$ by 8 and ab by 15. Thus,

$$a + b = 8, \quad \text{and} \quad ab = 15.$$

We want the two numbers a and b whose sum is 8 and whose product is 15. We check all pairs of numbers whose product is 15:

(a) $1 \times 15 = 15$; thus $a = 1$, $b = 15$, and $ab = 15$.

 $1 + 15 = 16$; therefore we reject these values because $a + b \neq 8$.

(b) $3 \times 5 = 15$; thus $a = 3$, $b = 5$, and $ab = 15$.

 $3 + 5 = 8$; therefore $a + b = 8$, and we accept these values.

Hence, $x^2 + 8x + 15 = 0$ is equivalent to

$$0 = x^2 + (3 + 5)x + 3 \times 5 = (x + 3)(x + 5)$$

Hence, $x + 5 = 0$ or $x + 3 = 0$.

Since the product of these two numbers is 0, one of the numbers must be 0. Hence, $x = -5$, or $x = -3$, and the solution set is $x = \{-5, -3\}$.

The student should note that $x = -5$ or $x = -3$. We are certainly not making the statement that $x = -5$, and $x = -3$. Also, the student should check that both these numbers do actually satisfy the given equations and hence are solutions.

Check: Replacing x by (-5) in the original equation:

$$x^2 + 8x + 15 = 0$$
$$(-5)^2 + 8(-5) + 15 = 0$$
$$25 - 40 + 15 = 0$$
$$-15 + 15 = 0$$
$$0 = 0$$

Replacing x by (-3) in the original equation:

$$x^2 + 8x + 15 = 0$$

$$(-3)^2 + 8(-3) + 15 = 0$$
$$9 - 24 + 15 = 0$$
$$-15 + 15 = 0$$
$$0 = 0$$

PROBLEM

Solve the following equations by factoring.

(1) $2x^2 + 3x = 0$ (2) $y^2 - 2y - 3 = y - 3$

(3) $z^2 - 2z - 3 = 0$ (4) $2m^2 - 11m - 6 = 0$

Solution

(1) $2x^2 + 3x = 0$. Factoring out the common factor of x from the left side of the given equation,

$$x(2x + 3) = 0.$$

Whenever a product $ab = 0$, where a and b are any two numbers, either $a = 0$ or $b = 0$. Then, either

$$x = 0 \quad \text{or} \quad 2x + 3 = 0$$
$$2x = -3$$
$$x = -^3/_2$$

Hence, the solution set to the original equation $2x^2 + 3x = 0$ is $\{-^3/_2, 0\}$.

(2) $y^2 - 2y - 3 = y - 3$. Subtract $(y - 3)$ from both sides of the given equation:

$$y^2 - 2y - 3 - (y - 3) = y - 3 - (y - 3)$$
$$y^2 - 2y - 3 - y + 3 = y - 3 - y + 3$$
$$y^2 - 2y - 3 - y + 3 = y - 3 - y + 3$$
$$y^2 - 3y = 0$$

Factor out a common factor of y from the left side of this equation:

$$y(y - 3) = 0$$

Thus, $y = 0$ or $y - 3 = 0$, $y = 3$.

Therefore, the solution set to the original equation $y^2 - 2y - 3 = y - 3$ is $\{0, 3\}$.

(3) $z^2 - 2z - 3 = 0$. Factor the original equation into a product of two polynomials:

$$z^2 - 2z - 3 = (z - 3)(z + 1) = 0$$

Hence,

$$(z - 3)(z + 1) = 0; \text{ and } z - 3 = 0 \quad \text{or} \quad z + 1 = 0$$
$$z = 3 \qquad\qquad z = -1$$

Therefore, the solution set to the original equation $z^2 - 2z - 3 = 0$ is $\{-1, 3\}$.

(4) $2m^2 - 11m - 6 = 0$. Factor the original equation into a product of two polynomials:

$$2m^2 - 11m - 6 = (2m + 1)(m - 6) = 0$$

Thus,

$$2m + 1 = 0 \quad \text{or} \quad m - 6 = 0$$
$$2m = -1 \qquad\qquad m = 6$$
$$m = -^1/_2$$

$-6 \pm \sqrt{b^2 - 4ac)}$

Therefore, the solution set to the original equation $2m^2 - 11m - 6 = 0$ is $\{-^1/_2, 6\}$.

Drill 6: Quadratic Equations

DIRECTIONS: Solve for all values of *x*.

1. $x^2 - 2x - 8 = 0$

   (A) 4 and -2

   (C) 4

   (E) -2

   (B) 4 and 8

   (D) -2 and 8

2. $x^2 + 2x - 3 = 0$

   (A) -3 and 2

   (C) 3 and 1

   (E) -3

   (B) 2 and 1

   (D) -3 and 1

$\dfrac{-B \pm \sqrt{B^2 - 4(ac)}}{2(a)}$

$-(-2) \pm \sqrt{(-2)^2 - 4(1 \cdot -8)}$

$2(1)$

$2 \pm \sqrt{4 - (4(-8))}$

$2 \pm \sqrt{4 + (+32)}$

$2 \pm \sqrt{4 + 32}$

$2 \pm \sqrt{36}$

4 and -2

$\dfrac{2 \pm 6}{2}$

$\dfrac{8}{2} \quad \dfrac{-4}{2}$

117

3. $x^2 - 7x = -10$

   (A) -3 and 5 (B) 2 and 5

   (C) 2 (D) -2 and -5

   (E) 5

4. $x^2 - 8x + 16 = 0$

   (A) 8 and 2 (B) 1 and 16

   (C) 4 (D) -2 and 4

   (E) 4 and -4

5. $3x^2 + 3x = 6$

   (A) 3 and -6 (B) 2 and 3

   (C) -3 and 2 (D) 1 and -3

   (E) 1 and -2

6. $x^2 + 7x = 0$

   (A) 7 (B) 0 and -7

   (C) -7 (D) 0 and 7

   (E) 0

7. $x^2 - 25 = 0$

   (A) 5 (B) 5 and -5

   (C) 15 and 10 (D) -5 and 10

   (E) -5

8. $2x^2 + 4x = 16$

   (A) 2 and -2 (B) 8 and -2

   (C) 4 and 8 (D) 2 and -4

   (E) 2 and 4

9. $6x^2 - x - 2 = 0$

   (A) 2 and 3 (B) $\frac{1}{2}$ and $\frac{1}{3}$

(C) $-\frac{1}{2}$ and $\frac{2}{3}$ (D) $\frac{2}{3}$ and 3

(E) 2 and $-\frac{1}{3}$

10. $12x^2 + 5x = 3$

(A) $\frac{1}{3}$ and $-\frac{1}{4}$ (B) 4 and -3

(C) 4 and $\frac{1}{6}$ (D) $\frac{1}{3}$ and -4

(E) $-\frac{3}{4}$ and $\frac{1}{3}$

7. INEQUALITIES

An inequality is a statement where the value of one quantity or expression is greater than ($>$), less than ($<$), greater than or equal to ($\geq$), less than or equal to ($\leq$), or not equal to ($\neq$) that of another.

EXAMPLE

$5 > 4$

The expression above means that the value of 5 is greater than the value of 4.

A **conditional inequality** is an inequality whose validity depends on the values of the variables in the sentence. That is, certain values of the variables will make the sentence true, and others will make it false. $3 - y > 3 + y$ is a conditional inequality for the set of real numbers, since it is true for any replacement less than 0 and false for all others.

$x + 5 > x + 2$ is an **absolute inequality** for the set of real numbers, meaning that for any real value x, the expression on the left is greater than the expression on the right.

The solution of a given inequality in one variable x consists of all values of x for which the inequality is true.

The graph of an inequality in one variable is represented by either a ray or a line segment on the real number line.

The endpoint is not a solution if the variable is strictly less than or greater than a particular value.

EXAMPLE

$x > 2$

2 is not a solution and should be represented as shown.

The endpoint is a solution if the variable is either (1) less than or equal to or (2) greater than or equal to a particular value.

EXAMPLE

$5 > x \geq 2$

In this case 2 is the solution and should be represented as shown.

Properties of Inequalities

If x and y are real numbers then one and only one of the following statements is true.

$$x > y, x = y, \text{ or } x < y$$

This is the order property of real numbers.

If a, b, and c are real numbers:

A)   If $a < b$ and $b < c$, then $a < c$.

B)   If $a > b$ and $b > c$, then $a > c$.

This is the **transitive property of inequalities**.

If a, b, and c are real numbers and $a > b$, then $a + c > b + c$ and $a - c > b - c$. This is the **addition property of inequality**.

Two inequalities are said to have the same **sense** if their signs of inequality point in the same direction.

The sense of an inequality remains the same if both sides are multiplied or divided by the same positive real number.

EXAMPLE

$4 > 3$

If we multiply both sides by 5 we will obtain:

$4 \times 5 > 3 \times 5$

$20 > 15$

The sense of the inequality does not change.

The sense of an inequality becomes opposite if each side is multiplied or divided by the same negative real number.

EXAMPLE

$4 > 3$

If we multiply both sides by -5 we would obtain:

$4 \times -5 < 3 \times -5$

$-20 < -15$

The sense of the inequality becomes opposite.

If $a > b$ and a, b, and n are positive real numbers, then:

$a^n > b^n$ and $a^{-n} < b^{-n}$

If $x > y$ and $q > p$ then $x + q > y + p$.

If $x > y > 0$ and $q > p > 0$ then $xq > yp$.

Inequalities that have the same solution set are called **equivalent inequalities**.

PROBLEM

Solve the inequality $2x + 5 > 9$.

Solution

$2x + 5 + (-5) > 9 + (-5)$	Adding -5 to both sides
$2x + 0 > 9 + (-5)$	Additive inverse property
$2x > 9 + (-5)$	Additive identity property
$2x > 4$	Combining terms
$\frac{1}{2}(2x) > \frac{1}{2} \times 4$	Multiplying both sides by $\frac{1}{2}$
$x > 2$	

The solution set is

$X = \{x \mid 2x + 5 > 9\}$

$= \{x \mid x > 2\}$

(that is all x, such that x is greater than 2).

PROBLEM

Solve the inequality $4x + 3 < 6x + 8$.

Solution

In order to solve the inequality $4x + 3 < 6x + 8$, we must find all values of x which make it true. Thus, we wish to obtain x alone on one side of the inequality.

Add -3 to both sides:

$$\begin{array}{r} 4x + 3 < 6x + 8 \\ -3 \quad\quad -3 \\ \hline 4x < 6x + 5 \end{array}$$

Add $-6x$ to both sides:

$$\begin{array}{r} 4x < 6x + 5 \\ -6x \quad -6x \\ \hline -2x < 5 \end{array}$$

In order to obtain x alone we must divide both sides by (-2). Recall that dividing an inequality by a negative number reverses the inequality sign, hence

$$\frac{-2x}{2} > \frac{5}{-2}$$

Cancelling $-^2/_{-2}$ we obtain, $x > -^5/_2$.

Thus, our solution is $\{x \mid x > -^5/_2\}$ (the set of all x such that x is greater than $-^5/_2$).

Drill 7: Inequalities

DIRECTIONS: Find the solution set for each inequality.

1. $3m + 2 < 7$

    (A) $m \geq ^5/_3$ (B) $m \leq 2$

    (C) $m < 2$ (D) $m > 2$

    (E) $m < ^5/_3$

2. $^1/_2 x - 3 \leq 1$

    (A) $-4 \leq x \leq 8$ (B) $x \geq -8$

(C) $x \leq 8$ (D) $2 \leq x \leq 8$

(E) $x \geq 8$

3. $-3p + 1 \geq 16$

   (handwritten: $-1 \quad -1$)

   (handwritten: $\dfrac{-3p \geq 15}{-3 \quad -3}$)   *(handwritten: $p \leq -5$)*

   (A) $p \geq -5$ (B) $p \geq \dfrac{-17}{3}$

   (C) $p \leq \dfrac{-17}{3}$ (D) $p \leq -5$

   (E) $p \geq 5$

   (handwritten: $-6 < \frac{2}{3}r + 6 \leq 2$)

4. $-6 < {}^{2}/_{3} r + 6 \leq 2$ *(handwritten: $-12 < \frac{2}{3}r \leq -4$)*

   (A) $-6 < r \leq -3$ (B) $-18 < r \leq -6$

   (C) $r \geq -6$ (D) $-2 < r \leq -{}^{4}/_{3}$ *(handwritten: $-12 \cdot \frac{3}{2} < r \leq -4 \frac{3}{2}$)*

   (E) $r \leq -6$ *(handwritten: $\dfrac{-36}{2} < r \leq \dfrac{-12}{2}$)*

5. $0 < 2 - y < 6$ *(handwritten: $-2 < -y < 4$)*   *(handwritten: $-18 < r \leq -6$)*

   (handwritten: $-2 \quad -2$)

   (A) $-4 \leq y < 2$ *(handwritten: $\dfrac{}{-1}$)*   (B) $-4 < y < 0$

   (C) $-4 < y < -2$ *(handwritten: $\dfrac{-2}{-1} > \dfrac{y}{-1} > \dfrac{4}{-1}$)*   (D) $-2 < y < 4$

   (E) $0 < y < 4$ *(handwritten: $2 > y > -4$)*

   (handwritten: ※ mult./divide by a neg. # you turn sign around)

8. GRAPHS

Coordinate geometry refers to the study of geometric figures using algebraic principles.

The graph on the next page is called the Cartesian coordinate plane. The graph consists of a pair of perpendicular lines called **coordinate axes**. The **vertical axis** is the y-axis and the **horizontal axis** is the x-axis. The point of intersection of these two axes is called the **origin**; it is the zero point of both axes. Furthermore, points to the right of the origin on the x-axis and above the origin on the y-axis represent positive real numbers. Points to the left of the origin on the x-axis or below the origin on the y-axis represent negative real numbers.

The four regions cut off by the coordinate axes are, in counterclockwise direction from the top right, called the first, second, third, and fourth quadrant, respectively. The first quadrant contains all points with two positive coordinates.

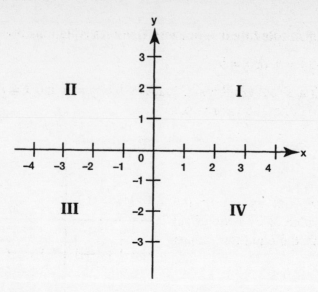

In the graph shown, two points are identified by the ordered pair (x, y) of numbers. The x-coordinate is the first number and the y-coordinate is the second number.

To plot a point on the graph when given the coordinates, draw perpendicular lines from the number-line coordinates to the point where the two lines intersect.

To find the coordinates of a given point on the graph, draw perpendicular lines from the point to the coordinates on the number line. The x-coordinate is written before the y-coordinate and a comma is used to separate the two.

In this case, point A has the coordinates (4, 2) and the coordinates of point B are (−3, −5).

Graphing simple linear equations involves equations like

$$y = mx, y = b, \text{ or } x = b$$

where m and b are real numbers. Equations like $y = b$ and $x = b$ represent lines parallel to either the x- or y-axis.

EXAMPLE

$$y = 3$$

Since x does not appear in the equation, the value of x has no effect on y. To satisfy the equation y must always be 3.

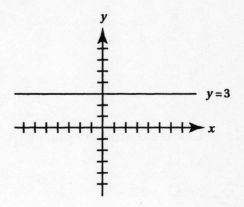

PROBLEM

Graph $y = 4x$.

Solution

Pick some values for x or y and substitute them in the equation to solve for the other variable. Try $y = 0$ and $y = 2$.

$$0 = 4x$$

$$0 = x$$

Therefore, (0, 0) satisfies the equation.

$$2 = 4x$$

$$^{1}/_{2} = x$$

$(^{1}/_{2}, 2)$ is another ordered pair which satisfies the equation.

Drill 8: Graphs

1. Which point shown has the coordinates (– 3, 2)?

    (A) A

    (B) B

    (C) C

    (D) D

    (E) E

2. Name the coordinates of point A.

    (A) (4, 3)

    (B) (3, – 4)

    (C) (3, 4)

    (D) (– 4, 3)

    (E) (4, – 3)

3. Which point shown has the coordinates (2.5, – 1)?

    (A) M

    (B) N

    (C) P

    (D) Q

    (E) R

4. The correct x-coordinate for point H is what number?

    (A) 3

    (B) 4

    (C) – 3

    (D) – 4

    (E) – 5

5. The correct *y*-coordinate for point R is what number?

(A) −7

(B) 2

(C) − 2

(D) 7

(E) 8

6. Which of the following is an equation of line ℓ?

(A) $x = 2$

(B) $y = 2$

(C) $x = 2y$

(D) $y = 2x$

(E) $x = y$

7. Which of the following equations gives a line parallel to the *x*-axis?

(A) $x = -y$ (B) $x = y$

(C) $y = 3x$ (D) $x + y = 0$

(E) $y = -6$

8. Which of the following is an equation of line *b*?

(A) $y = 1$

(B) $x = 2$

(C) $2y = x$

(D) $x + y = 2$

(E) $y = -2x$

ELEMENTARY ALGEBRA DRILLS

ANSWER KEY

Drill 1 – Operations with Polynomials

1.	(B)	6.	(B)	11.	(C)	16.	(C)
2.	(C)	7.	(C)	12.	(B)	17.	(D)
3.	(C)	8.	(E)	13.	(E)	18.	(E)
4.	(D)	9.	(A)	14.	(A)	19.	(B)
5.	(A)	10.	(D)	15.	(D)	20.	(B)

Drill 2 – Simplifying Algebraic Expressions

1.	(C)	4.	(A)	7.	(E)	10.	(E)
2.	(D)	5.	(D)	8.	(B)		
3.	(B)	6.	(B)	9.	(A)		

Drill 3 – Rational Expressions

1.	(B)	5.	(A)	9.	(C)	13.	(A)
2.	(C)	6.	(D)	10.	(A)	14.	(A)
3.	(A)	7.	(B)	11.	(C)	15.	(D)
4.	(E)	8.	(E)	12.	(E)		

Drill 4 – Linear Equations

1.	(C)	3.	(E)	5.	(B)
2.	(A)	4.	(D)		

Drill 5 – Two Linear Equations

1.	(E)	4.	(D)	7.	(D)	10.	(B)
2.	(B)	5.	(C)	8.	(E)		
3.	(A)	6.	(B)	9.	(A)		

Drill 6 – Quadratic Equations

1.	(A)	4.	(C)	7.	(B)	10.	(E)
2.	(D)	5.	(E)	8.	(D)		
3.	(B)	6.	(B)	9.	(C)		

Drill 7 – Inequalities

1.	(E)	3.	(D)	5.	(A)
2.	(C)	4.	(B)		

Drill 8 – Graphs

1.	(C)	3.	(B)	5.	(A)	7.	(E)
2.	(E)	4.	(D)	6.	(A)	8.	(C)

ELM

Entry Level Mathematics

Chapter 3
Geometry
Review

GEOMETRY
DIAGNOSTIC TEST

16 Questions

(Answer sheets appear at the back of the book.)

DIRECTIONS: Each question has five multiple-choice answers. Select the single best answer.

1. What is the area of the parallelogram as shown in the figure below?

    (A) 32 cm²   (B) 16 cm²

    (C) 24 cm²   (D) 28 cm²

    (E) Not enough information is given.

2. Find the area of a regular hexagon formed from 6 equilateral triangles with sides of 8 inches.

    (A) $16\sqrt{3}$ in²

    (B) $96\sqrt{2}$ in²

    (C) 64 in²

    (D) 128 in²

    (E) $96\sqrt{3}$ in²

3. Which of the following are not complementary or supplementary angles?

    (A) 45°, 45°

    (B) 123°, 57°

    (C) 84°, 96°

    (D) 39°, 51°

    (E) 73°, 117°

4. Find the total area of the 3 visible faces of the box below.

    6 in.

    14 in.

    10 in.

    (A) 284 in²

    (B) 420 in²

    (C) 568 in²

    (D) 840 in²

    (E) 192 in²

5. What is the length of the hypotenuse of a triangle having angles 45°, 45°, 90°, and the length of a leg 4 m?

    (A) 4 m

    (B) 16 m

    (C) 4√3 m

    (D) 4√2 m

    (E) 12 m

    45°

    4m

6. Find the area of the isosceles trapezoid.

    (A) 250√3

    (B) 150

    (C) 250

    (D) 125√3

    (E) Area cannot be found.

    10

    10

    60°

    60°

    30

7. In rhombus *ABCD*, which of the following are true?

I. ∠ *BAE* and ∠ *ECD* are congruent.

II. ∠*ADE* and ∠ *CDE* are congruent.

III. ∠ *ABE* and ∠ *ADE* are congruent.

(A) I only   (B) II only

(C) I and II only   (D) I and III only

(E) I, II, and III

8. If the angles of a triangle *ABC* are in the ratio of 3:5:7, then the triangle is

(A) acute.   (B) right.

(C) isosceles.   (D) obtuse.

(E) equilateral.

9. The area of this right-angled plane figure is

(A) 250.

(B) 162.

(C) 160.

(D) 150.

(E) 140.

10. If the diameter of a circle is 14 m, find the area of the circle.

(A) $49\pi \ m^2$ (B) $98\pi \ m^2$

(C) $14\pi \ m^2$ (D) $196\pi \ m^2$

(E) $28\pi \ m^2$

11. What is the height (altitude) of an equilateral triangle if the length of a side is 6 centimeters?

(A) $3\sqrt{2}$ cm

(B) $3\sqrt{3}$ cm

(C) 6 cm

(D) 9 cm

(E) 3 cm

12. How long of a metal bar do you need to make a basketball hoop with a diameter of 48 cm?

(A) 24π cm   (B) 48π cm

(C) 96π cm   (D) 192π cm

(E) 12π cm

13. If lines l, m, and n intersect at point P, express $x + y$ in terms of a.

(A) $180 - \dfrac{a}{2}$

(B) $\dfrac{a}{2} - 180$

(C) $90 - \dfrac{a}{2}$

(D) $a - 180$

(E) $180 - a$

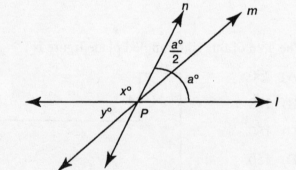

14. Find the area of a right triangle with a hypotenuse of 17 cm and a base of 8 cm.

(A) 45 cm^2 (B) 60 cm^2

(C) 68 cm^2 (D) 120 cm^2

(E) 138 cm^2

15. Find the area of a sector of a circle with a radius of 16 cm and a 45° arc.

    (A) 2π cm^2 (B) 32π cm^2

    (C) 720 cm^2 (D) 256π cm^2

    (E) 720π cm^2

16. In $\triangle ABC$, $AB = 6$, $BC = 4$, and $AC = 3$. What kind of triangle is it?

    (A) Right and scalene   (B) Obtuse and scalene

    (C) Acute and scalene   (D) Right and isosceles

    (E) Obtuse and isosceles

GEOMETRY
DIAGNOSTIC TEST

ANSWER KEY

1. (B)	5. (D)	9. (B)	13. (A)
2. (E)	6. (D)	10. (A)	14. (B)
3. (E)	7. (E)	11. (B)	15. (B)
4. (A)	8. (A)	12. (B)	16. (B)

DETERMINE YOUR STRENGTHS AND WEAKNESSES

GEOMETRY

Question Type	Question #	See Pages . . .
Points, Lines, and Angles	3, 7, 13	145–157
Triangles	1, 2, 5, 6, 7 8, 11, 14, 16	157–170
Quadrilaterals	1, 6, 7, 9	170–180
Circles	10, 12, 15	180–188
Solids	4	189–193

DETAILED EXPLANATIONS OF ANSWERS

DIAGNOSTIC TEST GEOMETRY

1. **(B)** The area of a parallelogram is

$$A = bh.$$

We know the base is 8 cm, but we must find the height. That is possible because we are given the measure of the angle. When the height is drawn in, we have a triangle with angles 30°–60°–90°. The hypotenuse of this is 4. Remember the relationship of the sides of a 30°–60°–90° triangle is $1:\sqrt{3}:2$. Since the hypotenuse is 4, the side opposite the 30° angle is 2. This is the height of the triangle and of the parallelogram. Now put this in the formula and get

$$A = (8)(2)$$

or the area is 16 cm².

2. **(E)** The area of the hexagon can be found by finding the area of one of the equilateral triangles. The height of one triangle can be found by using the Pythagorean Theorem.

$$h^2 + 4^2 = 8^2$$

$$h^2 + 16 = 64$$

$$h^2 = 48$$

$$h = 4\sqrt{3}$$

The area of one equilateral triangle

$$= \frac{1}{2}bh$$

$$= \frac{1}{2}(8)(4\sqrt{3})$$

$$A = 16\sqrt{3} \text{ in}^2$$

There are six triangles in the hexagon. The area of the hexagon

$$= 6(16\sqrt{3})$$

$$= 96\sqrt{3} \text{ in}^2$$

3. **(E)** Add the angles to see if the sum is 90° or 180°.

(A) 45° + 45° = 90°, complementary angle
(B) 123° + 57° = 180°, supplementary angle
(C) 84° + 96° = 180°, supplementary angle
(D) 39° + 51° = 90°, complementary angle
(E) 73° + 117° = 190°, not complementary or supplementary

4. **(A)** Compute the area of the front face: $6 \times 10 = 60$ in². Compute the area of the top face: $10 \times 14 = 140$ in². Compute the area of the side face: $6 \times 14 = 84$ in². Add these three areas together: 60 in² + 140 in² + 84 in² = 284 in².

5. **(D)** The hypotenuse is the longest side of the triangle. It is the side opposite of the right angle. A special relationship exists between the lengths of sides of a 45°–45°–90°, or isosceles right, triangle. The hypotenuse is always $\sqrt{2}$ times the length of a leg. So this one is $\sqrt{2} \times 4$ or $4\sqrt{2}$. Another method may be used to find this. The Pythagorean Theorem for right triangles is

$$a^2 + b^2 = c^2,$$

where a and b are the legs, and c is the hypotenuse.

$$4^2 + 4^2 = c^2 \text{ or } 32^2 = c^2 \text{ or } \sqrt{32} = c$$

$$\sqrt{16} \times \sqrt{2} = c$$

Therefore, $4\sqrt{2} = c$.

6. **(D)** The height of the trapezoid must be drawn inside the figure in order to use the formula for the area of a trapezoid

$$= \frac{1}{2}h(a + b)$$

where a and b are the bases. When h is drawn, a 30°–60°–90° triangle is formed with the hypotenuse given as 10 (the side of the trapezoid). The side opposite the 30° angle is 5, making the height (the side opposite the 60° angle) $= 5\sqrt{3}$. Base $b = 30$ as given and base $a = 30 - 10 = 20$.

$$\text{Area} = \frac{1}{2}5\sqrt{3}\,(20 + 30) = 25(5\sqrt{3}) = 125\sqrt{3}$$

7. **(E)** All three statements are true. Since a rhombus is a parallelogram, sides BA and CD are parallel. Using AC as a transversal, $\angle BAE$ and $\angle ECD$ are alternate interior angles and are therefore congruent making I true. The diagonals of a rhombus bisect the angles and so $\angle ADE$ and $\angle CDE$ are congruent making II true. In a rhombus, all four sides are congruent so triangle ABD is isosceles with congruent sides AB and AD. The angles opposite those congruent sides are congruent, so $\angle ABE$ and $\angle ADE$ are congruent making III true.

8. **(A)** Note that the ratio (3:5:7) of the angles in the triangle ABC can be represented as three distinct angles, $3x$, $5x$, and $7x$. Since the total number of degrees in a triangle is 180°, write and solve the equation.

$$3x + 5x + 7x = 180°$$

$$15x = 180°$$

$$x = 12°$$

Thus, the measures of the angles in triangle ABC are:

$$3x = 3(12°) = 36°,$$

$$5x = 5(12°) = 60°, \text{ and}$$

$$7x = 7(12°) = 84°,$$

respectively. Since each of the three angles is less than 90°, then triangle ABC is an acute triangle.

9. **(B)** Complete the diagram as shown to get two rectangles. The smaller rectangle has sides 3 and 4 and the larger has sides 6 and 25. The area of the figure

$$= 3 \times 4 + 6 \times 25 = 162.$$

10. **(A)**

$$\text{Area} = \pi r^2$$

The diameter is 14, and the radius is one-half of the diameter, which is 7.
   Substituting 7 for the radius,

$$A = \pi \times 7^2$$

$$A = \pi \times 49$$

$$A = 49\pi \text{ m}^2$$

11. **(B)** All sides of an equilateral triangle are congruent, or have the same measure. The altitude is the perpendicular bisector of the base and the bisector of the vertex angle. So the altitude divides the triangle into two triangles that have angles of 30°–60°–90°. The sides of this kind of triangle have the special relationship $1 : \sqrt{3} : 2$. This makes the length of the altitude of the triangle $3\sqrt{3}$ cm.

12. **(B)** To find the circumference multiply π times the diameter.

$$c = \pi \times 48, \, c = 48\pi \text{ cm}$$

13. **(A)** Since l, m, and n are lines intersecting at point P, adding $m \angle x$, $m \angle y$, and $m \angle {}^a/_2$ gives a straight angle, 180°.
   Thus,

$$x + y + {}^a/_2 = 180$$

$$x + y = 180 - {}^a/_2$$

14. **(B)** The formula for finding the area of a triangle is

Area = $^1/_2 \times$ base $\times$ height.

The base is given, but to find the height use the Pythagorean Theorem,

$$c^2 = a^2 + b^2.$$

Since the hypotenuse, c, equals 17, and the base, b, equals 8,

$$17^2 = a^2 + 8^2$$
$$289 = a^2 + 64$$
$$a^2 = 225$$

Taking the square root of both sides,

$$a = 15$$

The area of a triangle = $^1/_2$ (base) (height), so substituting 8 cm for the base and 15 cm for the height,

$$\text{Area} = {}^1/_2 \times 8 \text{ cm} \times 15 \text{ cm}$$
$$\text{Area} = 60 \text{ cm}^2$$

15. **(B)** The formula for finding the area of a sector

= (arc°/circle°) $\times \pi \times$ radius squared.

Substituting the information given,

$$A = \frac{45}{360} \times \pi \times 16^2$$

$$A = \frac{1}{8} \times \pi \times 256$$

$$A = 32 \times \pi$$

$$A = 32\pi \text{ cm}^2$$

16. **(B)** Since all the sides are of different lengths, the triangle is scalene. A triangle with sides of lengths 3, 4, and 5 is a right triangle. Thus, a triangle with sides of lengths 3, 4, and 6 is an obtuse triangle.

GEOMETRY REVIEW

1. POINTS, LINES, AND ANGLES

Geometry is built upon a series of undefined terms. These terms are those which we accept as known in order to define other undefined terms.

(A) **Point**: A point has no size, thickness, or width.

(B) **Line**: A line is a series of adjacent points which extends indefinitely. A line can be either curved or straight; however, unless otherwise stated, the term "line" refers to a straight line.

(C) **Plane**: A plane is a two-dimensional flat object which extends indefinitely in all directions.

A line is referred to by one small letter, i.e., l; or two letters with the symbol — on top, i.e., $\overline{CD}$.

If A and B are two points on a line, then the **line segment** AB is the set of points on that line between A and B and including A and B, which are endpoints. The line segment is referred to as AB; or two letters with the symbol — on top, i.e., $\overline{AB}$.

A **ray** is a series of points that lie to one side of a single endpoint. A ray is referred to by two letters with the symbol → on top, i.e., $\overrightarrow{EF}$.

A **straight line** can be uniquely determined by two points.

PROBLEM

How many lines can be found that contain (a) one given point, (b) two given points, and (c) three given points?

Solution

(a) *Given one point A*, there are an infinite number of distinct lines that contain the given point. To see this, consider line l_1 passing through point A. By rotating l_1 around A like the hands of a clock, we obtain different lines l_2, l_3, etc. Since we can rotate l_1 in infinitely many ways, there are infinitely many lines containing A.

(b) *Given two distinct points B and C*, there is one and only one distinct line. To see this, consider all the lines containing point B; l_5, l_6, l_7, and l_8. Only l_5 contains both points B and C. Thus, there is only one line containing both points B and C. Since there is always at least one line containing two distinct points and never more than one, the line passing through the two points is said to be determined by the two points.

(c) *Given three distinct points*, there may be one line or none. If a line exists that contains the three points, such as D, E, and F, then the points are said to be **colinear**. If no such line exists — as in the case of points G, H, and I, then the points are said to be **noncolinear**.

Intersecting Lines and Angles

An **angle** is a figure formed by two rays having the same endpoint. An angle such as the one illustrated below can be referred to in any of the following ways:

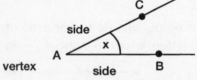

(A) by a capital letter which names its vertex, i.e., $\angle A$;

(B) by a lowercase letter or number placed inside the angle, i.e., $\angle x$;

(C) by three capital letters, where the middle letter is the vertex and the other two letters are not on the same ray, i.e., $\angle CAB$ or $\angle BAC$, both of which represent the angle illustrated in the figure.

Types of Angles

(A) A **right angle** is an angle whose measure is 90°.

(B) An **acute angle** is an angle whose measure is larger than 0° but less than 90°.

(C) An **obtuse angle** is an angle whose measure is larger than 90° but less than 180°.

(D) A **straight angle** is an angle whose measure is 180°. Such an angle is, in fact, a straight line.

(E) A **reflex angle** is an angle whose measure is greater than 180° but less than 360°.

(F) **Complementary angles** are two angles, the sum of the measures of which equals 90°.

(G) **Supplementary angles** are two angles, the sum of the measures of which equals 180°.

(H) **Congruent angles** are angles of equal measure.

(I) **Vertical angles** are formed when two lines intersect. These angles are equal.

$$\angle a = \angle b$$

(J) **Adjacent angles** are two angles with a common vertex and a common side, but no common interior points. In the following figure, $\angle DAC$ and $\angle BAC$ are adjacent angles. $\angle DAB$ and $\angle BAC$ are not.

PROBLEM

In the figure, we are given $l\ AB$ and triangle ABC. We are told that the measure of $\angle 1$ is five times the measure of $\angle 2$. Determine the measures of $\angle 1$ and $\angle 2$.

Solution

Since $\angle 1$ and $\angle 2$ are adjacent angles whose non-common sides lie on a straight line, they are, by definition, supplementary. As supplements, their measures must sum to 180°.

If x = the measure of $\angle 2$, then $5x$ = the measure of $\angle 1$.

To determine the respective angle measures, set $x + 5x = 180°$ and solve for x. $6x = 180°$. Therefore, $x = 30°$ and $5x = 150°$.

Therefore, the measure of $\angle 1 = 150°$ and the measure of $\angle 2 = 30°$.

Perpendicular Lines

Two lines are said to be **perpendicular** if they intersect and form right angles. The symbol for perpendicular (or, is therefore perpendicular to) is $\perp$; l_1 is perpendicular to l_2 is written $l_1 \perp l_2$.

PROBLEM

We are given straight lines l_1 and l_2 intersecting at point P. $l_3 \perp l_1$ and the measure of $\angle APD$ is 170°. Find the measures of $\angle 1$, $\angle 2$, $\angle 3$, and $\angle 4$.

Solution

This problem will involve making use of several of the properties of supplementary and vertical angles, as well as perpendicular lines.

$\angle APD$ and $\angle 1$ are adjacent angles whose non-common sides lie on a straight line, l_1. Therefore, they are supplements and their measures sum to 180°.

$$m \angle APD + m \angle 1 = 180°.$$

We know $m \angle APD = 170°$. Therefore, by substitution, $170° + m \angle 1 = 180°$. This implies $m \angle 1 = 10°$.

$\angle 1$ and $\angle 4$ are vertical angles because they are formed by the intersection of two straight lines, l_2 and l_1, and their sides form two pairs of opposite rays. As vertical angles, they are, by theorem, of equal measure. Since $m \angle 1 = 10°$, then $m \angle 4 = 10°$.

Since $l_3 \perp l_1$, at their intersection the angles formed must be right angles. Therefore, $\angle 3$ is a right angle and its measure is 90°. $m \angle 3 = 90°$.

The figure shows us that $\angle APD$ is composed of $\angle 3$ and $\angle 2$. Since the measure of the whole must be equal to the sum of the measures of its parts, $m \angle APD = m \angle 3 + m \angle 2$. We know the $m \angle APD = 170°$ and $m \angle 3 = 90°$; therefore, by substitution, we can solve for $m \angle 2$, our last unknown.

$$170° = 90° + m \angle 2$$

$$80° = m \angle 2$$

Therefore, $m \angle 1 = 10°$ $m \angle 2 = 80°$

$m \angle 3 = 90°$ $m \angle 4 = 10°$

PROBLEM

In the accompanying figure *SM* is the perpendicular bisector of *QR*, and *SN* is the perpendicular bisector of *QP*. Prove that *SR = SP*.

Solution

Every point on the perpendicular bisector of a segment is equidistant from the endpoints of the segment.

Since point *S* is on the perpendicular bisector of *QR*,

$SR = SQ$ \hfill (1)

Also, since point *S* is on the perpendicular bisector of *QP*,

$SQ = SP$ \hfill (2)

By the transitive property (quantities equal to the same quantity are equal), we have:

$SR = SP$ \hfill (3)

Parallel Lines

Two lines are called **parallel lines** if, and only if, they are in the same plane (coplanar) and do not intersect. The symbol for parallel, or is parallel to, is $\|$; l_1 is parallel to l_2 is written $l_1 \| l_2$.

The distance between two parallel lines is the length of the perpendicular segment from any point on one line to the other line.

$$l_1 \parallel l_2$$

Given a line l and a point P not on line l, there is one and only one line through point P that is parallel to line l.

Two coplanar lines are either intersecting lines or parallel lines.

If two (or more) lines are perpendicular to the same line, then they are parallel to each other.

If $l_1 \perp l_0$ and $l_2 \perp l_0$, then $l_1 \parallel l_2$.

If two lines are cut by a transversal so that alternate interior angles are equal, the lines are parallel.

If $\angle \alpha = \angle \beta$, then $l_1 \parallel l_2$.

If two lines are parallel to the same line, then they are parallel to each other.

If $l_1 \parallel l_0$ and $l_2 \parallel l_0$, then $l_1 \parallel l_2$.

If a line is perpendicular to one of two parallel lines, then it is perpendicular to the other line, too.

If $l_1 \parallel l_2$ and $l_1 \perp l_0$, then $l_0 \perp l_2$.

If two lines being cut by a transversal form congruent corresponding angles, then the two lines are parallel.

If $\angle \alpha = \angle \beta$, then $l_1 \parallel l_2$.

If two lines being cut by a transversal form interior angles on the same side of the transversal that are supplementary, then the two lines are parallel.

If $m \angle \alpha + m \angle \beta = 180°$, then $l_1 \parallel l_2$.

If a line is parallel to one of two parallel lines, it is also parallel to the other line.

If $l_1 \parallel l_2$ and $l_0 \parallel l_1$, then $l_0 \parallel l_2$.

If two parallel lines are cut by a transversal, then:

(A) the alternate interior angles are congruent.

(B) the corresponding angles are congruent.

(C) the consecutive interior angles are supplementary.

(D) the alternate exterior angles are congruent.

PROBLEM

Given: ∠2 is supplementary to ∠3.

Prove: $l_1 \parallel l_2$.

Solution

Given two lines intercepted by a transversal, if a pair of corresponding angles are congruent, then the two lines are parallel. In this problem, we will show that since ∠1 and ∠2 are supplementary and ∠2 and ∠3 are supplementary, ∠1 and ∠3 are congruent. Since corresponding angles are congruent, it follows $l_1 \parallel l_2$.

Statement	Reason
1. ∠2 is supplementary to ∠3.	1. Given.
2. ∠1 is supplementary to ∠2.	2. Two angles that form a linear pair are supplementary.
3. ∠1 ≅ ∠3.	3. Angles supplementary to the same angle are congruent.
4. $l_1 \parallel l_2$.	4. Given two lines intercepted by a transversal, if a pair of corresponding angles are congruent, then the two lines are parallel.

PROBLEM

If line l_1 is parallel to line l_2 and line l_3 is parallel to line l_4, prove that $m \angle 1 = m \angle 2$.

Solution

To show $\angle 1 \cong \angle 2$, we relate both to $\angle 3$. Because $l_3 \parallel l_4$, corresponding angles 1 and 3 are congruent. Since $l_1 \parallel l_2$, corresponding angles 3 and 2 are congruent. Because both $\angle 1$ and $\angle 2$ are congruent to the same angle, it follows that $\angle 1 \cong \angle 2$.

Statement	**Reason**
1. $l_3 \parallel l_4$.	1. Given.
2. $m \angle 1 = m \angle 3$.	2. If two parallel lines are cut by a transversal, corresponding angles are of equal measure.
3. $l_1 \parallel l_2$.	3. Given.
4. $m \angle 2 = m \angle 3$.	4. If two parallel lines are cut by a transversal, corresponding angles are equal in measure.
5. $m \angle 1 = m \angle 2$.	5. If two quantities are equal to the same quantity, they are equal to each other.

Drill 1: Points, Lines, and Angles

Intersecting Lines and Angles

1. Find a.

    (A) 38°

    (B) 68°

    (C) 78°

    (D) 90°

    (E) 112°

2. Find *c*.

(A) 32°

(B) 48°

(C) 58°

(D) 82°

(E) 148°

3. Determine *x*.

(A) 21°

(B) 23°

(C) 51°

(D) 102°

(E) 153°

$$27 + 2x + x = 180$$
$$-27 \qquad -27$$
$$\qquad\qquad 153$$

4. Find *x*.

(A) 8

(B) 11.75

(C) 21

(D) 23

(E) 32

$$3x = 153$$

$$3x + 12 + 5x - 16 = 180$$

$$8x - 4 = 180$$
$$+ 4 \quad + 4$$

$$8x = 184 \qquad 8\overline{)184}$$
$$\qquad\qquad \frac{16}{24}$$

5. Find *z*.

(A) 29°

(B) 54°

(C) 61°

(D) 88°

(E) 92°

$$\begin{array}{r} \overset{1}{6}\overset{3}{}\\ 29\\ \hline 92 \end{array}$$

$$\frac{180}{92}$$

Perpendicular Lines

6. $\vec{BA} \perp \vec{BC}$ and $m \angle DBC = 53°$. Find $m \angle ABD$.

   (A) 27°

   (B) 33°

   (C) 37°

   (D) 53°

   (E) 90°

$\dfrac{\cancel{90}\ \ \cancel{53}}{37}$

7. $m \angle 1 = 90°$. Find $m \angle 2. =$

   (A) 80°

   (B) 90°

   (C) 100°

   (D) 135°

   (E) 180°

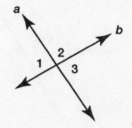

8. If $n \perp p$, which of the following statements is true?

   (A) $\angle 1 \cong \angle 2$

   (B) $\angle 4 \cong \angle 5$

   (C) $m \angle 4 + m \angle 5 > m \angle 1 + m \angle 2$

   (D) $m \angle 3 > m \angle 2$

   (E) $m \angle 4 = 90°$

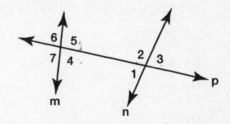

9. $CD \perp EF$. If $m \angle 1 = 2x$, $m \angle 2 = 30°$, and $m \angle 3 = x$, find x.

   (A) 5°

   (B) 10°

   (C) 12°

   (D) 20°

   (E) 25°

$2x + 30 + x = 90$
30
$3x = 60$

10. In the figure, $p \perp t$ and $q \perp t$. Which of the following statements is false?

(A) $\angle 1 \cong \angle 4$

(B) $\angle 2 \cong \angle 3$

(C) $m\angle 2 + m\angle 3 = m\angle 4 + m\angle 6$

(D) $m\angle 5 + m\angle 6 = 180°$

(E) $m\angle 2 > m\angle 5$

Parallel Lines

11. If $a \parallel b$, find z.

(A) 26°

(B) 32°

(C) 64°

(D) 86°

(E) 116°

12. In the figure, $p \parallel q \parallel r$. Find $m\angle 7$.

(A) 27°

(B) 33°

(C) 47°

(D) 57°

(E) 64°

13. If $m \parallel n$, which of the following statements is false?

(A) $\angle 2 \cong \angle 5$

(B) $\angle 3 \cong \angle 6$

(C) $m\angle 4 + m\angle 5 = 180°$

(D) $\angle 1 \cong \angle 8$

(E) $m\angle 7 + m\angle 1 = 180°$

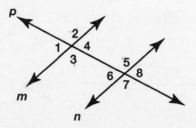

14. If $r \parallel s$, find $m \angle 2$.

    (A) 17°

    (B) 27°

    (C) 43°

    (D) 67°

    (E) 73°

15. If $a \parallel b$ and $c \parallel d$, find $m \angle 5$.

    (A) 55°

    (B) 65°

    (C) 75°

    (D) 95°

    (E) 125°

2. TRIANGLES

A closed three-sided geometric figure is called a **triangle**. The points of the intersection of the sides of a triangle are called the **vertices** of the triangle.

A side of a triangle is a line segment whose endpoints are the vertices of two angles of the triangle.

An interior angle of a triangle is an angle formed by two sides and includes the third side within its collection of points.

The sum of the interior angles of a triangle equals 180°.

The **perimeter** of a triangle is the sum of the measures of the sides of the triangle.

A triangle with no equal sides is called a **scalene triangle**.

157

A triangle having at least two equal sides is called an **isosceles triangle**. The third side is called the **base** of the triangle. The angles opposite the equal sides are equal.

$AB = AC$

An **equilateral triangle** is a triangle having three equal sides. The angles of an equilateral triangle are equal.

$AB = AC = BC$

A triangle with one obtuse angle greater than 90° is called an **obtuse triangle**.

An **acute triangle** is a triangle with three acute angles (less than 90°).

A triangle with a right angle is called a **right triangle**. The side opposite the right angle in a right triangle is called the **hypotenuse** of the right triangle. The other two sides are called **arms** or **legs** of the right triangle.

The **Pythagorean Theorem** is

$a^2 + b^2 = c^2$ in a right triangle.

a and *b* are the legs of the triangle and *c* is the hypotenuse.

In a 30°–60°–90° triangle, the hypotenuse is twice as long as the side opposite the 30° angle. The side opposite the 60° angle is equal to the length of the side opposite the 30° angle multiplied by $\sqrt{3}$. This gives a ratio of $1:\sqrt{3}:2$ for the sides of the triangle.

PROBLEM

Use the Pythagorean Theorem to show the special relationship in a 30°–60°–90° triangle.

Solution

Let the side opposite the 30° angle = 1. Then the hypotenuse = 2.

Using the Pythagorean Theorem,

$$a^2 + b^2 = c^2$$

$$1^2 + b^2 = 2^2$$

$$1 + b^2 = 4$$

$$b^2 = 4 - 1$$

$$b^2 = 3$$

$$b = \sqrt{3}$$

In a 45°–45°–90° triangle, the length of the hypotenuse is equal to the length of one of the legs multiplied by $\sqrt{2}$.

PROBLEM

Use the Pythagorean Theorem to show the special relationship in a 45°–45°–90° triangle.

Solution

Let the legs equal 1.

$$a^2 + b^2 = c^2$$

$$1^2 + 1^2 = c^2$$

$$1 + 1 = c^2$$

$$2 = c^2$$

$$\sqrt{2} = c$$

Two triangles are congruent if corresponding parts are congruent.

If $AB = DE$, $BC = EF$, $AC = DF$, $\angle A = \angle D$, $\angle B = \angle E$, and $\angle C = \angle F$, then $\triangle ABC \cong \triangle DEF$.

If two sides and the included angle of one triangle are equal respectively to two sides and the included angle of another triangle, then the two triangles are congruent. (S.A.S.)

If $AB = DE$, $AC = DF$, and $\angle A = \angle D$, then $\triangle ABC \cong \triangle DEF$.

If two angles and the included side of one triangle are equal respectively to two sides and the included side of another triangle, then the two triangles are congruent. (A.S.A.)

If $\angle A = \angle D$, $\angle B = \angle E$, and $AB = DE$, then $\triangle ABC \cong \triangle DEF$.

If three sides of one triangle are equal respectively to three sides of another triangle, then the triangles are congruent. (S.S.S.)

If $AB = DE$, $BC = EF$, and $AC = DF$, then $\triangle ABC \cong \triangle DEF$.

PROBLEM

Given figure *ABCDE* with straight line *ABCD*, *AB* = *CD*, *BE* = *CE*, and ∠ *EBA* = ∠ *ECD*, prove △*ABE* ≅ △*CED*.

Solution

Given a triangle with two sides and an included angle equal to another triangle, then the triangles are congruent.

Statement	Reason
1. *AB* = *CD*.	1. Given.
2. *BE* = *CE*.	2. Given.
3. ∠ *EBA* = ∠ *ECD*.	3. Given.
4. ∴ △*ABE* ≅ △*CED*.	4. S.A.S.

PROBLEM

Given figure *ABCD* with ∠ *x* = ∠ *y* and ∠ *r* = ∠ *s*, prove △*ABD* ≅ △*DBC*.

Solution

With the given information look for congruence between the triangles by having two angles and the included side equal.

Statement	Reason
1. ∠ *x* = ∠ *y*.	1. Given.
2. ∠ *r* = ∠ *s*.	2. Given.
3. *DB* = *DB*.	3. Any quantity equals itself (Identity).
4. ∴ △*ABD* ≅ △*DBC*.	4. A.S.A.

Two triangles are **similar** if corresponding angles are congruent and the corresponding sides are proportional segments.

Given $\angle A = \angle D$, $\angle B = \angle E$, and $\angle C = \angle F$. $\dfrac{AB}{DE} = \dfrac{BC}{EF} = \dfrac{AC}{DF}$ then $\triangle ABC \sim \triangle DEF$.

A line parallel to one side of a triangle that intersects the other two sides divides these two sides into proportional segments.

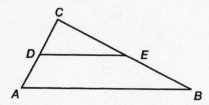

Given $\triangle ABC$ with $DE \parallel AB$, then $\dfrac{AD}{DC} = \dfrac{BE}{EC}$.

PROBLEM

Given $\triangle RST$, $UV \parallel RT$. If $SV = 3$, $VT = 2$, and $SU = 4$, then find UR.

Solution

Given $\triangle RST$, with $UV \parallel RT$, then

$$\frac{VT}{VS} = \frac{RU}{SU}$$

$$\frac{2}{3} = \frac{UR}{4}$$

$$UR = \frac{8}{3}$$

An **altitude** of a triangle is a line segment from a vertex of the triangle perpendicular to the opposite side.

A line segment connecting a vertex of a triangle and the midpoint of the opposite side is called a **median** of the triangle.

A line that bisects and is perpendicular to a side of a triangle is called a **perpendicular bisector** of that side.

An **angle bisector** of a triangle is a line that bisects an angle and extends to the opposite side of the triangle.

The line segment that joins the midpoints of two sides of a triangle is called a **midline** of the triangle.

An **exterior angle** of a triangle is an angle formed outside a triangle by one side of the triangle and the extension of an adjacent side.

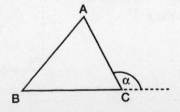

A triangle whose three interior angles have equal measure is said to be **equiangular**.

Three or more lines (or rays or segments) are concurrent if there exists one point common to all of them, that is, if they all intersect at the same point.

PROBLEM

The measure of the vertex angle of an isosceles triangle exceeds the measurement of each base angle by 30°. Find the value of each angle of the triangle.

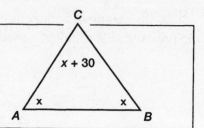

Solution

We know that the sum of the values of the angles of a triangle is 180°. In an isosceles triangle, the angles opposite the congruent sides (the base angles) are, themselves, congruent and of equal value.

Therefore,

(1)   Let x = the measure of each base angle.

(2)   Then $x + 30$ = the measure of the vertex angle.

We can solve for x algebraically by keeping in mind the sum of all the measures will be 180°.

$$x + x + (x + 30) = 180$$

$$3x + 30 = 180$$

$$3x = 150$$

$$x = 50$$

Therefore, the base angles each measure 50°, and the vertex angle measures 80°.

PROBLEM

Prove that the base angles of an isosceles right triangle measure 45°.

Solution

As drawn in the figure, $\triangle ABC$ is an isosceles right triangle with base angles BAC and BCA. The sum of the measures of the angles of any triangle is 180°. For $\triangle ABC$, this means

$$m \angle BAC + m \angle BCA + m \angle ABC = 180° \qquad (1)$$

But $m \angle ABC = 90°$ because $\triangle ABC$ is a right triangle. Furthermore, $m \angle BCA = m \angle BAC$, since the base angles of an isosceles triangle are congruent. Using these facts in equation (1),

$$m \angle BAC + m \angle BCA + 90° = 180°$$

or $\qquad 2m \angle BAC = 2m \angle BCA = 90°$

or $\qquad m \angle BAC = m \angle BCA = 45°$

Therefore, the base angles of an isosceles right triangle measure 45°.

The area of a triangle is given by the formula

$$A = \tfrac{1}{2}\, bh,$$

where b is the length of a base, which can be any side of the triangle and h is the corresponding height of the triangle, which is the perpendicular line segment that is drawn from the vertex opposite the base to the base itself.

$A = \tfrac{1}{2}\, bh$

$A = \tfrac{1}{2}\, (10)\,(3)$

$A = 15$

The area of a right triangle is found by taking $\tfrac{1}{2}$ the product of the lengths of its two arms.

$A = \tfrac{1}{2}\, (5)\,(12)$

$A = 30$

Drill 2: Triangles

Angle Measures

1.   In $\triangle PQR$, $\angle Q$ is a right angle. Find $m \angle R$.

     (A) 27°

     (B) 33°

     (C) 54°

     (D) 67°

     (E) 157°

$$\begin{array}{r} 90 \\ 23 \\ \hline 113 \end{array}$$

$$\begin{array}{r} 180 \\ 113 \\ \hline 67 \end{array}$$

2. $\triangle MNO$ is an isosceles triangle. If the vertex angle, $\angle N$, has a measure of 96°, find the measure of $\angle M$.

     (A) 21°

     (B) 42°

     (C) 64°

     (D) 84°

     (E) 96°

$$\begin{array}{r} 180 \\ 96 \\ \hline 84 \end{array}$$

$$42$$

3.   Find x.

     (A) 15°

     (B) 25°

     (C) 30°

     (D) 45°

     (E) 90°

$$3x + 2x = x$$

4.   Find $m \angle 1$.

     (A) 40°

     (B) 66°

     (C) 74°

     (D) 114°

     (E) 140°

$$\begin{array}{r} 180 \\ -114 \\ \hline 66 \end{array}$$

$$\begin{array}{r} 74 \\ 66 \\ \hline 140 \end{array}$$

5. $\triangle ABC$ is a right triangle with a right angle at B. $\triangle BDC$ is a right triangle with right angle $\angle BDC$. If $m \angle C = 36°$. Find $m \angle A$.

(A) 18°

(B) 36°

(C) 54°

(D) 72°

(E) 180°

Brittny 66

$\begin{array}{r} 90 \\ 36 \\ \hline 126 \end{array}$

Similar Triangles

6. The two triangles shown are similar. Find b.

(A) $2^2/_3$

(B) 3

(C) 4

(D) 16

(E) 24

$\begin{array}{r} 180 \\ 126 \\ \hline 54 \end{array}$

$\dfrac{6}{4} = \dfrac{4}{b}$

7. The two triangles shown are similar. Find $m \angle 1$.

(A) 48°

(B) 53°

(C) 74°

(D) 127°

(E) 180°

$\begin{array}{r} 85 \\ 42 \\ \hline 127 \end{array}$

$\begin{array}{r} 180 \\ 127 \\ \hline 53 \end{array}$

8. The two triangles shown are similar. Find a and b.

(A) 5 and 10

(B) 4 and 8

(C) $4^2/_3$ and $7^1/_3$

(D) 5 and 8

(E) $5^1/_3$ and 8

$\dfrac{3}{4} = \dfrac{4}{5} = \dfrac{6}{b}$

9. The perimeter of ΔLXR is 45 and the perimeter of ΔABC is 27. If LX = 15, find the length of AB.

    (A) 9

    (B) 15

    (C) 27

    (D) 45

    (E) 72

10. Find b.

    (A) 9

    (B) 15

    (C) 20

    (D) 45

    (E) 60

Area

11. Find the area of ΔMNO.

    (A) 22

    (B) 49

    (C) 56

    (D) 84

    (E) 112

12. Find the area of ΔPQR.

    (A) 31.5

    (B) 38.5

    (C) 53

    (D) 77

    (E) 82.5

13. Find the area of △*STU*.

    (A) $4\sqrt{2}$

    (B) $8\sqrt{2}$

    (C) $12\sqrt{2}$

    (D) $16\sqrt{2}$

    (E) $32\sqrt{2}$

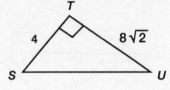

$\frac{1}{2} \cdot 4 \cdot 8\sqrt{2}$

$32\sqrt{2}$

14. Find the area of △*ABC*.

    (A) 54 cm²

    (B) 81 cm²

    (C) 108 cm²

    (D) 135 cm²

    (E) 180 cm²

$\frac{1}{2} b \cdot h$

$\begin{array}{r} \overset{2}{7}5 \\ 15 \\ \hline 75 \end{array}$

$\begin{array}{r} 11 \; 5^{-0} \\ \hline 225 \end{array}$

15. Find the area of △*XYZ*.

    (A) 20 cm²

    (B) 50 cm²

    (C) $50\sqrt{2}$ cm²

    (D) 100 cm²

    (E) 200 cm²

$\frac{1}{2} \cdot 9 \cdot 17$

12
9

$2\sqrt{118}$

$a^2 + b^2 = c^2$

$a^2 + 9^2 = 15^2 \quad a^2$

$a^2 + 81 = 225$
$\quad -81 = 81$
$\sqrt{144} = 12$

$\frac{1}{2} \cdot b \cdot h$

Congruent Triangles

DIRECTIONS: Determine whether or not the triangles are congruent and why. The answers are:

    (A) Congruent because of S.A.S.

    (B) Congruent because of A.S.A.

    (C) Congruent because of S.S.S.

    (D) Not congruent

16. Given $\triangle ADBC$ with $\angle x = \angle y$ and $\angle r = \angle s$, is $\triangle ABC \cong \triangle ADB$?

17. Given $\triangle ABC$ and $\triangle DEF$ with $\angle A = \angle D$, $AC = DF$, $AB = DE$, is $\triangle ABC \cong \triangle DEF$?

18. Given $\triangle ABC$ and $\triangle DEF$ with $\angle A = \angle E$, $BC = DF$, and $\angle C = \angle D$, is $\triangle ABC \cong \triangle ADEF$?

19. Given $AB = BC$ and $AD = DC$, is $\triangle ABD \cong \triangle BCD$?

20. Given $\angle A = \angle F$, $\angle C = \angle E$, and $CB = DE$, is $\triangle ABC \cong \triangle DEF$?

3. QUADRILATERALS

A **quadrilateral** is a polygon with four sides.

Parallelograms

A **parallelogram** is a quadrilateral whose opposite sides are parallel.

Two angles that have their vertices at the endpoints of the same side of a parallelogram are called **consecutive angles**.

The perpendicular segment connecting any point of a line containing one side of the parallelogram to the line containing the opposite side of the parallelogram is called the **altitude** of the parallelogram.

A diagonal of a polygon is a line segment joining any two non-consecutive vertices.

The area of a parallelogram is given by the formula $A = bh$, where b is the base and h is the height drawn perpendicular to that base. Note that the height equals the altitude of the parallelogram.

$A = bh$

$A = (10)(3)$

$A = 30$

Rectangles

A **rectangle** is a parallelogram with right angles.

The diagonals of a rectangle are equal. ($AC = DB$)

If the diagonals of a parallelogram are equal, the parallelogram is a rectangle.

If a quadrilateral has four right angles, then it is a rectangle.

The area of a rectangle is given by the formula $A = lw$, where l is the length and w is the width.

$A = lw$

$A = (3)(10)$

$A = 30$

Rhombi

A **rhombus** is a parallelogram with two adjacent sides equal.

All sides of a rhombus are equal.

The diagonals of a rhombus are perpendicular to each other.

The diagonals of a rhombus bisect the angles of the rhombus.

If the diagonals of a parallelogram are perpendicular, the parallelogram is a rhombus.

If a quadrilateral has four equal sides, then it is a rhombus.

A parallelogram is a rhombus if either diagonal of the parallelogram bisects the angles of the vertices it joins.

Squares

A **square** is a rhombus with a right angle.

A square is an equilateral quadrilateral.

A square has all the properties of parallelograms and rectangles.

A rhombus is a square if one of its interior angles is a right angle.

In a square, the measure of either diagonal can be calculated by multiplying the length of any side by the square root of 2.

$$AD = AB\sqrt{2}$$

The area of a square is given by the formula $A = s^2$, where s is the side of the square. Since all sides of a square are equal, it does not matter which side is used.

$A = s^2$

$A = 6^2$

$A = 36$

6

The area of a square can also be found by taking $^1/_2$ the product of the length of the diagonal squared.

$A = ^1/_2 \, d^2$

$A = ^1/_2 \, (8)^2$

$A = 32$

8

Trapezoids

A **trapezoid** is a quadrilateral with two and only two sides parallel. The parallel sides of a trapezoid are called **bases**.

The **median** of a trapezoid is the line joining the midpoints of the non-parallel sides.

A   B

median of trapezoid

C   D

The perpendicular segment connecting any point in the line containing one base of the trapezoid to the line containing the other base is the **altitude** of the trapezoid.

B

A

altitude

An **isosceles trapezoid** is a trapezoid whose non-parallel sides are equal. A pair of angles including only one of the parallel sides is called **a pair of base angles**.

Pairs of base angles

The median of a trapezoid is parallel to the bases and equal to one-half their sum.

The base angles of an isosceles trapezoid are equal.

The diagonals of an isosceles trapezoid are equal.

The opposite angles of an isosceles trapezoid are supplementary.

PROBLEM

Prove that all pairs of consecutive angles of a parallelogram are supplementary.

Solution

We must prove that the pairs of angles ∠ *BAD* and ∠ *ADC*, ∠ *ADC* and ∠ *DCB*, ∠ *DCB* and ∠ *CBA*, and ∠ *CBA* and ∠ *BAD* are supplementary. (This means that the sum of their measures is 180°.)

Because *ABCD* is a parallelogram, *AB* ∥ *CD*. Angles *BAD* and *ADC* are consecutive interior angles, as are ∠ *CBA* and ∠ *DCB*. Since the consecutive interior angles formed by two parallel lines and a transversal are supplementary, ∠ *BAD* and ∠ *ADC* are supplementary, as are ∠ *CBA* and ∠ *DCB*.

Similarly, *AD* ∥ *BC*. Angles *ADC* and *DCB* are consecutive interior angles, as are ∠ *CBA* and ∠ *BAD*. Since the consecutive interior angles formed by two parallel lines and a transversal are supplementary, ∠ *CBA* and ∠ *BAD* are supplementary, as are ∠ *ADC* and ∠ *DCB*.

PROBLEM

In the accompanying figure, Δ*ABC* is given to be an isosceles right triangle with ∠ *ABC* a right angle and *AB* ≅ *BC*. Line segment *BD*, which bisects *CA*, is extended to *E*, so that *BD* ≅ *DE*. Prove *BAEC* is a square.

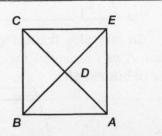

Solution

A square is a rectangle in which two consecutive sides are congruent. This definition will provide the framework for the proof in this problem. We will prove that *BAEC* is a parallelogram that is specifically a rectangle with consecutive sides congruent, namely a square.

Statement	Reason
1. $BD \cong DE$ and $AD \cong DC$.	1. Given (*BC* bisects *CA*).
2. *BAEC* is a parallelogram.	2. If diagonals of a quadrilateral bisect each other, then the quadrilateral is a parallelogram.
3. $\angle ABC$ is a right angle.	3. Given.
4. *BAEC* is a rectangle.	4. A parallelogram, one of whose angles is a right angle, is a rectangle.
5. $AB \cong BC$.	5. Given.
6. *BAEC* is a square.	6. If a rectangle has two congruent consecutive sides, then the rectangle is a square.

Drill 3: Quadrilaterals

Parallelograms, Rectangles, Rhombi, Squares, and Trapezoids

1. In parallelogram *wxyz*, $wx = 14$, $wz = 6$, $zy = 3x + 5$, and $xy = 2y - 4$. Find x and y.

   (A) 3 and 5
   (B) 4 and 5
   (C) 4 and 6
   (D) 6 and 10
   (E) 6 and 14

175

2. Quadrilateral *ABCD* is a parallelogram. If $m \angle B = (6x + 2)°$ and $m \angle D = 98°$, find x.

(A) 12

(B) 16

(C) $16^2/_3$

(D) 18

(E) 20

3. Find the area of parallelogram *STUV*.

(A) 56

(B) 90

(C) 108

(D) 162

(E) 180

4. Find the area of parallelogram *MNOP*.

(A) 19

(B) 32

(C) $32\sqrt{3}$

(D) 44

(E) $44\sqrt{3}$

5. Find the perimeter of rectangle *PQRS*.

(A) 31 in

(B) 38 in

(C) 40 in

(D) 44 in

(E) 121 in

6. In rectangle *ABCD*, *AD* = 6 cm and *DC* = 8 cm. Find the length of the diagonal *AC*.

    (A) 10 cm

    (B) 12 cm

    (C) 20 cm

    (D) 28 cm

    (E) 48 cm

7. Find the area of rectangle *UVXY*.

    (A) 17 cm²

    (B) 34 cm²

    (C) 35 cm²

    (D) 70 cm²

    (E) 140 cm²

8. Find *x* in rectangle *BCDE* if the diagonal *EC* is 17 mm.

    (A) 6.55 mm

    (B) 8 mm

    (C) 8.5 mm

    (D) 17 mm

    (E) 34 mm

9. In rhombus *DEFG*, *DE* = 7 cm. Find the perimeter of the rhombus.

    (A) 14 cm

    (B) 28 cm

    (C) 42 cm

    (D) 49 cm

    (E) 56 cm

10. In rhombus *RHOM*, the diagonal *RO* is 8 cm and the diagonal *HM* is 12 cm. Find the area of the rhombus.

    (A) 20 cm²

    (B) 40 cm²

    (C) 48 cm²

    (D) 68 cm²

    (E) 96 cm²

11. In rhombus *GHIJ*, *GI* = 6 cm and *HJ* = 8 cm. Find the length of *GH*.

    (A) 3 cm

    (B) 4 cm

    (C) 5 cm

    (D) 4√3 cm

    (E) 14 cm

12. In rhombus *CDEF*, *CD* is 13 mm and *DX* is 5 mm. Find the area of the rhombus.

    (A) 31 mm²

    (B) 60 mm²

    (C) 78 mm²

    (D) 120 mm²

    (E) 260 mm²

13. Quadrilateral *ATUV* is a square. If the perimeter of the square is 44 cm, find the length of *AT*.

    (A) 4 cm   (B) 11 cm

    (C) 22 cm   (D) 30 cm

    (E) 40 cm

14. The area of square *XYZW* is 196 cm². Find the perimeter of the square.

    (A) 28 cm

    (B) 42 cm

    (C) 56 cm

    (D) 98 cm

    (E) 196 cm

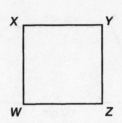

15. In square *MNOP*, *MN* is 6 cm. Find the length of diagonal *MO*.

    (A) 6 cm

    (B) $6\sqrt{2}$ cm

    (C) $6\sqrt{3}$ cm

    (D) $6\sqrt{6}$ cm

    (E) 12 cm

16. In square *ABCD*, *AB* = 3 cm. Find the area of the square.

    (A) 9 cm²

    (B) 12 cm²

    (C) 15 cm²

    (D) 18 cm²

    (E) 21 cm²

17. Find the area of trapezoid *RSTU*.

    (A) 80

    (B) 87.5

    (C) 140

    (D) 147

    (E) 175

$$a = \frac{h \cdot (b_1 + b_2)}{2}$$

18. *ABCD* is an isosceles trapezoid. Find the perimeter.

    (A) 21 cm

    (B) 27 cm

    (C) 30 cm

    (D) 50 cm

    (E) 54 cm

19. Find the area of trapezoid *MNOP*.

    (A) $(17 + 3\sqrt{3})$ mm^2

    (B) $^{33}/_2$ mm^2

    (C) $(33\sqrt{3})/2$ mm^2

    (D) 33 mm^2

    (E) $33\sqrt{3}$ mm^2

20. Trapezoid *XYZW* is isosceles. If $m \angle W = 58$ and $m \angle Z = (4x - 6)$, find *x*.

    (A) 8

    (B) 12

    (C) 13

    (D) 16

    (E) 58

4. CIRCLES

A **circle** is a set of points in the same plane equidistant from a fixed point called its center.

A **radius** of a circle is a line segment drawn from the center of the circle to any point on the circle.

A portion of a circle is called an **arc** of the circle.

A line that intersects a circle in two points is called a **secant.**

A line segment joining two points on a circle is called a **chord** of the circle.

A chord that passes through the center of the circle is called a **diameter** of the circle.

The line passing through the centers of two (or more) circles is called the **line of centers.**

An angle whose vertex is on the circle and whose sides are chords of the circle is called an **inscribed angle**.

The measure of an inscribed angle is half the measure of its intercepted arc.

$$m \angle CAB = \frac{1}{2} m \widehat{CB}$$

An angle inscribed in a semicircle is a right angle.

$$m \angle ABC = 90°$$

An angle whose vertex is at the center of a circle and whose sides are radii is called a **central angle.**

The measure of a minor arc is the measure of the central angle that intercepts that arc.

$$m \widehat{AB} = \alpha = m \angle AOB$$

Congruent circles are circles whose radii are congruent.

If $O_1A_1 \cong O_2A_2$, then $O_1 \cong O_2$.

The measure of a semicircle is 180°.

A **circumscribed circle** is a circle passing through all the vertices of a polygon.

Circles that have the same center and unequal radii are called **concentric circles.**

Concentric Circles

PROBLEM

A and *B* are points on circle *Q* such that $\triangle AQB$ is equilateral. If the length of side $AB = 12$, find the length of $\overset{\frown}{AB}$.

Solution

To find the arc length of $\overset{\frown}{AB}$, we must find the measure of the central angle $\angle AQB$ and the measure of the radius $\overline{QA}$. $\angle AQB$ is an interior angle of the equilateral triangle $\triangle AQB$. Therefore, $m \angle AQB = 60°$. Similarly, in the equilateral $\triangle AQB$,

$$AQ = AB = QB = 12.$$

Given the radius, r, and the central angle, n, the arc length is given by $^n/_{360} \times 2\pi r$. Therefore, by substitution of $m \angle AQB$,

$$\frac{60}{360} \times 2\pi \times 12 = \frac{1}{6} \times 2\pi \times 12 = 4\pi.$$

Therefore, the length of $\overset{\frown}{AB} = 4\pi$.

PROBLEM

In circle *O*, the measure of $\overset{\frown}{AB}$ is 80°. Find the measure of $\angle A$.

Solution

The accompanying figure shows that $\overset{\frown}{AB}$ is intercepted by central $\angle AOB$. By definition, we know that the measure of the central angle is the measure of its intercepted arc. In this case,

$$m \overset{\frown}{AB} = m \angle AOB = 80°.$$

Radius *OA* and radius *OB* are congruent and form two sides of $\triangle OAB$. By a theorem, the angles opposite these two congruent sides must, themselves, be congruent. Therefore, $m \angle A = m \angle B$.

The sum of the measures of the angles of a triangle is 180°. Therefore,

$$m \angle A + m \angle B + m \angle AOB = 180°.$$

Since $m \angle A = m \angle B$, we can write

$$m \angle A + m \angle A + 80° = 180°$$

or $2m \angle A = 100°$

or $m \angle A = 50°.$

Therefore, the measure of $\angle A$ is 50°.

Drill 4: Circles

1. Find the circumference of circle A if its radius is 3 mm.

   (A) 3π mm   (B) 6π mm

   (C) 9π mm   (D) 12π mm

   (E) 15π mm

2. The circumference of circle H is 20π cm. Find the length of the radius.

   (A) 10 cm   (B) 20 cm

   (C) 10π cm   (D) 15π cm

   (E) 20π cm

3. The circumference of circle A is how many millimeters larger than the circumference of circle B?

   (A) 3

   (B) 6

   (C) 3π

   (D) 6π

   (E) 7π

4. If the diameter of circle X is 9 cm, find the circumference of the circle.

    (A) 9 cm   (B) 4.5π cm

    (C) 6π cm   (D) 8π cm

    (E) 9π cm

5. Find the area of circle I.

    (A) 22 mm^2

    (B) 121 mm^2

    (C) 121π mm^2

    (D) 132 mm^2

    (E) 132π mm^2

6. The diameter of circle Z is 27 mm. Find the area of the circle.

    (A) 91.125 mm^2 (B) 182.25 mm^2

    (C) 191.5π mm^2 (D) 182.25π mm^2

    (E) 729 mm^2

7. The area of circle B is 225π cm^2. Find the length of the diameter of the circle.

    (A) 15 cm   (B) 20 cm

    (C) 30 cm   (D) 20π cm

    (E) 25π cm

8. The area of circle X is 144π mm^2 while the area of circle Y is 81π mm^2. Write the ratio of the radius of circle X to that of circle Y.

    (A) 3 : 4   (B) 4 : 3

    (C) 9 : 12   (D) 27 : 12

    (E) 18 : 24

$2\pi v = 18\pi$ $\dfrac{2v=18}{2 \quad 2}$

$\dfrac{}{\pi \quad \pi}$ $v=9$

9. The circumference of circle M is 18π cm. Find the area of the circle.

（A) 18π cm^2 （B) 81 cm^2 πr^2

（C) 36 cm^2 （D) 36π cm^2 81

（E) 81π cm^2

10. In two concentric circles, the smaller circle has a radius of 3 mm
    while the larger circle has a radius of 5 mm. Find the area of the
    shaded region.

（A) 2π mm^2 $\pi 3^2$

（B) 8π mm^2 $\pi 5^2$

（C) 13π mm^2 $\pi 9$

（D) 16π mm^2 $\pi 25$

（E) 26π mm^2

11. The radius of the smaller of two concentric circles is 5 cm while the
    radius of the larger circle is 7 cm. Determine the area of the shaded
    region.

（A) 7π cm^2 πr^2

（B) 24π cm^2 25π

（C) 25π cm^2 49π

（D) 36π cm^2

（E) 49π cm^2 $\dfrac{49}{25}$ $\dfrac{}{24}$

12. Find the measure of $\overarc{MN}$ if $m \angle MON = 62°$.

（A) $16°$

（B) $32°$

（C) $59°$

（D) $62°$

（E) $124°$

13. Find the measure of $\overarc{AXC}$.

    (A) 150°

    (B) 160°

    (C) 180°

    (D) 270°

    (E) 360°

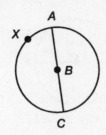

14. If $\overarc{MXP} = 236°$, find the measure of $\overarc{MP}$.

    (A) 62°

    (B) 124°

    (C) 236°

    (D) 270°

    (E) 360°

15. In circle S, major $\overarc{PQR}$ has a measure of 298°. Find the measure of the central $\angle PSR$.

    (A) 62°

    (B) 124°

    (C) 149°

    (D) 298°

    (E) 360°

16. Find the measure of $\overarc{XY}$ in circle W.

    (A) 40°

    (B) 120°

    (C) 140°

    (D) 180°

    (E) 220°

17. Find the area of the sector shown.

    (A) 4 cm²

    (B) 2π cm²

    (C) 16 cm²

    (D) 8π cm²

    (E) 16π cm²

18. Find the area of the shaded region.

    (A) 10

    (B) 5π

    (C) 25

    (D) 20π

    (E) 25π

19. Find the area of the sector shown.

    (A) $\dfrac{9\pi \text{ mm}^2}{4}$

    (B) $\dfrac{9\pi \text{ mm}^2}{2}$

    (C) 18 mm²

    (D) 6π mm²

    (E) 9π mm²

20. If the area of the square is 100 cm², find the area of the sector.

    (A) 10π cm²

    (B) 25 cm²

    (C) 25π cm²

    (D) 100 cm²

    (E) 100π cm²

5. SOLIDS

Solid geometry is the study of figures which consist of points not all in the same plane.

Rectangular Solids

A solid with lateral faces and bases that are rectangles is called a **rectangular solid**.

The surface area of a rectangular solid is the sum of the areas of all the faces.

The volume of a rectangular solid is equal to the product of its length, width, and height.

$$V = lwh$$

PROBLEM

What are the dimensions of a solid cube whose surface area is numerically equal to its volume?

Solution

The surface area of a cube of edge length a is equal to the sum of the areas of its 6 faces. Since a cube is a regular polygon, all 6 faces are congruent. Each face of a cube is a square of edge length a. Hence, the surface area of a cube of edge length a is

$$S = 6a^2.$$

The volume of a cube of edge length a is

$$V = a^3.$$

We require that $S = V$, or that

$$6a^2 = a^3 \quad \text{or} \quad a = 6$$

Hence, if a cube has edge length 6, its surface area will be numerically equal to its volume.

Cylinders

A solid with bases that are parallel circles and with cross sections parallel to the bases that are also circles is called a **circular cylinder** or a cylinder.

The altitude of a cylinder is the distance between two bases of the cylinder.

The lateral area of a cylinder is equal to the area of its curved cylindrical surface.

The total area of a cylinder is equal to the sum of its lateral area and the area of its bases.

The volume of any cylinder is the product of the area of its base and the altitude of its cylinder.

volume = (area of base) × (height)

$V = \pi r^2 h$

PROBLEM

Find, in terms of π, the volume of a right circular cylinder if the radius of its base measures 4 in. and its altitude measures 5 in.

Solution

If we picture the base of the cylinder having a depth of one unit of measure, we can then calculate the volume by determining the area of the base and multiplying it by the height of the cylinder. In effect, this multiplication amounts to stacking the bases up to the height of the cylinder.

Area of the bases $= \pi r^2$, where r is the radius of the circular base. Therefore, the volume is given by

$$V = \pi r^2 h.$$

By substitution,

$$V = \pi (4)^2 5 \text{ in}^3 = 80\pi \text{ in}^3.$$

Therefore, volume of the cylinder $= 80\pi \text{ in}^3$.

Spheres

A **sphere** is the set of points in space at a given distance from a given point, called the center of the sphere.

The area of a sphere is equal to the area of its curved spherical surface.

The volume of a sphere is equal to one-third the product of its area and the measure of its radius.

$$V = \frac{1}{3}Ar, \text{ or } V = \frac{4}{3}\pi r^3$$

$$(A = 4\pi r^2)$$

PROBLEM

A perfectly spherical planet Sandeep has a diameter of 6,000 km.

(a) Find its area.   (b) Find its volume.

Solution

(a) $d = 6,000$ km.

$$r = \frac{d}{2} = \frac{6,000}{2} = 3,000 \text{ km.}$$

$$= 3 \times 10^6 \text{ m}$$

Area $A = 4\pi r^2$

$$= 4\pi (3 \times 10^6)^2$$

$$A = 36 \times 10^{12} \pi \text{ m}^2$$

(b)   Volume $V = \dfrac{4}{3}\pi r^3$

$$= \dfrac{4}{3}\pi\,(3 \times 10^6)^3$$

$$V = 36 \times 10^{18}\pi \text{ m}^3$$

Drill 5: Solids

1. Find the total area of the rectangular prism shown.

    (A) 138 cm²

    (B) 336 cm²

    (C) 381 cm²

    (D) 426 cm²

    (E) 540 cm²

12 cm

5 cm

9 cm

2. Find the volume of the rectangular storage tank shown.

    (A) 24 m³

    (B) 36 m³

    (C) 38 m³

    (D) 42 m³

    (E) 45 m³

1.5 cm

4 cm

6 cm

3. The lateral area of a cube is 100 cm². Find the length of an edge of the cube.

    (A) 4 cm   (B) 5 cm

    (C) 10 cm   (D) 12 cm

    (E) 15 cm

4. Find the volume of a right circular cylinder of radius 4 inches and height 12 inches.

    (A) 192π in^3 (B) 144π in^3

    (C) 576π in^3 (D) 48π in^3

    (E) 196 in^3

$$\pi 4^2 \cdot h$$

$$\pi \, 16$$

$$\begin{array}{r} 16 \\ 2 \\ \hline 32 \\ 160 \\ \hline 192 \end{array}$$

REFERENCE TABLE FOR GEOMETRY FORMULAS

Triangles

$$\text{Perimeter} = AB + BC + AC$$

$$\text{Area} = \frac{1}{2}bh$$

Right Triangles

Pythagorean
Theorem $= a^2 + b^2 = c^2$

Quadrilaterals

$$\text{Perimeter} = AB + BC + CD + AD$$

$$\text{Area} = bh$$

Rectangles

$$\text{Perimeter} = 2l + 2w$$

$$\text{Area} = lw$$

Squares

$$\text{Perimeter} = 4s$$

$$\text{Area} = s^2$$

Circles

$$\text{Circumference} = 2\pi r$$

$$\text{Area} = \pi r^2$$

$$\text{Diameter} = 2r$$

Solids

Rectangular Solids

$$\text{Volume} = lwh$$

Cylinders

$$\text{Volume} = \pi r^2 h$$

Spheres

$$\text{Volume} = \frac{4}{3}\pi r^3$$

GEOMETRY DRILLS

ANSWER KEY

Drill 1 – Points, Lines, and Angles

1.	(B)	5.	(D)	9.	(D)	13.	(B)
2.	(A)	6.	(C)	10.	(E)	14.	(E)
3.	(C)	7.	(B)	11.	(C)	15.	(A)
4.	(D)	8.	(A)	12.	(D)		

Drill 2 – Triangles

1.	(D)	6.	(A)	11.	(C)	16.	(B)
2.	(B)	7.	(B)	12.	(B)	17.	(A)
3.	(C)	8.	(E)	13.	(D)	18.	(D)
4.	(E)	9.	(A)	14.	(A)	19.	(C)
5.	(C)	10.	(C)	15.	(B)	20.	(D)

Drill 3 – Quadrilaterals

1.	(A)	6.	(A)	11.	(C)	16.	(A)
2.	(B)	7.	(D)	12.	(D)	17.	(E)
3.	(D)	8.	(C)	13.	(B)	18.	(B)
4.	(E)	9.	(B)	14.	(C)	19.	(C)
5.	(C)	10.	(C)	15.	(B)	20.	(D)

Drill 4 – Circles

1.	(B)	6.	(D)	11.	(B)	16.	(C)
2.	(A)	7.	(C)	12.	(D)	17.	(B)
3.	(D)	8.	(B)	13.	(C)	18.	(D)
4.	(E)	9.	(E)	14.	(B)	19.	(A)
5.	(C)	10.	(D)	15.	(A)	20.	(C)

Drill 5 – Solids

1.	(D)	2.	(B)	3.	(C)	4.	(A)

ELM

Entry Level Mathematics

Chapter 4
Intermediate
Algebra

INTERMEDIATE ALGEBRA DIAGNOSTIC TEST

14 Questions

(Answer sheets appear at the back of the book.)

> **DIRECTIONS:** Each question has five multiple-choice answers. Select the single best answer.

1. If $x \neq 0$, then $(125^{2x})(5^x) =$

   (A) 5^{3x}.

   (B) 5^{4x}.

   (C) 5^{5x}.

   (D) 5^{7x}.

   (E) 5^{9x}.

2. If $\dfrac{5}{x-2} + \dfrac{2}{2x+1} = \dfrac{1}{x}$, then $x =$

   (A) $\dfrac{-1 \pm 2}{5}$.

   (B) $\dfrac{-2 \pm 2}{5}$.

   (C) $-1 \pm 2i$.

   (D) $-2 \pm 3i$.

   (E) $\dfrac{-1 \pm 2i}{5}$.

3. If a line contains the points $(2, 9)$ and $(-3, 1)$, then its y-intercept is

   (A) 1.

   (B) 2.

   (C) $\dfrac{19}{5}$.

   (D) $\dfrac{29}{5}$.

   (E) 8.

4. If $i^2 = -1$ and $y = 1 + 3i$, then $\dfrac{1}{y} =$

    (A) $\dfrac{1}{10} - \dfrac{3}{10}i.$

    (B) $\dfrac{1}{4} - \dfrac{3}{4}i.$

    (C) $\dfrac{1}{2} - \dfrac{3}{2}i.$

    (D) $1 - 3i.$

    (E) $1 + 9i.$

5. What are the coordinates of the midpoint between the points $(-2, 3)$ and $(4, -5)$?

    (A) $(2, -1)$

    (B) $(1, -1)$

    (C) $(0, -1)$

    (D) $(1, 1)$

    (E) $(1, 2)$

6. If $f(x) = 3x - 1$ and $g(f(x)) = x$, then $g(x) =$

    (A) $x.$

    (B) $\dfrac{x+1}{3}.$

    (C) $\dfrac{x-1}{3}.$

    (D) $3x + 1.$

    (E) $3x + 2.$

7. Which of the following is the graph of the equation $y = 2x + 1$?

    (A)

    (B)

(C)

(D)

(E)

8. If $|2x - 5|\omega = 3$, then

(A) $x = -2\dfrac{1}{2}$ or 3.

(B) $x = 2\dfrac{1}{2}$ or 4.

(C) $x = 1$ or 3.

(D) $x = 1$ or 4.

(E) $x = 0$ or -3.

9. For the following sequence of numbers,

$$\frac{1}{2}, \frac{1}{12}, \frac{1}{30}, \ldots,$$

the next number will be

(A) $\dfrac{1}{36}$.

(B) $\dfrac{1}{27}$.

(C) $\dfrac{1}{48}$.

(D) $\dfrac{1}{56}$.

(E) $\dfrac{1}{72}$.

10. In the following system

$$\begin{cases} 2x + 3y + 2z = 6 \\ 6x + 5y + 8z = 9 \\ x - 3y + 4z = -3 \end{cases}$$

x must equal

(A) 2.   (B) – 6.

(C) – 7.   (D) 8.

(E) – 10.

11. The first three terms of a progression are 3, 6, 12, ... What is the value of the tenth term?

(A) 1,200   (B) 2,468

(C) 188   (D) 1,536

(E) 3,272

12. If $\log_8 N = {}^2/_3$, what is the value of N?

(A) 2   (B) 4

(C) 8   (D) 10

(E) 12

13. In the equation $x^2 + 2x + 7 = 0$, the roots equal

(A) $-1 \pm i\sqrt{6}$.   (B) $-1 \pm \sqrt{6}$.

(C) $1 \pm i\sqrt{6}$.   (D) $-2 \pm \sqrt{6}$.

(E) $-2 \pm i\sqrt{6}$.

14. One solution to $x^3 - 16x = 0$ is

    (A) -2.   (B) 2.

    (C) 8.   (D) 4.

    (E) $^1/_4$.

INTERMEDIATE ALGEBRA
DIAGNOSTIC TEST

ANSWER KEY

1. (D)	5. (B)	9. (D)	13. (A)
2. (E)	6. (B)	10. (E)	14. (D)
3. (D)	7. (D)	11. (D)	
4. (A)	8. (D)	12. (B)	

DETERMINE YOUR STRENGTHS AND WEAKNESSES

INTERMEDIATE ALGEBRA

Question Type	Question #	See Pages . . .
Quadratic Equations	2, 13	212–217
Complex Numbers	4, 13, 2	218–220
Linear Equations and Rational Expressions	2, 10	221–225
Absolute Value Equations	8	225–228
Equations of Higher Degrees	14	228–231
Elementary Functions	6, 12	231–238
Fractional Exponents	1, 12	238–240
Sequences and Series	9, 11	240–242
Graphs	3, 5, 7	242–253

DETAILED EXPLANATIONS OF ANSWERS

INTERMEDIATE ALGEBRA DIAGNOSTIC TEST

1. **(D)**

$$(125^{2x})(5^x) = (5^3)^{2x} (5^x)$$
$$= (5^{6x}) (5^x)$$
$$= 5^{(6x + x)} = 5^{7x}$$

2. **(E)** Simplify the rational equation.

$$\frac{5}{x-2} + \frac{2}{2x+1} = \frac{1}{x}$$
$$\frac{5(2x+1) + 2(x-2)}{(x-2)(2x+1)} = \frac{1}{x}$$
$$\frac{10x + 5 + 2x - 4}{(x-2)(2x+1)} = \frac{1}{x}$$
$$\frac{12x + 1}{(x-2)(2x+1)} = \frac{1}{x}$$
$$x(12x + 1) = (x - 2)(2x + 1)$$
$$12x^2 + x = 2x^2 + x - 4x - 2$$
$$12x^2 + x = 2x^2 - 3x - 2$$
$$10x^2 + 4x + 2 = 0$$
$$5x^2 + 2x + 1 = 0$$

Use the quadratic formula to find the roots.

$$x = \frac{-2 \pm \sqrt{2^2 - 4(5)(1)}}{2(5)}$$
$$= \frac{-2 \pm \sqrt{-16}}{2(5)}$$

$$= \frac{-1 \pm \sqrt{-4}}{5}$$

$$= \frac{-1 \pm 2i}{5}$$

3.   **(D)**   The equation of the line is obtained from the point-slope equation:

$$\frac{y-1}{x-(-3)} = \frac{9-1}{2-(-3)}$$

$$\frac{y-1}{x+3} = \frac{8}{5}$$

$$y-1 = \frac{8}{5}(x+3)$$

$$y = \frac{8}{5}x + \frac{24}{5} + 1$$

$$y = \frac{8}{5}x + \frac{29}{5}$$

Therefore, the y-intercept is $\frac{29}{5}$.

4.   **(A)**   Multiply by complex conjugate to remove i from the denominator.

$$\frac{1}{y} = \frac{1}{1+3i} \times \frac{1-3i}{1-3i}$$

$$= \frac{1-3i}{1^2 - 3^2 i^2}$$

$$= \frac{1-3i}{10}$$

$$= \frac{1}{10} - \frac{3}{10}i$$

5. **(B)**

$$x = \frac{x_1 + x_2}{2}$$

$$= \frac{-2 + 4}{2}$$

$$= 1$$

$$y = \frac{y_1 + y_2}{2}$$

$$= \frac{3 + (-5)}{2}$$

$$= -1$$

The coordinates of the midpoint are $(x, y) = (1, -1)$.

6. **(B)** Since $g(f(x)) = x$, $g(x)$ is the inverse function of $f(x)$. Let

$$y = f(x) = 3x - 1.$$

Interchange x and y to obtain the inverse of $f(x)$.

$$x = 3y - 1$$

$$3y = x + 1$$

$$y = \frac{x + 1}{3}$$

7. **(D)**

$$y = 2x + 1 \rightarrow y\text{-intercept} = (0, 1), \quad \text{so we may eliminate (A) and (C)}.$$

We may also eliminate (E) since the slope of y is 2, which is positive. Graph (B) indicates that the point $(3, 2)$ is on the graph but if we substitute these values into the given equation we find the statement false. The only possibility, therefore, is Graph (D).

8. **(D)**

$$|2x - 5| = 3$$

$$2x - 5 = 3 \qquad\qquad 2x - 5 = -3$$

$$2x = 8 \qquad\qquad 2x = 2$$

$$x = 4 \qquad\qquad x = 1$$

Therefore, $x = 1$ or 4 is the solution to the given equation.

9. **(D)** To determine the next number, we look for a pattern among the previous terms. Only the denominators differ. We note by inspection that each denominator is equal to the product of two successive integers. For example, the first term:

$$\frac{1}{2} = \frac{1}{1 \times 2}$$

The second term:

$$\frac{1}{12} = \frac{1}{3 \times 4}$$

The third term:

$$\frac{1}{30} = \frac{1}{5 \times 6}$$

Thus, the next term in the sequence can be expected to be

$$\frac{1}{7 \times 8} \quad \text{or} \quad \frac{1}{56}.$$

10. **(E)** This is an example of a system of three equations in three unknowns. To solve for one unknown (x) we must eliminate the other two. We will first eliminate z. The given equations are:

$$2x + 3y + 2z = 6 \qquad\qquad (1)$$

$$6x + 5y + 8z = 9 \qquad\qquad (2)$$

$$x - 3y + 4z = -3 \qquad\qquad (3)$$

To eliminate z, we first multiply equation (1) by 4, and subtract from it equation (2):

$$4(2x + 3y + 2z = 6) = \quad 8x + 12y + 8z = 24$$
$$- (6x + 5y + 8z = 9)$$
$$\overline{2x + 7y = 15} \qquad (4)$$

Next we multiply equation (1) by 2 and subtract from it equation (3):

$$2(2x + 3y + 2z = 6) = \quad 4x + 6y + 4z = 12$$
$$- (x - 3y + 4z = - 3)$$
$$\overline{3x + 9y = 15} \qquad (5)$$

Thus, we are left with a system of two equations in two unknowns, namely equation (4) and equation (5). To find x, we must eliminate y. The best way to do this is to multiply equation (4) by 9 and equation (5) by 7, and then subtract the two equations:

$$9(2x + 7y = 15) = \quad 18x + 63y = 135$$
$$-(7 \, (3x + 9y = 15) = - (21x + 63y = 105)$$
$$\overline{- 3x = 30}$$

Solving for x: $x = - 10$.

11. **(D)** The progression given is a geometric progression. The expression for the nth term of a geometric progression is:

$$s_n = a_1 r^{n-1}$$

where a_1 is the first term and r is the common ratio between terms.

In the given sequence, the first term is 3. The common ratio is found to be:

$$\frac{6}{3} = \frac{12}{6} = 2 \, .$$

Therefore, letting $n = 10$ (for the tenth term), we have:

$$s_{10} = 3(2)^{10-1} = 3(2)^9.$$

Since $\qquad 2^9 = 512$

$$s_{10} = 3(512) = 1,536.$$

12. **(B)** To solve, the inverse of the logarithmic function must be used. This is stated as:

$$y = \log_a N$$

$$N = a^y.$$

Applying this to the given equation yields $N = 8^{2/3}$. So

$$N = \sqrt[3]{8^2} = \sqrt[3]{64} = 4 \,.$$

13. **(A)** To solve this quadratic equation, use the quadratic formula:

$$x = \frac{-b \pm \sqrt{b^2 - 4ac}}{2a}$$

The equation is

$$x^2 + 2x + 7 = 0.$$

So $a = 1$, $b = 2$, and $c = 7$. Substituting into the formula:

$$x = \frac{-2 \pm \sqrt{2^2 - 4(1)(7)}}{2(1)}$$

$$= \frac{-2 \pm \sqrt{4 - 28}}{2}$$

$$= -1 \pm \sqrt{-6}$$

Since $i = \sqrt{-1}$, $x = -1 \pm i\sqrt{-6}$.

14. **(D)**

$$x^3 - 16x = 0$$

$$x(x^2 - 16) = 0$$

$$x(x - 4)(x + 4) = 0$$

Factor the given equation. Find the solution set.

$$x = 0, \quad x - 4 = 0 \qquad \text{or} \qquad x + 4 = 0$$

$$x = 4 \qquad\qquad x = -4$$

$$x = \{-4, 0, 4\}$$

INTERMEDIATE ALGEBRA REVIEW

This section is a continuation of the algebra review. Basic operations are explained in the Elementary Algebra Review section.

1. QUADRATIC EQUATIONS

An equation in the form of

$$ax^2 + bx + c = 0,$$

where a, b, and c are real numbers and $a \neq 0$ is a **quadratic equation.** To solve a quadratic equation one can use several methods if factoring the equation is difficult and involves solutions that may not be whole numbers.

(A) **Completing the square** is one method that can be used. This method uses products based on

$$(x + a)^2 = x^2 + 2ax + a^2 \quad \text{and} \quad (x - a)^2 = x^2 - 2ax + a^2$$

1. Arrange the equation with the constant term on the right.

2. If the coefficient of x^2 is not 1, divide each term by the coefficient of x^2.

3. Complete the square:

    a. Find the x coefficient.

    b. Take one-half ($^1/_2$) of the coefficient and square it.

    c. Add the square to both sides of the equation.

4. Rewrite the left-hand terms as a perfect square.

5. Take the square root of both sides of the equation.

6. Solve the resulting equation.

7. Check in the original equation.

PROBLEM

Solve by completing the square, $x^2 - 6x + 8 = 0$.

Solution

$$x^2 - 6x = -8$$

Rearranging the constant term to the right-hand side of the equation.

$$(-6) \times (^1/_2) = -3$$

Taking one-half of the x coefficient.

$$(-3)^2 = 9$$

Squaring the coefficient.

$$x^2 - 6x + 9 = -8 + 9$$

Adding the square to both sides.

$$(x - 3)^2 = 1$$

$$x - 3 = \pm 1$$

Taking the square root of both sides.

$$x - 3 = 1 \qquad \text{and} \qquad x - 3 = -1$$

$$x = 4 \qquad\qquad\qquad x = 2$$

Check in the original equation.

$$4^2 - 6(4) + 8 = 0 \qquad \text{and} \qquad 2^2 - 6(2) + 8 = 0$$

$$16 - 24 + 8 = 0 \qquad\qquad 4 - 12 + 8 = 0$$

$$0 = 0 \qquad\qquad\qquad 0 = 0$$

(B) The **quadratic formula** is another way to solve quadratic equations that is faster than completing the square. Remember the general form of a quadratic equation is

$$ax^2 + bx + c = 0.$$

The quadratic formula is

$$\frac{-b \pm \sqrt{b^2 - 4ac}}{2a}$$

The expression $b^2 - 4ac$ under the square root symbol is called the **discriminant of the quadratic equation.** If the discriminant is 0, then both solutions or roots are the same.

If the discriminant is negative, then the roots are not real numbers; they are complex numbers. If the discriminant is positive, then there are two different real solutions.

PROBLEM

Solve by using the quadratic formula, $x^2 + 6x + 8 = 0$.

Solution

In this equation, $a = 1$, $b = 6$, and $c = 8$. Substitute into the quadratic formula.

$$x = \frac{-6 \pm \sqrt{6^2 - 4(1)(8)}}{2(1)}$$

$$= \frac{-6 \pm \sqrt{36 - 32}}{2}$$

$$= \frac{-6 \pm \sqrt{4}}{2}$$

$$= \frac{-6 \pm 2}{2}$$

$$x = \frac{-6 + 2}{2} \quad \text{or} \quad x = \frac{-6 - 2}{2}$$

$$= -2 \qquad\qquad = -4$$

Substitute in the original equation.

$$(-2)^2 + 6(-2) + 8 = 0 \qquad\qquad (-4)^2 + 6(-4) + 8 = 0$$

$$4 - 12 + 8 = 0 \qquad\qquad 16 - 24 + 8 = 0$$

$$0 = 0 \qquad\qquad\qquad 0 = 0$$

To solve quadratic inequalities the following steps can be used to find the solutions:

a. Put the inequality in a form where 0 is on one side.

b. Factor the quadratic equation.

c. Identify the critical points, the solutions to the factored equation.

d. Determine if the product of the two equations must be less than 0, greater than 0, or equal to or less/greater than 0.

(Remember that the product of two negative numbers or two positive numbers gives values greater than 0, and the product of a negative and positive number gives values less than 0.)

PROBLEM

Solve $x^2 - 5x + 4 \pounds 0$.

Solution

$$(x-1)(x-4) \leq 0$$

Factor the quadratic equation. Since the product is negative, one of the factors can be positive and then the other must be negative.

Therefore, either

	$x - 1 \geq 0$	and	$x - 4 \leq 0$	Case 1
or	$x - 1 \leq 0$	and	$x - 4 \geq 0$	Case 2

Solving for x in each inequality:

	$x \geq 1$	and	$x \leq 4$	Case 1
or	$x \leq 1$	and	$x \geq 4$	Case 2

The solution to the equation is the set of all x, such that $x \geq 1$ and $x \leq 4$, or $x \leq 1$ and $x \geq 4$. Therefore, $1 \leq x \leq 4$ is the solution set.

Drill 1: Quadratic Equations

Completing the Squares

DIRECTIONS: Solve the following equations.

1. $5x^2 + 8x + 2 = 0$

    (A) $(-4 \pm \sqrt{6})$ (B) $\frac{1}{5}(4 \pm \sqrt{6})$

    (C) $\frac{1}{5}(-4 \pm \sqrt{6})$ (D) $5(4 \pm \sqrt{6})$

    (E) $\frac{2}{5}(-4 \pm \sqrt{6})$

2. $2a^2 - a = 1$

    (A) $1, 2$ (B) $-1, -\frac{1}{4}$

    (C) $-\frac{1}{4}, 1$ (D) $1, -\frac{1}{2}$

    (E) $-1, -\frac{1}{2}$

3. $2t^2 + 4t + 1 = 0$

   (A) $\pm \frac{1}{2}$ (B) ± 1

   (C) $2 \pm \sqrt{2}$ (D) $\dfrac{2 \pm \sqrt{2}}{2}$

   (E) $\dfrac{-2 \pm \sqrt{2}}{2}$

4. $6s^2 + 11s + 3 = 0$

   (A) $-\frac{3}{2}, -\frac{1}{3}$ (B) $-\frac{3}{2}, -\frac{1}{4}$

   (C) $\frac{3}{2}, \frac{1}{3}$ (D) $-\frac{3}{2}, \frac{1}{3}$

   (E) $\frac{3}{2}, -\frac{1}{2}$

5. $8r^2 + 6r = 9$

   (A) $-\frac{3}{4}, \frac{2}{3}$ (B) $-\frac{3}{2}, \frac{3}{4}$

   (C) $\frac{2}{3}, \frac{3}{4}$ (D) $\frac{3}{4}, -\frac{2}{3}$

   (E) $\frac{4}{3}, -\frac{2}{3}$

Quadratic Formula

DIRECTIONS: Use the quadratic formula to solve the following equations.

6. $8x = -4x^2 - 3$

   (A) $-\frac{7}{8}, -\frac{1}{4}$ (B) $-\frac{1}{2}, -\frac{3}{2}$

   (C) $\frac{1}{2}, \frac{3}{2}$ (D) $\frac{7}{8}, \frac{1}{4}$

   (E) $-2, -\frac{2}{3}$

7. $3w^2 - 4w = \frac{5}{3}$

   (A) $-\frac{5}{3}, -\frac{1}{3}$ (B) $-\frac{5}{3}, \frac{1}{3}$

   (C) $\frac{5}{3}, -\frac{1}{3}$ (D) $3, -\frac{3}{5}$

   (E) $-1, \frac{1}{3}$

8. $3x^2 + 7x + 2 = 0$

   (A) $-2, -\frac{1}{3}$ (B) $2, \frac{1}{3}$

(C) $3, \frac{1}{2}$

(D) $-3, -\frac{1}{2}$

(E) $-2, \frac{1}{2}$

9. $2m^2 - 5m = 3$

(A) $1, \frac{3}{2}$

(B) $-1, -\frac{3}{2}$

(C) $3, -\frac{1}{2}$

(D) $-3, \frac{1}{2}$

(E) $-3, -\frac{1}{2}$

10. $2n^2 - 7n + 6 = 0$

(A) $-2, -\frac{3}{2}$

(B) $3, \frac{1}{2}$

(C) $-3, -\frac{1}{2}$

(D) $2, \frac{3}{2}$

(E) $-2, -\frac{2}{3}$

Quadratic Inequalities

DIRECTIONS: Solve the following inequalities.

11. $x^2 - 7x + 12 < 0$

(A) $3 < x < 4$

(B) $2 < x < 6$

(C) $x = 3$ or $x = 4$

(D) $x < 3$ or $x > 4$

(E) $3 \le x \le 4$

12. $x^2 + 5x + 6 < 0$

(A) $-3 < x$ or $x > -2$

(B) $2 < x < 3$

(C) $-6 < x < -1$

(D) $-3 \le x \le -2$

(E) $-3 < x < -2$

13. $x^2 - 5x + 6 \ge 0$

(A) $2 \le x \le 3$

(B) $x < 2$ or $x > 3$

(C) $x \le 2$ or $x \ge 3$

(D) $1 < x < 6$

(E) $x < 1$ or $x > 6$

2. COMPLEX NUMBERS

A **complex number** is a number that can be written in the form $a + bi$, where a and b are real numbers and $i = \sqrt{-1}$. The number a is the **real part**, and the number b is the **imaginary part** of the complex number.

To add, subtract, or multiply complex numbers, compute in the usual way, replace i^2 with -1 and simplify.

$$(a + bi) + (c + di) = (a + c) + (b + d)i$$

$$(a + bi) - (c + di) = (a - c) + (b - d)i$$

$$(a + bi)(c + di) = ac + adi + bci + bdi^2 = ac - bd + (ad + bc)i$$

PROBLEM

Simplify the following $(3 + i)(2 + i)$.

Solution

$$(3 + i)(2 + i) = 3(2 + i) + i(2 + i)$$

$$= 6 + 3i + 2i + i^2$$

$$= 6 + (3 + 2)i + (-1)$$

$$= 5 + 5i$$

Complex numbers, $a + bi$, may be obtained when using the quadratic formula to solve quadratic equations.

PROBLEM

Solve the equation $x^2 - x + 1 = 0$.

Solution

In this equation, $a = 1$, $b = -1$, and $c = 1$. Substitute into the quadratic formula.

$$x = \frac{-(-1) \pm \sqrt{(-1)^2 - 4(1)(1)}}{2(1)}$$

$$= \frac{1 \pm \sqrt{1 - 4}}{2}$$

$$= \frac{1 \pm \sqrt{-3}}{2}$$

$$= \frac{1 \pm \sqrt{-3}i}{2}$$

$$x = \frac{1 + \sqrt{3}i}{2} \quad \text{or} \quad x = \frac{1 - \sqrt{3}i}{2}$$

Drill 2: Complex Numbers

DIRECTIONS: Simplify the following.

1. $3i^3 =$

    (A) $-3i$ (B) $3i$

    (C) $9i$ (D) $-i$

    (E) 3

2. $2i^7 =$

    (A) $-128i$ (B) $2i$

    (C) $14i$ (D) $-14i$

    (E) $-2i$

3. $-4i^4 =$

    (A) 4 (B) -4

    (C) $4i$ (D) $-4i$

    (E) -14

4. $-5i^6 =$

    (A) -5 (B) $-5i$

    (C) $-i$ (D) $30i$

    (E) 5

5. $(3 + 2i)(2 + 3i) =$

    (A) $12 + 13i$ (B) $-12 - 13i$

(C) $13i$

(D) $-13i$

(E) $-i$

6. $(2-i)(2+i) =$

(A) -5

(B) $5i$

(C) $-5i$

(D) 5

(E) 3

7. $(5-4i)^2 =$

(A) $9-40i$

(B) $-9-40i$

(C) $41-40i$

(D) $9+40i$

(E) $-9+40i$

DIRECTIONS: Solve the following equations.

8. $x^2 + 16 = 0$

(A) ± 4

(B) $\pm 4i$

(C) $4 \pm i$

(D) $-4 \pm i$

(E) $i \pm 4$

9. $4y^2 + 1 = 0$

(A) $\pm \frac{1}{2}$

(B) $i \pm \frac{1}{2}$

(C) $-i \pm \frac{1}{2}$

(D) $\frac{1}{2} \pm i$

(E) $\pm \frac{1}{2}i$

10. $x^2 - 4x + 13 = 0$

(A) $3 \pm 2i$

(B) $\pm 6i$

(C) $\pm 5i$

(D) $2 \pm 3i$

(E) $-2 \pm 3i$

3. LINEAR EQUATIONS AND RATIONAL EXPRESSIONS

A system of three linear equations in three unknowns is solved by eliminating one unknown from any two of the three equations and solving them. After finding two unknowns, substitute them in any of the equations to find the third unknown.

PROBLEM

Solve the system.

$$2x + 3y - 4z = -8 \tag{1}$$

$$x + y - 2z = -5 \tag{2}$$

$$7x - 2y + 5z = 4 \tag{3}$$

Solution

We cannot eliminate any variable from two pairs of equations by a single multiplication. However, both x and z may be eliminated from equations (1) and (2) by multiplying equation (2) by -2. Then

$$2x + 3y - 4z = -8 \tag{1}$$

$$\underline{-2x - 2y + 4z = 10} \tag{4}$$

$$y = 2$$

Although we may now eliminate either x or z from another pair of equations, we can more conveniently substitute $y = 2$ in equations (2) and (3) to get two equations in two variables. Thus, making the substitution $y = 2$ in equations (2) and (3), we have

$$x - 2z = -7 \tag{5}$$

$$7x + 5z = 8 \tag{6}$$

Multiply equation (5) by 5 and multiply equation (6) by 2. Then add the two new equations. Then $x = -1$. Substitute x in either equation (5) or (6) to find z.

$$5x - 10z = -35 \tag{7}$$

$$\underline{14x + 10z = 16} \tag{8}$$

$$19x = -19 \tag{9}$$

$$x = -1$$

Substitute x into equation (5).

$$-1 - 2z = -7$$
$$-2z = -6$$
$$z = 3$$

The solution of the system is $x = -1$, $y = 2$, and $z = 3$. Check by substitution.

A system of equations, as shown below, that has all constant terms, $b_1, b_2, \ldots, b_n$ equal to 0 is said to be a homogeneous system:

$$\begin{cases} a_{11}x_1 + a_{12}x_2 + \ldots + a_{1n}x_m = b_1 \\ a_{21}x_1 + a_{22}x_2 + \ldots + a_{2n}x_m = b_2 \\ \quad m \quad\quad m \quad\quad\quad m \quad\quad m \\ a_{n1}x_1 + a_{n2}x_2 + \ldots + a_{nn}x_m = b_n \end{cases}$$

A homogeneous system always has at least one solution which is called the trivial solution that is

$$x_1 = 0, \ x_2 = 0, \ \ldots, \ x_m = 0.$$

For any given homogeneous system of equations, in which the number of variables is greater than or equal to the number of equations, there are non-trivial solutions.

Equations with Rational Expressions

Rational equations contain fractions that have numerators and denominators that are polynomials. Solving rational equations uses the same rules as linear and quadratic equations. Start by clearing the equation of fractions, usually using the lowest common denominator of the fractions that appear in the equation.

PROBLEM

Solve the following equation.

$$\frac{x+1}{5} - 2 = -\frac{4}{x} \qquad (x \neq 0)$$

Solution

$$\frac{x+1}{5} - 2 = -\frac{4}{x} \qquad (x \neq 0)$$

Multiply both sides by $5x$.

$$x(x + 1) - 5x(2) = - 4(5)$$

$$x^2 + x - 10x = - 20$$

Combine terms and add 20 to both sides.

$$x^2 - 9x + 20 = 0$$

Factor the quadratic equation.

$$(x - 4)(x - 5) = 0$$

Solve for x.

$$x - 4 = 0 \quad \text{or} \quad x - 5 = 0$$

$$x = 4 \qquad\qquad x = 5$$

Multiplying both sides of an equation by a quantity that contains a variable sometimes leads to a false solution or an **extraneous solution**. This happens if the solution would make one of the denominators equal to 0. Any value that would cause the denominator of a rational expression to equal 0 is excluded from the solution set.

Drill 3: Linear Equations and Rational Expressions

DIRECTIONS: Solve the following systems of equations.

1. $x + y + z = 4$
    $2x + y - z = 1$
    $2x - 3y + z = 1$
    Find the value of z.

    (A) -1 (B) 1

    (C) 0   (D) 2

    (E) -2

2. $x + y + 2z = 7$
    $x + 2y + z = 8$
    $2x + y + z = 9$
    Find the value of x.

    (A) 1   (B) 2

    (C) -3 (D) 3

    (E) -1

3. $2x - y + 3z = 9$
   $x + y + 2z = 4$
   $y + z = 1$
   Find the value of y.

   (A) -1 (B) 0

   (C) 1 (D) 2

   (E) No solution

4. $2x + y - z = 1$
   $x + 2y + 2z = 2$
   $4x + 5y + 3z = 3$
   Find the value of x.

   (A) -1 (B) 1

   (C) 2 (D) 3

   (E) No solution

Equations Containing Rational Expressions

DIRECTIONS: Solve the following equations.

5. $\dfrac{a+2}{a+1} = \dfrac{a-4}{a-3}$ Solve for a.

   (A) -2 (B) 4

   (C) 1 (D) -1

   (E) 0

6. $\dfrac{x+4}{x+7} - \dfrac{x}{x+3} = \dfrac{3}{8}$ Solve for x.

   (A) $-1, 11$ (B) $-11, 1$

   (C) $3, 8$ (D) $1, 5$

   (E) $2, 1$

7. $\dfrac{3}{x+1} - \dfrac{x-2}{2} = \dfrac{x-2}{x+1}$ Solve for x.

(A) 2, 0   (B) − 3, 4

(C) 3, 2   (D) − 4, 3

(E) No solution

8. $\dfrac{5}{x+4} + \dfrac{1}{x+4} = x - 1$ Solve for x.

(A) − 2, 5   (B) 1, 0

(C) − 5, 2   (D) − 5, − 2

(E) No solution

4. ABSOLUTE VALUE EQUATIONS

The absolute value of a, $|a|$, is defined as:

$|a| = a$ when $a > 0$,

$|a| = -a$ when $a < 0$,

$|a| = 0$ when $a = 0$.

When the definition of absolute value is applied to an equation, the quantity within the absolute value symbol is considered to have two values. This value can be either positive or negative before the absolute value is taken. As a result, each absolute value equation actually contains two separate equations.

When evaluating equations containing absolute values, proceed as follows.

EXAMPLE

$|5 - 3x| = 7$ is valid if either

$$5 - 3x = 7 \qquad \text{or} \qquad 5 - 3x = -7$$
$$-3x = 2 \qquad\qquad\qquad -3x = -12$$
$$x = -\frac{2}{3} \qquad\qquad\qquad x = 4$$

The solution set is therefore $x = (-\frac{2}{3}, 4)$.

Remember, the absolute value of a number cannot be negative. So, for the equation $|5x + 4| = -3$, there would be no solution.

EXAMPLE

Solve for x in $|2x - 6| = |4 - 5x|$

There are four possibilities here. $2x - 6$ and $4 - 5x$ can be either positive or negative. Therefore,

$$2x - 6 = 4 - 5x \tag{1}$$

$$-(2x - 6) = 4 - 5x \tag{2}$$

$$2x - 6 = -(4 - 5x) \tag{3}$$

$$-(2x - 6) = -(4 - 5x) \tag{4}$$

Equations (2) and (3) result in the same solution, as do equations (1) and (4). Therefore, it is necessary to solve only for equations (1) and (2). This gives:

$$2x - 6 = 4 - 5x \qquad \text{or} \qquad -(2x - 6) = 4 - 5x$$
$$7x = 10 \qquad\qquad\qquad -2x + 6 = 4 - 5x$$
$$x = {}^{10}/_7 \qquad\qquad\qquad x = -{}^2/_3$$

The solution set is therefore $({}^{10}/_7, -{}^2/_3)$.

Absolute value inequalities have the following relationship:

a. $|x| < k$ is equal to $-k < x < k$.

b. $|x| > k$ is equal to $x < -k$ or $x > k$.

If the value of k is included in the interval depends on if the symbol greater than, less than, or equal to is used.

PROBLEM

Solve $|2 - 3x| \geq 8$.

Solution

Write as two separate inequalities and solve each one for x.

$$2 - 3x \leq -8 \qquad \text{or} \qquad 2 - 3x \geq 8$$

Add (-2) to both sides.

$$-3x \leq -10 \qquad\qquad -3x \geq 6$$

Multiply both sides by (-1). (Note that inequalities reverse when multiplied or divided by a negative number.)

$$3x \geq 10 \qquad\qquad 3x \leq -6$$

Divide both sides by 3.

$$x \geq {}^{10}/_3 \qquad \text{or} \qquad x \leq -2$$

Drill 4: Absolute Value Equations

DIRECTIONS: Solve the equations.

1. $|4x - 2| = 6$

   (A) -2 and -1 (B) -1 and 2

   (C) 2   (D) $^1/_2$ and -2

   (E) No solution

2. $|3 - {}^y/_2| = -7$

   (A) -8 and 20   (B) 8 and -20

   (C) 2 and -5 (D) 4 and -2

   (E) No solution

3. $2|x + 7| = 12$

   (A) -13 and -1 (B) -6 and 6

   (C) -1 and 13   (D) 6 and -13

   (E) No solution

4. $|5x| - 7 = 3$

   (A) 2 and 4   (B) $^4/_5$ and 3

   (C) -2 and 2   (D) 2

   (E) No solution

5. $\left|\dfrac{3m}{4}\right| = 9$

   (A) 24 and -16 (B) $^4/_{27}$ and $-^4/_3$

   (C) $^4/_3$ and 12   (D) -12 and 12

   (E) No solution

DIRECTIONS: Solve each inequality.

6. $|3x + 2| > 14$

    (A) $x > 4$ or $x < -\,{}^{16}/_3$ (B) $-\,{}^{16}/_3 < x < 4$

    (C) $x < 4$ (D) $x > {}^{14}/_3$ or $x < -\,{}^{14}/_3$

    (E) $x > 4$ or $x < -4$

7. $3\,|2x + 5| \geq 9$

    (A) $-4 < x < -1$ (B) $1 < x < 4$

    (C) $x \geq -1$ or $x \leq -4$ (D) $x \geq -3$ or $x \leq -12$

    (E) $x > -1$ or $x < -4$

8. $|3 - 2x| < 7$

    (A) $x < -2$ or $x > 5$ (B) $-2 < x < 5$

    (C) $-\,{}^{7}/_2 < x < {}^{7}/_2$ (D) $-10 < x < 4$

    (E) $-4 < x < 10$

9. $|8x - 2| > 0$

    (A) $x > 4$ or $x < 4$ (B) $x > 2$ or $x < -2$

    (C) $x > {}^{1}/_4$ or $x < -\,{}^{1}/_4$ (D) $x > {}^{1}/_4$ or $x < {}^{1}/_4$

    (E) $-\,{}^{1}/_4 < x < {}^{1}/_4$

5. EQUATIONS OF HIGHER DEGREES

Polynomial equations of $n \geq 1$ have n roots (although some roots may be the same). Let polynomial equation

$$a_n x^n + a_{n-1} x^{n-1} + \ldots + a_1 x + a_0 = 0$$

have integral coefficients. If the equation has a rational root p/q (where p and q are integers with no common factor other than ± 1), then p is a factor of a_0 and q is a factor of a_n. If no such root exists the roots of the equation are irrational or imaginary.

PROBLEM

Find the roots of $x^3 - 3x^2 - 10x = 0$.

Solution

$$x^3 - 3x^2 - 10x = 0$$

Factor x.

$$x(x^2 - 3x - 10) = 0$$

Factor $(x^2 - 3x - 10)$.

$$x(x - 5)(x + 2) = 0$$

$$x = 0 \qquad x - 5 = 0 \qquad x + 2 = 0$$

$$x = 5 \qquad x = -2$$

The roots are 0, 5, and –2.

Binomial Theorem

The **binomial theorem** expands $(a + b)^n$ as follows:

$$(a + b)^n = a^n + \frac{n!}{1!(n-1)!}a^{n-1}b + \frac{n!}{2!(n-2)!}a^{n-2}b^2 + \ldots$$

$$+ \frac{n!}{r!(n-r)!}a^{n-r}b^r + \ldots + b^n$$

$n!$ is **factorial notation** which is defined as

$$n! = n(n-1)(n-2)(n-3)\ldots(3)(2)(1).$$

Note that by definition $0! = 1$.

EXAMPLE

$$3! = (3)(2)(1) = 6$$

PROBLEM

Use the binomial theorem to expand $(2x - y)^3$.

Solution

Let $a = 2x$, $b = -y$, and $n = 3$.

$$(a + b)^3 = a^3 + \frac{3!}{1!(3-1)!}a^{3-1}b + \frac{3!}{2!(3-2)!}ab^2 + b^3$$

$$= a^3 + \frac{3 \times 2!}{2!}a^2b + \frac{3 \times 2!}{2!}ab^2 + b^3$$

$$= a^3 + 3a^2b + 3ab^2 + b^3$$
$$= (2x)^3 + 3(2x)^2(-y) + 3(2x)(-y)^2 + (-y)^3$$
$$= 8x^3 - 3(4)x^2y + 6xy^2 - y^3$$
$$= 8x^3 - 12x^2y + 6xy^2 - y^3$$

Drill 5: Equations of Higher Degrees

<u>DIRECTIONS</u>: Find a root to the following equations.

1. $x^3 - 5x^2 - x + 5 = 0$

    (A) -5 (B) 0

    (C) $-\frac{1}{5}$ (D) $\frac{1}{5}$

    (E) -1

2. $x^3 - 2x^2 - 9x + 18 = 0$

    (A) 9 (B) 2

    (C) 0 (D) -6

    (E) 6

3. $x^4 - 6x^3 + 8x^2 = 0$

    (A) 0 (B) -2

    (C) -4 (D) 1

    (E) -1

<u>DIRECTIONS</u>: Use the binomial theorem to expand each binomial.

4. $(a + b)^4 =$

    (A) $a^4 + 3a^3b + 2a^2b^2 + 3ab^4 + b^5$

    (B) $a^4 + 2a^2b^2 + b^4$

    (C) $a^4 + 12a^3b + 8a^2b^2 + 12ab^4 + b^5$

    (D) $a^4 - 4a^3b + 6a^2b^2 - 4ab^3 + b^5$

    (E) $a^4 + 4a^3b + 6a^2b^2 + 4ab^3 + b^5$

5. $(x + 1)^5 =$

    (A) $x^5 + 10x^4 + 20x^3 + 1$

    (B) $x^5 + 6x^4 + 12x^3 + 13x^2 + 9x + 1$

    (C) $x^5 + 5x^4 + 10x^3 + 10x^2 + 5x + 1$

    (D) $x^5 + 10x^4 + 5x^3 + 5x^2 + 10x + 1$

    (E) $x^5 + 5x^4 + 10x^2 + 1$

6. $(x - y)^3 =$

    (A) $x^3 - 3x^2y + 3xy^2 - y^3$

    (B) $x^3 + 3x^2y + 3xy + y^3$

    (C) $x^3 - y^3$

    (D) $x^3 - 2xy - y^3$

    (E) $x^3 - 6x^2y + 6xy^2 - y^3$

6. ELEMENTARY FUNCTIONS

A **function** is any process that assigns a single value to y to each number of x. Because the value of x determines the value of y, y is called the **dependent variable** and x is called the **independent variable**. The set of all the values of x which the function is defined is called the **domain** of the function. The set of corresponding values of y is called the **range** of the function.

PROBLEM

Is $y^2 = x$ a function?

Solution

Graph the equation. Note that x can have two values of y. Therefore $y^2 = x$ is not a function.

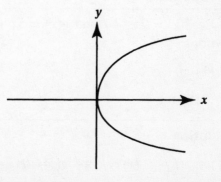

PROBLEM

Find the domain and range for $y = 5 - x^2$.

Solution

First determine if there are any values that would make the function undefined (i.e., dividing by 0). There are none. The domain is the set of real numbers. The range can be found by putting some values in for x.

x	2	1	0	-1	-2
y	1	4	5	4	1

The range is the set of real numbers less than or equal to 5.

PROBLEM

Evaluate $f(1)$ for $y = f(x) = 5x + 2$.

Solution

$$f(x) = 5x + 2$$
$$f(1) = 5(1) + 2$$
$$= 5 + 2$$
$$= 7$$

Functions can be added, subtracted, multiplied, or divided to form new functions.

a. $(f + g)(x) = f(x) + g(x)$

b. $(f - g)(x) = f(x) - g(x)$

c. $(f \cdot g)(x) = f(x) g(x)$

d. $(f / g)(x) = f(x) / g(x)$

PROBLEM

Let $f(x) = 2x^2 - 1$ and $g(x) = 5x + 3$. Determine the following functions:

(1) $f + g$ (2) $f - g$

(3) $f \times g$ (4) f / g

Solution

(1) $(f + g)(x) = f(x) + g(x) = 2x^2 - 1 + 5x + 3$
$$= 2x^2 + 5x + 2$$

(2) $(f - g)(x) = f(x) - g(x) = 2x^2 - 1 - (5x + 3)$

$$= 2x^2 - 1 - 5x - 3$$

$$= 2x^2 - 5x - 4$$

(3) $(f \times g)(x) = f(x)\, g(x) = (2x^2 - 1)(5x + 3)$

$$= 10x^3 + 6x^2 - 5x - 3$$

(4) $(f / g)(x) = f(x) / g(x) = (2x^2 - 1) / (5x + 3)$

Note the domain of (d) is for all real numbers except $- \, ^3/_5$

The **composite function** $f \circ g$ is defined $(f \circ g)(x) = f(g(x))$.

PROBLEM

Given $f(x) = 3x$ and $g(x) = 4x + 2$.

Find $(f \circ g)(x)$ and $(g \circ f)(x)$.

Solution

$$(f \circ g)(x) = f(g(x)) = 3(4x + 2)$$

$$= 12x + 6$$

$$(g \circ f)(x) = g(f(x)) = 4(3x) + 2$$

$$= 12x + 2$$

Note that $(f \circ g)(x) \neq (g \circ f)(x)$.

PROBLEM

Find $(f \circ g)(2)$ if

$f(x) = x^2 - 3$ and $g(x) = 3x + 1$

Solution

$$(f \circ g)(2) = f(g(2))$$

$$g(x) = 3x + 1$$

Substitute the value of x.

$$g(2) = 3(2) + 1$$

$$= 7$$

$$f(x) = x^2 - 3$$

Substitute the value of $g(2)$ in $f(x)$.

$$f(7) = (7)^2 - 3$$
$$= 49 - 3$$
$$= 46$$

The **inverse** of a function, f^{-1}, is obtained from f by interchanging the x and y and then solving for y.

Two functions f and g are inverses of one another if $g \circ f = x$ and $f \circ g = x$. To find g when f is given, interchange x and g in the equation $y = f(x)$ and solve for $y = g(x)$.

PROBLEM

Find the inverse of the functions

(1) $f(x) = 3x + 2$ (2) $f(x) = x^2 - 3$

Solution

(1) $f(x) = y = 3x + 2$

To find $f^{-1}(x)$, interchange x and y.

$$x = 3y + 2$$
$$3y = x - 2$$

Solve for y.

$$y = \frac{x - 2}{3}$$

(2) $f(x) = y = x^2 - 3$.

To find $f^{-1}(x)$, interchange x and y.

$$x = y^2 - 3$$
$$y^2 = x + 3$$

Solve for y.

$$y = \sqrt{x + 3}$$

Logarithms and Exponential Functions and Equations

An equation

$$y = b^x$$

(with $b > 0$ and $b \neq 1$) is called an **exponential function**. The exponential function with base b can be written as

$$y = f(x) = b^x.$$

The inverse of an exponential function is the **logarithmic function**,

$$f^{-1}(x) = \log_b x.$$

PROBLEM

Write the following equations in logarithmic form:

$$3^4 = 81 \text{ and } M^k = 5.$$

Solution

The expression $y = b^x$ is equivalent to the logarithmic expression $\log_b y = x$. Therefore, $3^4 = 81$ is equivalent to the logarithmic expression

$$\log_3 81 = 4$$

and $M^k = 5$ is equivalent to the logarithmic expression

$$\log_M 5 = k.$$

PROBLEM

Find the value of $\log_5 25$ and $\log_4 x = 2$.

Solution

$\log_5 25$ is equivalent to $5^x = 25$. Thus $x = 2$, since $5^2 = 25$.

$\log_4 x = 2$ is equivalent to $4^2 = x$. $x = 16$.

Logarithm Properties

If M, N, p, and b are positive numbers and $b = 1$, then

a. $\log_b 1 = 0$

b. $\log_b b = 1$

c. $\log_b b^x = x$

d. $\log_b M\,N = \log_b M + \log_b N$

e. $\log_b M\,/\,N = \log_b M - \log_b N$

f. $\log_b M^p = p\,\log_b M$

PROBLEM

If $\log_{10}3 = .4771$ and $\log_{10}4 = .6021$, find $\log_{10}12$.

Solution

Since $12 = 4(3)$, $\log_{10}12 = \log_{10}(4)\,(3)$

Remember

$\log_b M\,N = \log_b M + \log_b N.$

Therefore

$$\log_{10}12 = \log_{10}4 + \log_{10}3$$
$$= .6021 + .4771$$
$$= 1.0792$$

Drill 6: Elementary Functions

Logarithms and Exponentials

<u>DIRECTIONS</u>: Find the value of x.

1. $\log_7 1 = x$

   (A) 1   (B) 7

   (C) $1/7$ (D) 0

   (E) .1

2. $\log_2 8 = x$

   (A) 2   (B) 3

   (C) 4   (D) 16

   (E) 64

3. $\log_x 16 = 4$

   (A) 2   (B) 4

   (C) $^1/_4$ (D) 16

   (E) 64

4. $\log_3 x = 2$

   (A) $^2/_3$ (B) $^3/_2$

   (C) 6   (D) 8

   (E) 9

5. Given $\log_{10} 2 = 0.3010$ and $\log_{10} 3 = 0.4771$, find $\log_{10} 6 = x$.

   (A) 0.1761   (B) 0.1436

   (C) 0.6020   (D) 0.7781

   (E) 0.9542

DIRECTIONS: Evaluate each expression when $f(x) = 2x + 1$ and $g(x) = x^2 - 1$.

6. $(f \circ g)(2)$

   (A) 7   (B) 8

   (C) 10   (D) 15

   (E) 24

7. $(g \circ f)(-3)$

   (A) −40   (B) 3

   (C) 13   (D) 17

   (E) 24

8. $(g + f)(2)$

   (A) −2   (B) 2

   (C) 7   (D) 8

   (E) 15

9. $f^{-1}(x)$

    (A) $1 - 2x$ (B) $(x - 1)/2$

    (C) $x - \frac{1}{2}$ (D) x^2

    (E) $\frac{x}{2}$

10. $g^{-1}(x)$

    (A) $\sqrt{x}$ (B) $1 - x^2$

    (C) $x + 1$ (D) $(x + 1)^{1/2}$

    (E) $(x + 1)^2$

7. FRACTIONAL EXPONENTS

The properties that govern integral exponents extend to fractional exponents.

$$a^p a^q = a^{p + q}$$

$$(a^p)^q = a^{pq}$$

$$\frac{a^p}{a^q} = a^{p - q}$$

$$(ab)^p = a^p b^p$$

$$\left(\frac{a}{b}\right)^p = \frac{a^p}{b^p}$$

$$a^0 = 1, \text{ if } a \neq 0$$

$$a^{-n} = \frac{1}{a^n}$$

$$a^{m/n} = \sqrt[n]{a^m}$$

A **fractional exponent** is defined as

$$a^{1/n} = \sqrt[n]{a}$$

where $n > 1$ and a is a real number (non-negative if n is even), i.e.,

$$3^{1/2} = \sqrt{3}.$$

PROBLEM

Reduce $16^{3/4}$.

Solution

$$16^{3/4} = \sqrt[4]{16^3}$$
$$= \sqrt[4]{4,096}$$
$$= 8$$

Note $16 = 2 \times 2 \times 2 \times 2 = 2^4$

so $(2^4)^{3/4} = 2^3 = 8.$

Drill 7: Fractional Exponents

<u>DIRECTIONS</u>: Simplify the following.

1. $4^{1/2}$

(A) 16   (B) 2

(C) 4   (D) 8

(E) 6

2. $(4^{1/5})^3$

(A) $12^{1/5}$ (B) $4^{2/5}$

(C) $4^{4/5}$ (D) $4^{3/5}$

(E) $4^{1/15}$

3. $\dfrac{x^{a/4}}{x^{a/3}}$

(A) $\dfrac{1}{x^{a/12}}$ (B) $x^{a/12}$

(C) $x^{2a/7}$ (D) $x^{1/4}$

(E) x^a

4. $16^{-3/2}$

   (A) 64   (B) 4

   (C) $1/64$ (D) $1/4$

   (E) $1/16$

8. SEQUENCES AND SERIES

A **sequence** is a set of numbers in order, i.e.,

$$2, 4, 6, ..., 2n, ...$$

Two important types of sequences are the arithmetic sequence and geometric sequence.

Arithmetic progression is a sequence of the form

$$a, a + d, a + 2d, a + 3d, ..., a + (n - 1)d, ...$$

where a is the first term, $a + (n - 1)d$ is the nth term, and d is the common difference.

The formula to find the sum of the first n terms is

$$S_n = \frac{n(a + 1)}{2}$$

n is the number of terms, a is the first term, and l is the last (n^{th}) term.

PROBLEM

Find the sum of the first 20 terms in the series, 3, 8, 13, ...

Solution

To use the formula find the values for a, n, d, and l.

The number of terms $n = 20$ and the first term $a = 3$.

The difference

$$d = 8 - 3 = 5.$$

The last term

$$l = a + (n - 1)d = 3 + (20 - 1)5 = 98.$$

Substitute into the formula

$$S_{20} = \frac{(20(3+98))}{2}$$

$$= 10(101) = 1{,}010$$

Geometric progression is a sequence of the form

$$a,\ ar,\ ar^2,\ ar^3,\ \ldots,\ ar^{n-1},\ \ldots$$

where a is the first term and r is the common ratio. The formula to find the sum of the first n terms is

$$S_n = \frac{a - ar^n}{1 - r},\quad r \neq 1$$

and n is the number of terms, a is the first term, and r is the common ratio.

PROBLEM

Find the sum of the first six terms of the geometric progression $1 + \frac{1}{2} + \frac{1}{4} + \ldots$

Solution

$$a = 1,\ n = 6,\ \text{and } r = \frac{1}{2}$$

Substitute into the formula to obtain

$$S_6 = \frac{(1 - 1(\frac{1}{2})^6)}{1 - \frac{1}{2}}$$

$$= \frac{(1 - \frac{1}{64})}{\frac{1}{2}}$$

$$= \frac{63}{32}$$

Drill 8: Sequences and Series

1. Find the sum of the first 100 positive odd numbers.

    (A) 10,100

    (B) 10,000

    (C) 5,050

    (D) 9,900

    (E) 100,000

2. Find the sum of the first 20 terms for the series – 10, 10, 30, ...

    (A) 4,000   (B) 1,700

    (C) 2,100   (D) 3,600

    (E) 3,900

3. Find the sum of the first six terms of the series 8, 4, 2, ...

    (A) $63/_4$ (B) $63/_8$

    (C) $126/_8$ (D) 16

    (E) $31/_2$

4. Find the sum of the first five terms of the series 4, 8, 16, ...

    (A) 128   (B) 64

    (C) 124   (D) 62

    (E) 120

9. GRAPHS

This section is a continuation of the review started in the Elementary Algebra Review section. Graphs and number lines illustrate answers that were solved by algebraic means. Information about two points can be obtained and an equation connecting the points can be found.

(A) The distance from A to B with coordinates (x_A, y_A) and (x_B, y_B), respectively, is:

$$AB = d = \sqrt{(x_A - x_B)^2 + (y_A - y_B)^2}$$

This is known as the **distance formula**.

PROBLEM

Find the distance between the point $A(1, 3)$ and $B(5, 3)$.

Solution

In this case, where the ordinate of both points is the same, the distance between the two points is given by the absolute value of the difference between the two abscissas. In fact, this case reduces to merely counting boxes as the figure shows.

Let,

x_1 = abscissa of A y_1 = ordinate of A

x_2 = abscissa of B y_2 = ordinate of B

d = the distance

Therefore,

$$d = |x_1 - x_2|.$$

By substitution,

$$d = |1 - 5| = |-4| = 4.$$

This answer can also be obtained by applying the general formula for distance between any two points

$$d = \sqrt{(x_1 - x_2)^2 + (y_1 - y_2)^2}$$

By substitution,

$$d = \sqrt{(1 - 5)^2 + (3 - 3)^2}$$

$$= \sqrt{(-4)^2 + (0)^2}$$

$$= \sqrt{16}$$

$$= 4$$

The distance is 4.

To find the **midpoint** of a segment between the two given endpoints, use the formula

$$MP = \left(\frac{x_1 + x_2}{2}, \frac{y_1 + y_2}{2} \right)$$

where x_1 and y_1 are the coordinates of one point; x_2 and y_2 are the coordinates of the other point.

The **slope** of the line from (x_1, y_1) to (x_2, y_2) is

$$m = \frac{y_2 - y_1}{x_2 - x_1}$$

The equation of the line from (x_1, y_1) to (x_2, y_2) is

$$y - y_1 = m(x - x_1)$$

where m is the slope. This reduces to a form of

$$y = mx + b$$

with slope = m and y-intercept = b.

Lines are parallel if the slopes of each line are equal. Lines are perpendicular if their slopes are negative reciprocals.

PROBLEM

Find the slope and the y-intercept of the line with equation

$$2(x - 3) = -3(y + 5).$$

Solution

Write the equation in the form

$$y = mx + b$$

to find the slope, m, and y-intercept, b.

$$2(x - 3) = -3(y + 5)$$
$$2x - 6 = -3y - 15$$
$$3y = -2x + 6 - 15$$

Simplify.

$$3y = -2x - 9$$

Divide both sides by 3.

$$y = -\tfrac{2}{3}x - 3$$

$$m = -\tfrac{2}{3} \text{ and } b = -3$$

Inequalities can be represented on number lines and graphs. Solve for the unknown and graph.

The results can be **bounded intervals** between two numbers.

Interval	Graph and Inequality
(a, b) :	$a < x < b$

An open interval

$[a, b]$: $a \leq x \leq b$

A closed interval

$(a, b]$: $a < x \leq b$

A half-open or half-closed interval

Note that a parenthesis in $(a, b]$ means a is not included in the interval and a bracket means b is included in the interval. In the three examples the numbers a and b are the boundaries for the values of x.

The results can be **unbounded intervals**. The results can be numbers less than or greater than a certain number.

Interval	Graph and Inequality
(a, ∞) :	$a < x$

An open unbounded interval

$(-\infty, b]$: $x \leq b$

A closed unbounded interval

PROBLEM

Solve $3(x + 2) < 5x$ and graph.

Solution

$$3(x + 2) < 5x$$

$$3x + 6 < 5x$$

Add $(-3x)$ to both sides.

$$6 < 5x - 3x$$

$$6 < 2x$$

Divide both sides by 2.

$$3 < x$$

$x = 3$ is not included in the solution set.

PROBLEM

Solve and graph $|3x + 2| \le 5$.

Solution

$$|3x + 2| \le 5$$

Rewrite without absolute signs.

$$-5 \le 3x + 2 \le 5$$

Add -2 to all sides.

$$-7 \le 3x \le 3$$

Divide all sides by 3.

$$-7/3 \le x \le 1$$

The solution set includes both $-7/3$ and 1.

A graph of a linear inequality, graphs all ordered pairs (x, y) that satisfy the inequality. A broken line means that the ordered pair that satisfies the linear equation is not included in the solution.

PROBLEM

Solve and graph $2x - 3y \geq 6$.

Solution

The $\geq$ sign means that the graph includes

$$2x - 3y = 6$$

and values

$$2x - 3y > 6.$$

Find the x-intercept. Set $y = 0$.

$$2x - 3y = 6$$

$$2x = 6$$

$$x = 3 \text{ or } \{3, 0\}$$

Find the y-intercept. Set $x = 0$.

$$-3y = 6$$

$$y = -2 \text{ or } \{0, -2\}$$

Determine the region for which

$$2x - 3y > 6$$

is true. Try two points on either side of the line. Try the points $(0, 0)$ and $(5, 1)$.

For $(0, 0)$	For $(5, 1)$
$2x - 3y > 6$	$2x - 3y > 6$
$2(0) - 3(0) > 6$	$2(5) - 3(1) > 6$
$0 - 0 > 6$	$10 - 3 > 6$
$0 > 6$	$7 > 6$
False	True

The shaded region represents the solution to the inequality.

Graphs of quadratic equations are parabolas. The graph of

$$y = a(x - h)^2 + k$$

is a parabola with vertex (h, k). The parabola opens upward when $a > 0$ and downward when $a < 0$. The axis of symmetry is the line $x = h$. The graph of

$$y = ax^2 + bx + c$$

has vertex coordinates of

$$\left(-\frac{b}{2a}, c - \frac{b^2}{4a} \right).$$

PROBLEM

Graph $y = -x^2 + 2x + 1$.

Solution

The vertex $= \left(-\dfrac{b}{2a}, c - \dfrac{b^2}{4a} \right).$

$a = -1, b = 2, c = 1$

$$-\frac{b}{2a} = -\frac{2}{2(-1)}$$

$$= \frac{-2}{-2} = 1$$

$$c - \frac{b^2}{4a} = 1 - \frac{2^2}{4(-1)}$$

$$= 1 - \frac{4}{-4}$$

$$= 1 + 1 = 2$$

The vertex is $(1, 2)$ and the parabola points downward since $a = -1$.

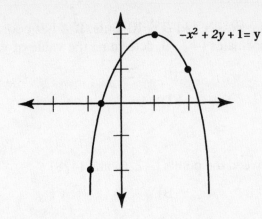

x	y
−1	−2
0	1
1	2
2	1

Drill 9: Graphs

1. Find the distance between $(4, -7)$ and $(-2, -7)$.

   (A) 4   (B) 6

   (C) 7   (D) 14

   (E) 15

2. Find the distance between $(3, 8)$ and $(5, 11)$.

   (A) 2   (B) 3

   (C) $\sqrt{13}$ (D) $\sqrt{15}$

   (E) $3\sqrt{3}$

3. How far from the origin is point $(3, 4)$?

   (A) 3   (B) 4

   (C) 5   (D) $5\sqrt{3}$

   (E) $4\sqrt{5}$

4. Find the distance between the points $(-4, 2)$ and $(3, -5)$.

   (A) 3   (B) $3\sqrt{3}$

   (C) 7   (D) $7\sqrt{2}$

   (E) $7\sqrt{3}$

5. The distance between points A and B is 10 units. If A has coordinates $(4, -6)$ and B has coordinates $(-2, y)$, determine the value of y.

   (A) -6 (B) -2

   (C) 0 (D) 1

   (E) 2

6. Find the midpoint between the points $(-2, 6)$ and $(4, 8)$.

   (A) $(3, 7)$ (B) $(1, 7)$

   (C) $(3, 1)$ (D) $(1, 1)$

   (E) $(-3, 7)$

7. Find the coordinates of the midpoint between the points $(-5, 7)$ and $(3, -1)$.

   (A) $(-4, 4)$ (B) $(3, -1)$

   (C) $(1, -3)$ (D) $(-1, 3)$

   (E) $(4, -4)$

8. The y-coordinate of the midpoint of segment AB if A has coordinates $(-3, 7)$ and B has coordinates $(-3, -2)$ is what value?

   (A) $5/2$ (B) 3

   (C) $7/2$ (D) 5

   (E) $15/2$

9. One endpoint of a line segment is $(5, -3)$. The midpoint is $(-1, 6)$. What is the other endpoint?

   (A) $(7, 3)$ (B) $(2, 1.5)$

   (C) $(-7, 15)$ (D) $(-2, 1.5)$

   (E) $(-7, 12)$

10. The point $(-2, 6)$ is the midpoint for which of the following pair of points?

   (A) $(1, 4)$ and $(-3, 8)$ (B) $(-1, -3)$ and $(5, 9)$

   (C) $(1, 4)$ and $(5, 9)$ (D) $(-1, 4)$ and $(3, -8)$

   (E) $(1, 3)$ and $(-5, 9)$

11. Which line is parallel to $y = 3x + 4$?

    (A) $y = 4x - 3$ (B) $y = 3x - 7$

    (C) $y = 7x + 4$ (D) $y = -\frac{1}{3}x + 8$

    (E) $3y = x + 4$

12. What is the slope of the line through $(3, 4)$ and $(0, -3)$?

    (A) $\frac{3}{7}$ (B) -1

    (C) $\frac{3}{4}$ (D) 3

    (E) $\frac{7}{3}$

13. What is the y-intercept of the line determined by $3x - 2y = 8$?

    (A) -4 (B) 8

    (C) -8 (D) 4

    (E) 3

14. What is the equation that has $m = -3$ and passes through $(2, -4)$?

    (A) $y = -3x$ (B) $y = -3x - 10$

    (C) $y = -3x + 2$ (D) $y = -3x - 4$

    (E) $y = -3x + 6$

15. What is the slope of the line through $(5, 2)$ and $(-1, 1)$?

    (A) $-\frac{1}{6}$ (B) $-\frac{1}{5}$

    (C) $\frac{1}{2}$ (D) $\frac{1}{6}$

    (E) 6

16. Solve for x and graph $x + 4 < 0$.

    (A)

    (B)

    (C)

(D)

(E)

17. Solve for x and graph $2x + 7 \le 5 - 6x$.

(A)

(B)

(C)

(D)

(E)

18. Which of the following correspond to the graph shown?

(A) $-3x + 2y > 6$

(B) $3x - 2y > 6$

(C) $3x + 2y > 6$

(D) $3x + 2y \ge 6$

(E) $3x + 2y < 6$

19. Graph the solution set to $|2 - 3x| \ge 8$.

(A)

(B)

(C)

(D)

$-2 \qquad 0 \qquad \dfrac{10}{3}$

(E)

$-2 \qquad 0 \qquad \dfrac{10}{3}$

20. The graph of $y = x^2 + 1$ might look like which of the following?

(A)

(B)

(C)

(D)

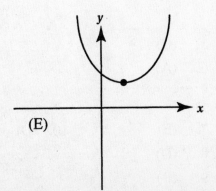

(E)

INTERMEDIATE ALGEBRA DRILLS

ANSWER KEY

Drill 1 – Quadratic Equations

1. (C)	5. (B)	9. (C)	13. (C)
2. (D)	6. (B)	10. (D)	
3. (E)	7. (C)	11. (A)	
4. (A)	8. (A)	12. (E)	

Drill 2 – Complex Numbers

1. (A)	4. (E)	7. (A)	10. (D)
2. (E)	5. (C)	8. (B)	
3. (B)	6. (D)	9. (E)	

Drill 3 – Linear Equations and Rational Expressions

1. (D)	3. (A)	5. (C)	7. (D)
2. (D)	4. (E)	6. (B)	8. (C)

Drill 4 – Absolute Value Equations

1. (B)	4. (C)	7. (C)
2. (E)	5. (D)	8. (B)
3. (A)	6. (A)	9. (D)

Drill 5 – Equations of Higher Degrees

1. (E)	3. (A)	5. (C)
2. (B)	4. (E)	6. (A)

Drill 6 – Elementary Functions

1. (D)	4. (E)	7. (E)	10. (D)
2. (B)	5. (D)	8. (D)	
3. (A)	6. (A)	9. (B)	

Drill 7 – Fractional Exponents

1. (B)	2. (D)	3. (A)	4. (C)

Drill 8 – Sequences and Series

1. (B)	2. (D)	3. (A)	4. (C)

Drill 9 – Graphs

1. (B)	6. (B)	11. (B)	16. (D)
2. (C)	7. (D)	12. (E)	17. (E)
3. (C)	8. (A)	13. (A)	18. (C)
4. (D)	9. (C)	14. (C)	19. (E)
5. (E)	10. (E)	15. (D)	20. (A)

ELM

Entry Level Mathematics

Chapter 5
Other Topics

OTHER TOPICS
DIAGNOSTIC TEST

19 Questions

(Answer sheets appear at the back of the book.)

DIRECTIONS: Each question has five multiple-choice answers. Select the single best answer.

1. In how many different ways can the letters in the word "bananas" be arranged to form a different combination of letters?

   (A) 35   (B) 84

   (C) 360   (D) 420

   (E) 5,040

2. From a deck of cards, two cards are drawn, one at a time, with no replacement. What is the probability of getting a 3 or a 4 of any suit for both cards?

   (A) .02   (B) .05

   (C) .08   (D) .12

   (E) .15

3. Marie went bowling and scored 160, 145, and 151 in her first three games. What score will she need in her fourth game so that the mean of all four games is 155?

   (A) 166   (B) 164

   (C) 162   (D) 160

   (E) 158

4. A single die is tossed 18 times. What is the expected number of times the number 2 will appear?

(A) 2   (B) 3

(C) 4   (D) 6

(E) 9

5. Julia has a total of eight necklaces, seven bracelets, and six rings in her jewelry box. She will randomly select two necklaces, two bracelets, and two rings. How many different combinations are possible?

(A) 2,097,152   (B) 112,896

(C) 8,820   (D) 336

(E) 44

6. If an ordinary six-sided dice is tossed 3 times, what is the probability of getting a sum higher than 16?

(A) .02   (B) .06

(C) .11   (D) .16

(E) .19

Questions 7 and 8 refer to the chart below.

Year	Tuition	Average Textbook Price
1985	$3,000	$32.50
1986	$3,200	$31.75
1987	$3,800	$39.62
1988	$3,800	$41.94
1989	$4,500	$40.79
1990	$4,700	$45.21
1991	$5,000	$44.97
1992	$5,700	$49.52
1993	$6,100	$53.10

7. If the average textbook price increased by the same percentage rate that tuition rose between the years 1991 and 1992, what would have been the average textbook price in 1992? (Round to the nearest hundredth.)

    (A) $50.11   (B) $50.49

    (C) $51.27   (D) $52.33

    (E) $52.67

8. Using the same chart, assume the percent increase from 1993 to 1994 will be the same as the percent increase from 1992 to 1993. What is the projected cost of tuition for 1994?

    (A) $6,527   (B) $6,500

    (C) $6,432   (D) $6,400

    (E) $6,377

9. How much time is left on the parking meter pictured below?

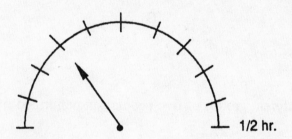

1/2 hr.

    (A) 8 minutes   (B) 9 minutes

    (C) 10 minutes   (D) 12 minutes

    (E) 15 minutes

10. A math instructor determines a student's final grade as follows: The quiz average accounts for 20%, the exam average accounts for 30%, homework accounts for 10%, and the final exam accounts for 40%. Steve has a quiz average of 80, an exam average of 90, a homework average of 70, and a final exam grade of 75. What is his final grade?

    (A) 72   (B) 74

(C) 76   (D) 78

(E) 80

11. A bag contains five white marbles, three red marbles, and two blue marbles. Four marbles are drawn, one at a time, with no replacement. Given that the first three marbles drawn were blue, red, and white, what is the probability that the fourth marble drawn will be white?

(A) $1/10$ (B) $1/2$

(C) $4/7$ (D) $3/4$

(E) $5/6$

12. Mrs. Jones wishes to seat two boys and three girls in a row with five seats so that the two boys do not sit in adjacent seats. One of the boys, Josh, must sit in either the first or the second seat from the front of the room. In how many different ways can the boys be seated?

(A) 6   (B) 5

(C) 4   (D) 3

(E) 2

13. How many different groups of five people can be formed from eight people?

(A) 13   (B) 20

(C) 35   (D) 40

(E) 56

14. A coin is tossed seven times. How many different sequences of heads and tails are possible, excluding the sequences of all tails or all heads?

(A) 14   (B) 49

(C) 64   (D) 126

(E) 208

15. At a local school, 70% of the students take accelerated math, 60% take accelerated English, and 45% take both accelerated math and English. If a student at this school is randomly selected, what is the probability that he or she does not take accelerated math or English?

    (A) .40   (B) .35

    (C) .25   (D) .15

    (E) .05

16. An ordinary coin is tossed four times. What is the probability of getting tails exactly twice?

    (A) .250   (B) .375

    (C) .500   (D) .625

    (E) .750

17. If the numbers 4, 20, 8, 12, and x have a median of 8, what is the value of x?

    (A) 5   (B) 9

    (C) 12   (D) 15

    (E) 21

18. Which group of numbers has a single mode of 13?

    (A) 12, 13, 13, 15, 16, 16, 17   (B) 12, 13, 15, 16, 17, 18, 19

    (C) 12, 12, 13, 13, 13, 16, 16   (D) 12, 12, 13, 13, 16, 16, 18

    (E) 12, 12, 12, 13, 14, 14, 14

The table below refers to question 19.

	Freshman	Sophomore	Junior	Senior	Graduate
	$180	$158	$179	$166	$116
	195	191	194	189	153
	168	202	210	190	98
	184	173	203	157	121
	205	187	183	203	92
	208	212	177	171	118
	184	197	192	180	126
	178	181	169	164	114
	193	166	198	188	119
	196	180	204	170	96
Total	$1,891	$1,847	$1,909	$1,778	$1,153

19. Which of the following is the best approximation (to the nearest dollar) of the average amount of money spent on textbooks by any senior class student in the school's bookstore in August?

(A) $193

(B) $183

(C) $178

(D) $173

(E) $168

OTHER TOPICS
DIAGNOSTIC TEST

ANSWER KEY

1. (D)	6. (A)	11. (C)	16. (B)
2. (A)	7. (C)	12. (B)	17. (A)
3. (B)	8. (A)	13. (E)	18. (C)
4. (B)	9. (B)	14. (D)	19. (C)
5. (C)	10. (E)	15. (D)	

DETERMINE YOUR STRENGTHS AND WEAKNESSES

OTHER TOPICS

Question Type	Question #	See Pages . . .
Counting	1, 5, 12, 13, 14	273-276
Probability	2, 6, 11, 15, 16	277-282
Statistics	3, 4, 10, 17, 18	283-286
Data Interpretation	7, 8, 9, 19	287-293

DETAILED EXPLANATIONS OF ANSWERS

OTHER TOPICS DIAGNOSTIC TEST

1.   **(D)**   In "bananas," there are three identical a's and two identical n's. The number of arrangements, or permutations, is given by

$$\frac{7!}{[(3!)(2!)]} =$$

$$\frac{5,040}{12} = 420.$$

2.   **(A)**   Since there are four 3s and four 4s within the entire deck, the probability of picking either a 3 or a 4 on the first try is $^8/_{52}$ or .1538. Assuming a 3 or a 4 was picked on the first try, a total of 7 3s and 4s. 4s remain in a total of 51 cards. The probability of picking a 3 or a 4 the second time is $^7/_{51}$ or .1372. To find the combined probability, multiply both probabilities:

$$.1538 \times .1372 \approx .02$$

Therefore, the combined probability is .02.

3.   **(B)**   The required total for all four games is

$$(4)(155) = 620.$$

Marie's current game total needs to be subtracted from the required total for all four games.

$$620 - (160 + 145 + 151) = 164$$

Marie needs a score of 164 in her fourth game in order to have an average of 155.

4. **(B)** The expected number of times is found by multiplying the probability of getting a 2 on any one toss by the number of tosses.

$$(\tfrac{1}{6})(18) = 3$$

5. **(C)** First, the number of combinations possible within the individual groups of necklaces, bracelets, and rings must be found. The combination formula must be applied to the three groups in order to find out how many different combinations are possible.

$$n^c r = \frac{n!}{r!(n-r)!}$$

There are 8 different necklaces and any combination of 2 may be picked.

$$8^c 2 = \frac{8!}{2!(8-2)!}$$

$$8^c 2 = \frac{8!}{(2!)(6!)}$$

$$8^c 2 = 28$$

There are 7 different bracelets and any combination of 2 may be picked.

$$7^c 2 = \frac{7!}{2!(7-2)!}$$

$$7^c 2 = \frac{7!}{(2!)(5!)}$$

$$7^c 2 = 21$$

There are 6 different rings and any combination of 2 may be picked.

$$6^c 2 = \frac{6!}{2!(6-2)!}$$

$$6^c 2 = \frac{6!}{(2!)(4!)}$$

$$6^c 2 = 15$$

Now the counting rule must be applied to the number of possible combinations of necklaces, bracelets, and rings.

$$(28)(21)(15) = 8,820$$

Thus, there are 8,820 different possibilities.

6. **(A)** To get a sum greater than 16, the sequences 5-6-6, 6-5-6, 6-6-5, or 6-6-6 are necessary. Since there is a total of 216 different sequences possible for the three tosses, the probability of the four specific sequences being rolled is $4/216 \approx .02$.

7. **(C)** Tuition increased from \$5,000 to \$5,700 from 1991 to 1992. Therefore, tuition increased by

$$\frac{700}{5,000} = 14\%.$$

If textbooks cost 14% more in 1992 than in 1991, than the cost of textbooks in 1992 is

$$\$44.97 \times 1.14 \approx \$51.27.$$

8. **(A)** The percent increase for tuition is

$$\frac{400}{5,700} = 7\%.$$

Therefore, if tuition in 1993 is \$6,100 then the tuition for 1994 will be

$$\$6,100 \times 1.07 = \$6,527.$$

9. **(B)** The meter shows that $3/10$ of the total time on the meter is left. However, this is a $1/2$-hour meter. Since

$$\frac{3}{10} \times \frac{1}{2} = \frac{3}{20},$$

this means that there is $3/20$ of an hour left on the meter, and $3/20$ of an hour is 9 minutes.

There are 10 calibrations for a half hour or 30 minutes. Each calibration is therefore $30/10 = 3$ minutes. Since the arrow is on the 3rd calibration, $3 \times 3 = 9$ minutes left.

10. **(E)** $(80)(.20) + (90)(.30) + (70)(.10) + (75)(.40) = 80$

11. **(C)** After the first three draws, there are seven marbles left, only four of which are white. So, $4/7$ equals the probability that the fourth marble drawn will be white.

12. **(B)** If Josh sits in the first seat, the other boy can sit in the third, fourth, or fifth seats. If Josh sits in the second seat, the other boy can only sit in the fourth or fifth seat. Thus, there are five different seating arrangements for the boys.

13. **(E)** Use the formula for combinations:

$$n^C r = \frac{n!}{r!(n-r)!}$$

$$8^C 5 = \frac{8!}{5!(8-5)!}$$

$$8^C 5 = \frac{8!}{(5!)(3!)}$$

$$8^C 5 = \frac{8 \times 7 \times 6 \times 5 \times 4 \times 3 \times 2 \times 1}{(5 \times 4 \times 3 \times 2 \times 1)(3 \times 2 \times 1)}$$

$$8^C 5 = 56$$

14. **(D)** There are two different possibilities each time a coin is tossed: It can land heads up or tails up. First, the number of possible sequences must be determined.

$$2^7 = 128$$

There are 128 different sequences possible.

Since there are two sequences which are all tails or all heads, two must now be subtracted from the total number of possible sequences.

$$128 - 2 = 126$$

There are 126 different sequences possible.

15. **(D)** Let A = accelerated math and let B = accelerated English.

  $P(A) = .70$

  $P(B) = .60$

  $P(A \text{ and } B) = .45$

The probability of a student taking either A or B or both is

  $P(A \text{ or } B \text{ or both}) = (.70 + .60) - .45 = .85.$

Therefore, the probability of a student taking neither A nor B is

  $1 - .85 = .15.$

16. **(B)** The answer is given by $(nCr) \times (p)^r \times (1 - p)^{n-r}$. The letter n is the number of trials, r is the number of successes, and p is the probability of success on any single trial.

  $(4C2) \times (.5)^2 \times (.5)^2 = .375$

17. **(A)** The four given numbers, in order, are 4, 8, 12, 20. In order for 8 to be the median, we need two numbers less than 8 and two numbers greater than 8. The sequence already has two numbers greater than 8: 12 and 20. Thus, we chose the number 5, (A), since it is the only option less than 8.

18. **(C)** The mode is the most frequently occurring number in a set of numbers. The number 13 occurs most frequently in (C). In selection (C), 13 appears 3 times.

19. **(C)** The average (arithmetic mean), $\bar{x}$, of a set of numbers is equal to the sum of the numbers divided by the number of numbers, n. That is,

  $$\bar{x} = \frac{\text{sum of number}}{n}.$$

Thus, this question can be answered by calculating the average of the amounts of money spent in the school's bookstore on textbooks only. These amounts are listed in the column headed "Senior" in the table shown. They are:

166, 189, 190, 157, 203, 171, 180, 164, 188, and 170.

The sum of these numbers is also given in the table as 1,778. Since there are 10 numbers, it follows that

$$\ddot{x} = \frac{1.778}{10} = 177.8.$$

Thus, the best approximation of the average amount of money spent by any senior class student is $178.

OTHER TOPICS REVIEW AND DRILLS

1. THE FUNDAMENTAL COUNTING PRINCIPLE

The fundamental counting principle deals with identifying the number of outcomes of a given experiment and can be broken down into the following three areas.

The Counting Rule

If one experiment can be performed in m ways, and a second experiment can be performed in n ways, then there are $m \times n$ distinct ways both experiments can be performed in this specified order. The counting principle (also known as the multiplication principle) can be applied to more than two experiments.

EXAMPLE

A new line of children's clothing is color-coordinated. Niki's mother bought her five tops, three shorts, and two pairs of shoes for the summer. How many different outfits can Niki choose from?

How many choices are there for a top?   5
How many choices are there for shorts?   3
How many choices are there for shoes?   2

Apply the counting principle: $5 \times 3 \times 2 = 30$.

Thus, Niki has 30 different outfits.

PROBLEM

Suppose a man has four ways to travel from New York to Chicago, three ways to travel from Chicago to Denver, and six ways to travel from Denver to San Francisco. In how many ways can he go from New York to San Francisco via Chicago and Denver?

Solution

If we let A_1 be the event "going from New York to Chicago," A_2 be the event "going from Chicago to Denver," and A_3 be the event "going from Denver to San Francisco," then because there are four ways to accomplish A_1, three ways to accomplish A_2, and six ways to accomplish A_3, the number of routes the man can take is

$4 \times 3 \times 6 = 72.$

Permutations

A permutation is an arrangement of specific objects where order is of particular importance. To determine the number of possible permutations, the following formula can be used:

$_nP_r = \dfrac{n!}{(n-r)!}$ (where n is the number of objects in the given set, r is the number of objects being ordered, and ! is the notation used for factorial)

Or, more simply, use the counting rule described above.

Remember, a factorial of a positive integer is written "$n!$". The factorial of 0 equals 1 ($0! = 1$).

$n! = n \times (n-1) \times (n-2) \times \ldots \times 3 \times 2 \times 1$

For example, the factorial of 4 is written 4!.

$4! = 4 \times (4-1) \times (4-2) \times (4-3) \times 1$
$4! = 4 \times 3 \times 2 \times 1$
$4! = 24$

EXAMPLE

Ten children in Ms. Berea's fifth grade class competed in the school's science fair. First, second, and third place trophies will go to the top three projects. In how many ways can the trophies be awarded?

Order is of definite importance here.

How many children have a chance at the first place trophy? 10
How many children have a chance at the second place trophy? 9
How many children have a chance at the third place trophy? 8

Apply the counting principle: $10 \times 9 \times 8 = 720$.

Thus, there are 720 ways these 10 children could finish first, second, or third.

PROBLEM

Suppose a class consists of five students. The instructor calls on exactly three students out of the five during each class period to answer three different questions. How many ways can the student be called on?

Solution

$$\text{Average} = \frac{1(70) + 1(90) + 3(85)}{1 + 1 + 3} = \frac{415}{83}$$

PROBLEM

Using any letter of the alphabet, in how many ways can any five different letters be placed in a row so that a different combination of letters appears?

Solution

The answer is found in $26^P5 = 26!/21! = 26 \times 25 \times 24 \times 23 \times 22 = 7,893,600$.

Combinations

A combination is an arrangement of specific objects where order is NOT of particular importance. To determine the number of possible combinations, use the following formula:

$$n^C r = \frac{n!}{r!(n-r)!}$$

(where n is the number of objects in the given set, r is the number of objects being ordered, and ! is the notation used for factorial)

EXAMPLE

Simon has ten compact discs and his player holds three discs at a time. How many combinations of three discs are possible?

$$10^C 3 = \frac{10!}{3!(10-3)!}$$

$$= \frac{10!}{3! \times 7!}$$

$$= \frac{10 \times 9 \times 8 \times 7 \times 6 \times 5 \times 4 \times 3 \times 2 \times 1}{(3 \times 2 \times 1)(7 \times 6 \times 5 \times 4 \times 3 \times 2 \times 1)}$$

$$= \frac{720}{6} = 120$$

Thus, there are 120 combinations of discs taken three at a time.

PROBLEM

How many groups of 4 students each can be selected from a class of 20 students?

Solution

Group means combination. Thus, we want $20^C4 = \dfrac{20!}{(16!)(4!)} = 4,845.$

Drill 1: The Fundamental Counting Principle

1. A local developer has five different floor plans, and each plan has two different elevations. How many different homes are available?

    (A) 5   (B) 7

    (C) 10   (D) 25

    (E) 30

2. A radio station is running a contest. They have eight phone lines, all of which light up instantly when the word "PYRAMID" is broadcast. The first caller will win $1,000, the second caller will win $250, and the third caller will win $25. In how many different ways can the callers be selected to win the prizes?

    (A) 21   (B) 56

    (C) 336   (D) 6,720

    (E) 40,320

3. From six sections of college algebra and four sections of calculus, a researcher will choose two college algebra sections and two calculus sections to be the subjects of a research study. How many different groupings can be selected?

    (A) 6   (B) 24

    (C) 40   (D) 90

    (E) 360

4. At the Ranch House Diner there are three different soups, seven different main dishes, and four different desserts. If a customer orders a soup, a main dish, and a dessert, how many different combinations are there?

(A) 14   (B) 40

(C) 60   (D) 84

(E) 96

5. At Pop's Diner there are five soups, twelve main dishes, and an unknown amount of desserts. A customer will choose a soup, a main dish, and a dessert. Suppose there are 1,080 different combinations of these three dishes. How many different desserts are available?

(A) 15   (B) 18

(C) 24   (D) 30

(E) 45

6. How many different ways can eight people arrange themselves in a waiting line?

(A) 32   (B) 64

(C) 128   (D) 10,080

(E) 40,320

2. PROBABILITY

Probability

Before discussing the actual calculation of a probability, examine the following probability facts.

(1) Probabilities are values ranging from 0 to 1 inclusive: $0 \leq P(E) \leq 1$. Probabilities cannot be negative or greater than 1.

    a. A probability of 0 means that the event cannot or did not occur.

    b. A probability of 1 means that the event must occur or always occurred.

(2) The sum of the probabilities of all possible events in any given experiment is 1.

(3) The notation used for the probability of an event E not happening is: $P(E')$, where E' is read E compliment.

(4) Combining facts (2) and (3), we then see that: $P(E) + P(E') = 1$. That is, the probability of an event happening or its compliment happening is 1. This formula may also be applied in the following form: $1 - P(E) = P(E')$, depending on the context of the problem.

EXAMPLE

Past records indicate that 25% of the students drop college algebra. What is the probability that a student does not drop college algebra?

25% means $^{25}/_{100}$ or $^1/_4$ of the students drop algebra.

Those who do drop algebra and those who do not drop it constitute the entire universal set.

Apply the formula: $\quad 1 - P(E) = P(E')$.
$$1 - ^1/_4 = ^3/_4$$

Thus, $^3/_4$ or .75 is the probability that a student does not drop college algebra.

The mathematical formula associated with the probability of a simple event is: $P(E) = ^m/_n$, where m is the number of favorable outcomes relative to event E, and n is the total number of possible outcomes.

EXAMPLE

Given that Jeffrey gets two hits out of three times at bat at every T-ball game, what is the probability that Jeffrey will get a hit his next time up to bat?

The number of favorable outcomes, i.e., the number of hits, is two. The number of possible outcomes is three. Thus, the probability of a hit is $^2/_3$.

The mathematical formula that allows us to find the probability of obtaining either event A or event B is:

$$P(A \text{ or } B) = P(A) + P(B) - P(A \text{ and } B).$$

Note: If events A and B are mutually exclusive, $P(A \text{ and } B) = 0$, then the formula above simplifies to $P(A \text{ or } B) = P(A) + P(B)$.

EXAMPLE

On a field trip, the teachers counted the orders for a snack and sent in the information with a few people. The orders were for 94 colas and 56 fries. If there were 133 orders, what was the probability of an order for a cola and fries?

Before using the formula presented above, we must determine P(cola), P(fries), and P(cola or fries).

$$P(\text{cola}) = {}^{94}\!/_{133}$$
$$P(\text{fries}) = {}^{56}\!/_{133}$$
$$P(\text{cola or fries}) = {}^{133}\!/_{133}$$

$$P(A \text{ or } B) = P(A) + P(B) - P(A \text{ and } B)$$
$$ {}^{133}\!/_{133} = {}^{94}\!/_{133} + {}^{56}\!/_{133} - P(\text{cola and fries})$$
$$ {}^{133}\!/_{133} = {}^{150}\!/_{133} - P(\text{cola and fries})$$
$$P(\text{cola and fries}) = {}^{150}\!/_{133} - {}^{133}\!/_{133}$$

$$P(\text{cola and fries}) = {}^{17}\!/_{133}$$

PROBLEM

If the probability of Event A is .40, the probability of Events A and B is .08, and the probability of Event A or B is .57, what is the probability of Event B?

Solution

$$P(A) = \text{Probability of } A$$
$$P(B) = \text{Probability of } B$$
$$P(A \cap B) = P(A) + P(B) - P(A \cap B)$$
$$.57 = .40 + P(B) - .08$$
$$P(B) = .25$$

Conditional Probability and Independence

From the conditional probability formula: $P(A \mid B) = \dfrac{P(A \text{ and } B)}{P(B)}$.

we can derive the multiplication rule: $P(A \text{ and } B) = P(A \mid B) \times P(B)$. It is not necessary to fully understand what conditional probability is as long as you are able to apply the counting rules discussed earlier.

EXAMPLE

If Kyle has eight pairs of socks, four white, two black, one blue, and one red, what is the probability that he randomly chooses two pairs of white socks to wear on consecutive days?

What is the probability of selecting one pair of white socks? $\frac{4}{8}$

Given that Kyle already chose a pair of white socks, what is the probability that he chooses another pair of white socks? $\frac{3}{7}$ Why?

How many pairs of white socks are left to choose? 3

How many total pairs of socks are left? 7

Thus, the probability of drawing two pairs of white socks is: $\frac{4}{8} \times \frac{3}{7}$ or $\frac{3}{14}$.

PROBLEM

> Two cards are drawn from an ordinary deck, one at a time with no replacements. What is the probability of getting a jack on the first draw and a queen on the second draw?

Solution

The probability of getting a jack is $\frac{4}{52}$ or $\frac{1}{13}$. On the second draw, only 51 cards are left, so that $\frac{4}{51}$ is the probability of drawing a queen on the second draw. The required probability is $\frac{1}{13} \times \frac{4}{51} = \frac{4}{663}$.

If the occurrence of event A in no way affects the occurrence or nonoccurrence of event B, then events A and B are said to be independent. If events A and B are independent, then $P(A \text{ and } B) = P(A) \times P(B)$.

EXAMPLE

The probability that a child born is male is 0.5. What is the probability that the next three children born at Memorial Hospital to unrelated parents are all boys?

The birth of three children to unrelated parents would be considered independent events.

$$P(3 \text{ males}) = (0.5)(0.5)(0.5)$$
$$P(3 \text{ males}) = 0.125$$

Thus, the probability of three males is 0.125 which is 12.5%.

Probability Word Problems

As with all prior real-world problems, the context of the problems is vast. A table or graph will provide the necessary information to calculate a single outcome, multiple outcomes or conditional probability or an expected value.

EXAMPLE

The students at a local college voted for a new student body president. The following table is a breakdown of the vote for the student who won the election.

	Freshman	Sophomore	Junior	Senior
Male	9%	17%	10%	9%
Female	16%	13%	15%	11%

Question 1: If a student who voted for the winner is selected at random, what is the probability that that person is a sophomore and a male?

Solution: By locating the correct cell in the table, we see that 17% of votes were from sophomore males. This gives a probability of 0.17.

Question 2: What is the probability of a randomly selected student not being a senior?

Solution: Locate the senior cells.
9% males + 11% females = 20% seniors

Nonseniors: 100% − 20% = 80%

Thus, the probability of not being a senior is 0.80.

Question 3: Knowing that a selected person is a junior, what is the probability that the person is a female?

Solution: This is a conditional probability problem.

To solve such a problem, we need to identify how many are in the given category, in this case juniors.

Locate the junior cells.

10% males + 15% females = 25% juniors

The numerical value associated with the given, the person is a junior, is the denominator for the fraction.

Of the juniors, identify the percent that are females: 15%. This is the numerator.

Thus, the probability that the person is female given that the person is a junior is $^{15}\!/_{25}$ or 0.60.

Question 4: If in this election there were 500 votes for the winner, how many females cast votes for the winner?

Solution: Total number of females: $16\% + 13\% + 15\% + 11\% = 55\%$

55% of 500 is $^{55}/_{100} \times 500 = 275$

Thus, 275 females cast votes for the winner.

Drill 2: Probability

1. A note card manufacturer discovered that the packaging machine was sometimes inserting nine cards into a box that was to contain eight cards. The company opened 10 boxes and discovered that three contained the additional card. What is the probability that a randomly selected box would have nine cards?

    (A) $^{1}/_{10}$ (B) $^{3}/_{10}$
    (C) $^{4}/_{10}$ (D) $^{8}/_{10}$
    (E) $^{9}/_{10}$

2. Refer back to problem 1. If 30% of the boxes contain nine cards, what is the probability of selecting two boxes with nine cards from a shipping crate containing 100 boxes?

    (A) $^{29}/_{330}$ (B) $^{9}/_{100}$
    (C) $^{1}/_{15}$ (D) $^{9}/_{50}$
    (E) $^{1}/_{6}$

3. If the probability that a student is selected to be a National Merit Scholar is 0.02 and that the student is a female is 0.40, what is the probability that a female is selected to be a National Merit Scholar?

    (A) 0.42   (B) 0.40

    (C) 0.38   (D) -0.20

    (E) 0.008

Mr. Bennett's sixth grade mathematics class is collecting data on eye color and gender. They organize the data they collected into the following table.

	Brown	Blue	Green
Male	22%	18%	10%
Female	18%	20%	12%

4. If a student is chosen at random, what is the probability that the student is a female with brown eyes?

   (A) 0.18   (B) 0.40

   (C) 0.45   (D) 0.50

   (E) 0.68

5. What is the probability of a randomly selected student not having green eyes?

   (A) 0.12   (B) 0.22

   (C) 0.88   (D) 0.78

   (E) 0.90

6. Given that the student selected has blue eyes, what is the probability that the student is a male?

   (A) 0.18   (B) 0.20

   (C) 0.47   (D) 0.53

   (E) 0.80

3. STATISTICS

Mean

The mean is the arithmetic average. It is the sum of the data points divided by the number of items in the sample.

EXAMPLE

Find the mean salary for four company employees who make $5/hr., $8/hr., $12/hr., and $15/hr.

The mean salary is the average.

$5 + 8 + 12 + 15 = 40$ Sum of the salaries.

$40/4 = \$10/hr$ Divide by the number of items.

EXAMPLE

Find the mean length of five fish with lengths (in inches) of 7.5, 7.75, 8.5, 8.5, and 8.25.

The mean length is the average length.

$$7.5 + 7.75 + 8.5 +$$
$$8.5 + 8.25 = 40.5 \qquad \text{Sum of the lengths.}$$
$$40.5/_5 = 8.1 \text{ in} \qquad \text{Divide by the number of items.}$$

Weighted Average

In averaging a set of observations, it is often necessary to compute the so-called weighted average to arrive at the desired measure of central location.

EXAMPLE

If a final examination in a course is weighted 3 times as much as the quizzes are, and if a student has a final examination grade of 85 and quiz grades of 70 and 90, what is the weighted average?

$$\text{Average} = \frac{1(70) + 1(90) + 3(85)}{1+1+3} = \frac{415}{83} = 83$$

PROBLEM

In a class, scores earned on quizzes, a midterm, and a final exam determine the final grade. The quiz average counts for 15%, the midterm average for 40%, and the final exam for 45%. If a person's quiz average is 70, has an 80 on the midterm, and scores 90 on the final exam, what is this student's final grade?

Solution

The weighted average is $(70)(.15) + (80)(.40) + (90)(.45) = 83$

Median

The median is the middle value in a set of items that is arranged in ascending or descending order.

To find the median,

(1) arrange the items in ascending or descending order and

(2) count in from each end the same number of items until one or two items remain.

If one item remains, that value is the median.

If two items remain, average the two values to find the median.

EXAMPLE

Find the median of the following set of numbers:

5, 2, 8, 9, 3

Arrange in ascending order: 2 3 5 8 9
Count in toward the center: 2̶ 3̶ 5 8̶ 9̶
One item remains, 5, and that is the median.

EXAMPLE

Find the median of the following set of numbers:

9, 5, 11, 10, 2, 3
Arrange in ascending order: 2 3 5 9 10 11
Count in toward the center: 2̶ 3̶ 5 9 1̶0̶ 1̶1̶
Two items remain, 5 and 9.
Average the two values: $(5 + 9)/2 = 7$
Thus, 7 is the median.

Mode

The mode is the most frequently occurring value in the set of items. It is possible that a set of items could have no mode or have a number of modes. A set with two modes is said to be bimodal.

EXAMPLE

Find the mode of the following set of numbers:

4, 5, 8, 3, 8, 2

Since 8 occurs twice while the other values occur only once, 8 is the mode.

EXAMPLE

For the given data, find the mean, median, and mode.

500, 600, 800, 800, 900, 900, 900, 900, 900, 1000, 1100

To find the mean:

500 + 600 + 800 + 800 + 900 + 900 + 900 + 900 + 900 +

$1,000 + 1,100 = 9,300$

$9300/11 = 845.45$

To find the median:

The items are already in ascending order, so count toward the middle. We arrive at one item, 900.

To find the mode:

See which item appears most frequently. That would be 900, which appears five times.

Expected Value

The expected value is found by taking each possibility, multiplying by the associated probability, and then adding the results.

EXAMPLE

An ordinary die is rolled once. What is the expected value?

The expected value is found by taking each possibility, multiplying by the associated probability, then adding results. In this example, $(1)(^1/_{16}) + (2)(^1/_6) + (3)(^1/_{16}) + (4)(^1/_6) + (5)(^1/_6) + 6(^1/_6) = {^{21}/_6}$ or 3.5.

Drill 3: Statistics

1. What is the mean of the data in the following sample?
   12, 15, 18, 24, 31

   (A) 18   (B) 19.3

   (C) 20   (D) 21.5

   (E) 25

2. What is the median of the data in the following sample?
   19, 15, 21, 27, 12

   (A) 12   (B) 15

   (C) 19   (D) 21

   (E) 27

3. What is the mode of the data in the following sample?
16, 14, 12, 16, 30, 28

(A) 6   (B) 14

(C) 16   (D) $19.\overline{3}$

(E) 28

4. Mrs. Brandish cans tomatoes. She finds that most often she gets 10 tomatoes in each jar. Sometimes she can squeeze 11 in and once she managed to get 12 in one jar. Select the statement that is true about the number of tomatoes in each jar.

(A) The mode equals the mean.

(B) The mean is less than the mode.

(C) The median is greater than the mean.

(D) The mode is more than the median.

(E) The mode is less than the median.

5. In a small company of only six employees, one employee earns $40,000 per year, two each earn $35,000 per year, and the remaining three employees each earn $20,000 per year. What is the average salary for all six employees?

(A) $31,667   (B) $29,250

(C) $28,750   (D) $28,333

(E) $27,500

4. DATA INTERPRETATION

Graphs

The information requested from reading the graph and performing a calculation or two will be limited to obtaining:

A. sums and differences of frequencies;

B. a percent of the whole; and

C. a frequency from a percent.

EXAMPLE

Examine the bar graph below.

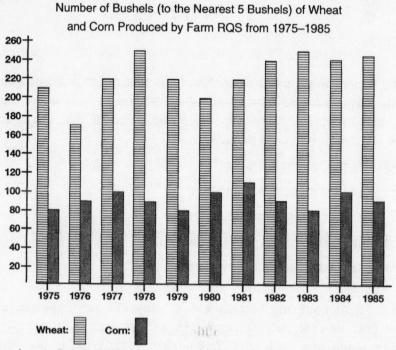

Number of Bushels (to the Nearest 5 Bushels) of Wheat and Corn Produced by Farm RQS from 1975–1985

Wheat: ▤ Corn: ■

Question 1: In which year was the least number of bushels of wheat produced?

Solution: The number of bushels of wheat produced is represented by the vertical columns, as indicated in the legend below the graph.

By inspection of the graph, we find that the shortest bar representing wheat production is the one for 1976.

Thus, the least number of bushels of wheat was produced in 1976.

Question 2: How many more bushels of corn were produced in 1981 than in 1975?

Solution: The number of bushels of corn produced is represented by the dotted vertical columns, as indicated by the legend under the graph.

By reading the height of the vertical column for corn for the year 1981, we see that approximately 110 bushels were produced. The reading for 1975 is approximately 80 bushels. This is a difference of 110 – 80 or 30.

Thus, there were 30 more bushels of corn produced in 1981 than in 1975.

Question 3: What was the total number of bushels of wheat produced from 1983 to 1985?

Solution: The readings for wheat production in 1983, 1984, and 1985 are approximately 250, 240, and 245, respectively.

Since the question asks for the total number of bushels, add the three values: $250 + 240 + 245 = 735$.

Thus, there was a total of 735 bushels of wheat produced from 1983 to 1985.

EXAMPLE

Examine the line graph below.

Amount of Scholarship Money Awarded to Graduating Seniors
West High — 1981–1990

Question 1: Between what two years did scholarship money increase the most?

Solution: With a visual inspection, one can see that the greatest increase occurred between the years of 1983 and 1984.

Question 2: In what year(s) did scholarship money actually decrease from the year before?

Solution: A decrease would be indicated by a data point for a particular year below the data point for the previous year. Through visual inspection, we see that scholarship money decreased in 1983, again in 1986, and again in 1987.

EXAMPLE

Examine the pie chart below.

Sample Family Budget

Auto – 15%

Food – 25%

Medical Insurance – 6%

Miscellaneous – 8%

Clothing – 8%

Gifts / Charity – 8%

Housing – 30%

Question 1: Using the budget shown, a family with an income of $2,000 a month would plan to spend what amount on food?

Solution: We see from the chart that the budget allocates 25% of the monthly income to food.

Thus, we need to calculate 25% of $2,000.

$2,000 \times {}^{25}/_{100} = 2,000 \times {}^{1}/_{4} = 500$

Answer: $500

Question 2: A family with a monthly income of $1,200 spends $72 on clothing. What percent of their monthly income are they actually spending on clothing?

Solution: To calculate the percentage, we will set up a proportion as covered in a previous skill area.

$$
\begin{aligned}
{}^{72}/_{1,200} &= {}^{P}/_{100} \\
72 \times 100 &= 1,200 \times P \qquad \text{Cross multiply.} \\
7,200 &= 1,200 \times P \qquad \text{Simplify.} \\
6 &= P
\end{aligned}
$$

Answer: 6%

Question 3: Using the budget shown, a family with an income of $2,000 a month would plan to spend what amount on medical insurance or auto?

Solution: The combined percentage allocated to medical insurance and auto is 6% + 15% or 21%.

Thus, we need to calculate 21% of $2,000.
$2,000 \times 21/100 = 20 \times 21 = 420$

Answer: $420

Predictions from Statistical Data

In this skill area, a table, histogram, broken line graph, scatter diagram, or line graph will be given. From this information, you will be asked to infer relationships and/or make predictions. More precisely, the types of questions that may be asked include:

A. commenting on the relationship between two variables;

A most critical concept to remember is that just because two variables appear to be related, there is no justification in presuming that one variable *causes* the other.

B. commenting on the trend of a single variable;

C. interpolating; and

D. extrapolating.

EXAMPLE

Tuition and average textbook price are given in the following table. Which statement best describes the relationship between tuition and average textbook price?

Year	Tuition	Average Textbook Price
1985	$3,000	$32.50
1986	$3,200	$31.75
1987	$3,800	$39.62
1988	$3,800	$41.94
1989	$4,500	$40.79
1990	$4,700	$45.21
1991	$5,000	$44.97
1992	$5,700	$49.52
1993	$6,100	$53.10

(A) An increase in the tuition caused an increase in textbook price.

(B) An increase in textbook price caused an increase in tuition.

(C) There appears to be a positive association between tuition and textbook price.

(D) There appears to be a negative association between tuition and textbook price.

Solution: Be cautious of cause-and-effect relationships. Unless there is a direct link between two variables, the relationship can be coincidental. Eliminate choices (A) and (B).

Examine the tuition column and the textbook price column. Both columns are effectively increasing over time. If two variables change in the same direction, both increase or both decrease, we say this is a positive relationship. If one increases while the other decreases, we say this is a negative relationship. Thus, we can eliminate (D) and realize that (C) is the correct choice.

EXAMPLE

Consider the following line graph. Which of the following best describes the trend in pledge money?

Amount of Money Pledged to Public Television during Telethons
1981-1990

(A) Pledge money has fluctuated but has in general increased over time.

(B) There is no trend in pledge money for any time.

(C) Pledge money actually decreased from 1987 to 1990.

(D) There was more pledge money available in the early 1980s than in the latter part of the decade.

Solution: Visually, we can see that pledge money has in general increased over time. Thus, we can eliminate (B).

Choice (C) is incorrect because pledge money increased from 1987 to 1990.

Choice (D) is incorrect because there was more money in the later 1980s than in the earlier 1980s.

This leaves choice (A). Even though pledge money has not consistently increased, it has in general over time.

EXAMPLE

Using the same line graph from the previous example, between what two years was the increase in pledge money the most significant?

(A) 1981 – 1982   (C) 1985 – 1986

(B) 1983 – 1984   (D) 1987 – 1988

Solution: To determine the greatest increase, we must compare the differences between each two-year period.

1981 – 1982	$80{,}000 - 40{,}000 = 40{,}000$
1983 – 1984	$150{,}000 - 50{,}000 = 100{,}000$
1985 – 1986	$120{,}000 - 175{,}000 = -55{,}000$
1987 – 1988	$150{,}000 - 70{,}000 = 80{,}000$

We can see that the greatest increase came between 1983 – 1984, and this is choice (B).

Drill 4: Data Interpretation

Questions 1–3 refer to the following bar graph.

Changes in Average Mileage

1. By how much did the mileage increase for Car 2 when the new product was used?

    (A) 5 mpg

    (B) 6 mpg

    (C) 7 mpg

    (D) 10 mpg

    (E) 11 mpg

2. Which car's mileage increased the most in this test?

    (A) Car 2

    (B) Car 3

    (C) Car 1

    (D) Cars 1 and 2

    (E) Cars 2 and 3

3. According to the bar graph, if your car averages 25 mpg, what mileage might you expect with the new product?

    (A) 21 mpg

    (B) 29 mpg

    (C) 31 mpg

    (D) 35 mpg

    (E) 40 mpg

4. Family income and food cost are given in the following table. Which statement best describes the relationship between family income and food cost?

Year	Family Income	Food Cost as a Percent of Income
1985	$23,000	25%
1986	$25,200	23%
1987	$28,800	20%
1988	$30,800	19%
1989	$34,500	17%
1990	$34,700	17%
1991	$35,000	16%
1992	$35,700	16%
1993	$38,100	15%

(A) As a family's income increases, they spend less money on food.

(B) An increase in income causes a decrease in the percent of that income spent on food.

(C) There appears to be a positive association between a family's income and the percent spent on food.

(D) There appears to be a negative association between a family's income and the percent spent on food.

(E) There is no relationship between a family's income and the percent spent on food.

5. Refer to the table in problem 4 above. Which of the following best describes the percent of income spent on food beyond 1993?

(A) Provided the family continues in the same trend, the percent of income spent on food will continue to decrease slightly.

(B) The percent spent on food will never drop below 15%.

(C) It is not possible to predict what will happen beyond 1993 because the trends represented here are unstable.

(D) Since 15% is such a small percent to pay for food, one would expect the percent to begin increasing independent of income.

(E) The percent spent on food will begin to increase.

6. Refer to the following scatter diagram showing students' scores on the math and science sections of a test. If a student scored 550 on the math section, what would you estimate the science score to be?

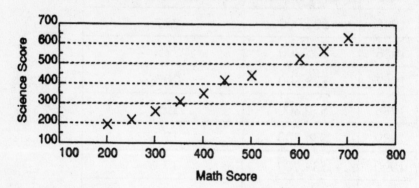

(A) Around 200   (B) Around 340

(C) Around 480   (D) Around 600

(E) Impossible to predict

7. Using the same scatter diagram in Question 6, if a student scored 600 on the math section, what would you expect that same student to score on the verbal section?

(A) Around 400   (B) Around 550

(C) Around 650   (D) Around 700

(E) Impossible to predict

OTHER TOPICS DRILLS

ANSWER KEY

Drill 1 – The Fundamental Counting Principle

1.	(C)	3.	(D)	5.	(B)
2.	(C)	4.	(D)	6.	(E)

Drill 2 – Probability

1.	(B)	3.	(E)	5.	(D)
2.	(A)	4.	(A)	6.	(C)

Drill 3 – Statistics

1.	(C)	3.	(C)	5.	(D)
2.	(C)	4.	(E)		

Drill 4 – Data Interpretation

1.	(B)	3.	(B)	5.	(A)	7.	(E)
2.	(E)	4.	(D)	6.	(C)		

Entry Level Mathematics

Chapter 6
Word Problems
Review

WORD PROBLEMS DIAGNOSTIC TEST

11 Questions

(Answer sheets appear at the back of the book.)

> **DIRECTIONS:** Each question has five multiple-choice answers. Select the single best answer.

1. John bought a $250 radio. The salesman gave him a 10% discount. How much did he pay for the radio?

   (A) $25   (B) $125

   (C) $175   (D) $225

   (E) $275

2. An airplane travels 1,800 miles in 3 hours flying with the wind. On the return trip, flying against the wind, it takes 4 hours to travel 2,000 miles. Find the rate of the plane in still air.

   (A) 425 mph   (B) 500 mph

   (C) 542 mph   (D) 550 mph

   (E) 600 mph

3. How long must a rectangular bin be to hold 1,800 cubic meters, if the width is 10 meters and the height is 6 meters?

   (A) 30 m   (B) 45 m

   (C) 60 m   (D) 10,800 m

   (E) Cannot be determined

4. Lynsey is 5 years older than Gretta. The sum of their ages is 95. How old is Lynsey?

    (A) 5   (B) 40

    (C) 45   (D) 50

    (E) 55

5. In the Daly Auto Factory, robots assemble cars. If 3 robots assemble 17 cars in 10 minutes, how many cars can 14 robots assemble in 45 minutes if all robots work at the same rate all the time?

    (A) 357   (B) 340

    (C) 705   (D) 150

    (E) 272

6. John wishes to contribute $2,500 to his favorite charities A and B in the ratio of 2 to 3. The amount he should contribute to charity A is

    (A) $500.   (B) $1,000.

    (C) $1,250.   (D) $1,500.

    (E) $2,000.

7. Emile receives a flat weekly salary of $240 plus 12% commission of the total volume of all sales he makes. What must his dollar volume be in a week if he is to make a total weekly salary of $540?

    (A) $2,880   (B) $3,600

    (C) $6,480   (D) $2,500

    (E) $2,000

8. Ms. Jones received a 10% salary increase each of the last two years. If her annual salary this year is $41,745, what was her annual salary two years ago?

    (A) $34,500   (B) $33,813.45

(C) $33,396   (D) $34,000

(E) $34,750

9. A man has $20,000 to invest. He invests $5,000 at 5% and $7,000 at 7%. In order to have a yearly income of $1,500, he must invest the remainder at

(A) 8%.   (B) 8.5%.

(C) 9%.   (D) 9.5%.

(E) 10%.

10. A doctor has 44 cc of 2% tincture of iodine. If the iodine is boiled, alcohol is evaporated away and the strength of tincture is raised. How much alcohol must be boiled away in order to raise the strength of the tincture to 8%?

(A) 33 cc   (B) 32 cc

(C) 30 cc   (D) 24 cc

(E) 10 cc

11. If the cost of five apples is $3.25, and if the cost of an orange and one of these apples together is $1.05, what is the cost of an orange alone?

(A) $0.35   (B) $0.40

(C) $0.45   (D) $0.50

(E) $0.55

WORD PROBLEMS
DIAGNOSTIC TEST

ANSWER KEY

1. (D)	4. (D)	7. (D)	10. (A)
2. (D)	5. (A)	8. (A)	11. (B)
3. (A)	6. (B)	9. (D)	

DETERMINE YOUR STRENGTHS AND WEAKNESSES

WORD PROBLEMS

Question Type	Question #	See Pages . . .
Algebraic	4, 11	311, 312
Rate	2	313, 314
Work	5	315
Mixture	10, 11	316, 317
Interest	8, 9	318-320
Discount	1	321
Profit	7	322, 323
Ratios and Proportions	5, 6	324-326
Geometry	3	327

DETAILED EXPLANATIONS OF ANSWERS

WORD PROBLEMS DIAGNOSTIC TEST

1.   **(D)**   Since the salesman has given John a discount, we need to figure out the amount of money deducted from John's bill. Ten percent of the cost of the radio must be subtracted from the original cost to compute the new cost. Ten percent of $250 is .10 × 250 or $25. Subtracting the $25 discount from the original $250 price yields $225.

2.   **(D)**   Using the formula

$$\text{Distance} = \text{Rate} \times \text{Time},$$

which can be rewritten as

$$\text{Rate} = \frac{\text{Distance}}{\text{Time}} = \text{Speed}$$

(Actual speed of plane in still air)

= (Apparent speed of plane) − (wind speed)

Traveling *with* the wind produces a *positive* wind speed, while traveling *against* the wind produces a *negative* wind speed. Therefore,

Let w = wind speed

x = actual speed of plane in still air

$$x = \left(\frac{1,800 \text{ mi}}{4 \text{ hr}}\right) - (w) \text{ with the wind}$$

$$x = \left(\frac{2,000 \text{ mi}}{4 \text{ hr}}\right) - (-w) \text{ against the wind}$$

Setting these equations equal,

$$(600 \text{ mi/hr}) - (w) = (500 \text{ mi/hr}) - (-w)$$

$$600 \text{ mi/hr} - w = 500 \text{ mi/hr} + w$$

Solving for w,

$$2w = 100 \text{ mi/hr}.$$

$$w = 50 \text{ mi/hr}.$$

Substituting this into either initial equation gives

$$x = (600 \text{ mi/hr} - 50 \text{ mi/hr}) = (500 \text{ mi/hr} + 50 \text{ mi/hr}) = 550 \text{ mi/hr}.$$

3.   **(A)**   The formula for the volume is $v = lwh$. Substitute 1,800 for the volume, v, l for the length, 10 for the width, w, and 6 for the height, h.

$$1,800 = l \times 10 \times 6$$

$$1,800 = 60l$$

$$30 = l$$

The length is 30 meters.

4.   **(D)**   Set up an algebraic relationship. Let x = Gretta's age, and $(x + 5)$ = Lynsey's age, since Lynsey is 5 years older.
The sum of their ages is 95, so

$$(x) + (x + 5) = 95$$

$$2x + 5 = 95$$

$$2x = 90$$

$$x = 45.$$

Since x = Gretta's age which is 45, and Lynsey is 5 years older, Lynsey is $45 + 5$, or 50 years old.

5.   **(A)**   One method for attacking this problem is to let x be the number of cars that 14 robots can assemble in 45 minutes. Because the robots work at the same rate all the time, we can express this rate by using the information that 3 robots can assemble 17 cars in 10 minutes.
Now, if 3 robots can assemble 17 cars in 10 minutes, then 3 robots can assemble $17/10$ cars in 1 minute. Consequently, 1 robot assembles

$$\frac{1}{3}\left(\frac{17}{10}\right) \text{ or } \frac{17}{30}$$

of a car in 1 minute.

Similarly, if 14 robots assemble x cars in 45 minutes, then the 14 robots assemble $x/45$ cars in 1 minute. Thus, 1 robot assembles

$$\frac{1}{14}\left(\frac{x}{45}\right), \text{ or } \frac{x}{14(45)}.$$

of a car in 1 minute. Because the rates are equal, we have the proportion

$$\frac{x}{14(45)} = \frac{17}{30}$$

$$\frac{x}{630} = \frac{17}{30}.$$

Solving this proportion for x yields,

$$30x = (630)(17)$$

$$30x = 10,710$$

$$x = \frac{10,710}{30} = 357.$$

6. **(B)** If John contributes $2X$ to A and $3X$ to B, then his contributions to A and B will be in the ratio of 2 to 3. Then

$$2X + 3X = 2,500, \text{ or } X = 500.$$

Therefore, he should contribute $2(500) = \$1,000$ to charity A.

7. **(D)** Since we do not know Emile's dollar volume during the week in question, we can assign this amount the value of x.

Now, Emile's total salary of $540 can be divided into two parts: One part is his flat salary of $240, and the other part is his salary from commissions, which amounts to $540 − $240 = $300. This part of his salary is equal to 12% of his dollar volume, x. Thus, 12% of x = $300. This means

$$(0.12)x = 300$$

$$x = 300/0.12 = \$2,500.$$

8.   **(A)**   Let x be Ms. Jones' salary two years ago. Then $x + 10\%x$ was her salary last year and

$$(x + 10\%x) + 10\%(x + 10\%x)$$

is an expression for her salary this year.

$$(x + 10\%x) + 10\%(x + 10\%x) = 41,745$$
$$1.1x + .11x = 41,745$$
$$1.21x = 41,745$$
$$x = 34,500$$

9.   **(D)**   Of the $20,000 he has to invest, the man invests $5,000 at 5% giving him

$$\$5,000(.05) = \$250$$

in interest. He invests $7,000 at 7% giving him

$$\$7,000(.07) = \$490$$

in interest. The remaining amount of interest needed to reach $1,500 a year is, therefore,

$$\$1,500 - \$740 = \$760.$$

The remaining amount of principal is

$$\$20,000 - \$12,000 = \$8,000.$$

Letting x be the rate of interest, we have

$$8,000x = 760 \text{ or } 760/8,000 = .095 = 9.5\%.$$

10. **(A)**

Solution	Amount	%	Amount of Iodine
Original Amount	44	2	44(.02)
Boiled Away	x	0	0
New Solution	$(44 - x)$	8	$(44 - x)(.08)$

The amount of iodine in the original solution less the amount of iodine in the alcohol evaporated (which is 0) equals the amount of iodine in the new solution.

$$.02(44) - 0 = .08(44 - x)$$

Solve for *x*.

$$.88 - 0 = 3.52 - .08x$$

$$.08x = 3.52 - .88$$

$$.08x = 2.64$$

$$x = 33$$

11. **(B)**   Cost of an apple

$$= \frac{\$3.25}{5} = \$0.65.$$

Cost of an orange

$$= \$1.05 - \$0.65 = \$0.40.$$

WORD PROBLEMS REVIEW AND DRILLS

One of the main difficulties students have in mathematics is in solving word problems. The secret to solving these problems is being able to convert words into numbers and variables in the form of an algebraic equation. To help you in this regard, our drill items in this section are answered in detail.

The easiest way to approach a word problem is to read the question and ask yourself what you are trying to find. This unknown quantity can be represented by a variable.

Next, determine how the variable relates to the other quantities in the problem. More than likely, these quantities can be explained in terms of the original variable. If not, a separate variable may have to be used to represent a quantity.

Using these variables and the relationships determined among them, an equation can be written. Solve for a particular variable and then substitute this number in for each relationship that involves this variable in order to find any unknown quantities.

Lastly, re-read the problem to be sure that you have answered the questions correctly and fully.

1. ALGEBRAIC

Here's how to formulate an equation and solve the problem.

PROBLEM

Find two consecutive odd integers whose sum is 36.

Solution

Let x = the first odd integer

Let $x + 2$ = the second odd integer

The sum of the two numbers is 36. Therefore,

$$x + (x + 2) = 36.$$

Simplifying,

$$2x + 2 = 36$$
$$2x + 2 + (-2) = 36 + (-2)$$
$$2x = 34$$
$$x = 17$$

Substituting 17 in for x, we find the second odd integer =

$$(x + 2) = (17 + 2) = 19.$$

Therefore, we find that the two consecutive odd integers whose sum is 36 are 17 and 19, respectively.

Drill 1: Algebraic

1. The sum of two numbers is 41. One number is one less than twice the other. Find the larger of the two numbers.

   (A) 13   (B) 14

   (C) 21   (D) 27

   (E) 41

2. The sum of two consecutive integers is 111. Three times the larger integer less two times the smaller integer is 58. Find the value of the smaller integer.

   (A) 55   (B) 56

   (C) 58   (D) 111

   (E) 112

3. The difference between two integers is 12. The sum of the two integers is 2. Find both integers.

   (A) 7 and 5   (B) 7 and – 5

   (C) – 7 and 5   (D) 2 and 12

   (E) – 2 and 12

2. RATE

One of the formulas you will use for rate problems will be

Rate × Time = Distance.

PROBLEM

> If a plane travels five hours from New York to California at a speed
> of 600 miles per hour, how many miles does the plane travel?

Solution

Using the formula rate × time = distance, multiply

600 mph × 5 hours = 3,000 miles.

The average rate at which an object travels can be solved by dividing
the total distance traveled by the total amount of time.

PROBLEM

> On a 40-mile bicycle trip, Cathy rode half the distance at 20 mph and
> the other half at 10 mph. What was Cathy's average speed on the bike
> trip?

Solution

First you need to break down the problem. On half of the trip, which
would be 20 miles, Cathy rode 20 mph. Using the rate formula,

$$\frac{\text{distance}}{\text{rate}} = \text{time},$$

you would compute,

$$\frac{20 \text{ miles}}{20 \text{ miles per hour}} = 1 \text{ hour}$$

to travel the first 20 miles. During the second 20 miles, Cathy traveled at
10 miles per hour, which would be

$$\frac{20 \text{ miles}}{10 \text{ miles per hour}} = 2 \text{ hours}.$$

Thus, the average speed Cathy traveled would be $^{40}/_3 = 13.34$ miles per
hour.

In solving for some rate problems you can use cross multiplication involving ratios to solve for *x*.

PROBLEM

If two pairs of shoes cost $52, then what is the cost of 10 pairs of shoes at this rate?

Solution

$$\frac{2}{52} = \frac{10}{x}, \quad 2x = 52 \times 10, \quad x = \frac{520}{2}, \quad x = \$260.$$

Drill 2: Rate

1. Two towns are 420 miles apart. A car leaves the first town traveling toward the second town at 55 mph. At the same time, a second car leaves the other town and heads toward the first town at 65 mph. How long will it take for the two cars to meet?

    (A) 2 hours　　　　　　　　　(B) 3 hours

    (C) 3.5 hours　　　　　　　　(D) 4 hours

    (E) 4.25 hours

2. A camper leaves the campsite walking due east at a rate of 3.5 mph. Another camper leaves the campsite at the same time but travels due west. In two hours the two campers will be 15 miles apart. What is the walking rate of the second camper?

    (A) 2.5 mph　　　　　　　　　(B) 3 mph

    (C) 3.25 mph　　　　　　　　(D) 3.5 mph

    (E) 4 mph

3. A bicycle racer covers a 75 mile training route to prepare for an upcoming race. If the racer could increase his speed by 5 mph, he could complete the same course in 3/4 of the time. Find his average rate of speed.

    (A) 15 mph　　　　　　　　　(B) 15.5 mph

    (C) 16 mph　　　　　　　　　(D) 18 mph

    (E) 20 mph

3. WORK

In work problems, one of the basic formulas is

$$\frac{1}{x} + \frac{1}{y} = \frac{1}{z}$$

where x and y represent the number of hours it takes two objects or people to complete the work and z is the total number of hours when both are working together.

PROBLEM

Otis can seal and stamp 400 envelopes in 2 hours while Elizabeth seals and stamps 400 envelopes in 1 hour. In how many hours can Otis and Elizabeth, working together, complete a 400-piece mailing at these rates?

Solution

$$\frac{1}{2} + \frac{1}{1} = \frac{1}{z}, \quad \frac{1}{2} + \frac{2}{2} = \frac{3}{2}, \quad \frac{3}{2} = \frac{1}{z}, \quad 3z = 2$$

$z = \frac{2}{3}$ of an hour or 40 minutes. Working together, Otis and Elizabeth can seal and stamp 400 envelopes in 40 minutes.

Drill 3: Work

1. It takes Marty three hours to type the address labels for his club's newsletter. It only takes Pat $2\frac{1}{4}$ hours to type the same amount of labels. How long would it take them working together to complete the address labels?

   (A) $\frac{7}{9}$ hr   (B) $1\frac{2}{7}$ hr

   (C) $1\frac{4}{5}$ hr   (D) $2\frac{5}{8}$ hr

   (E) $5\frac{1}{4}$ hr

2. It takes Troy three hours to mow his family's large lawn. With his little brother's help, he can finish the job in only two hours. How long would it take the little brother to mow the entire lawn alone?

   (A) 4 hr   (B) 5 hr

(C) 5.5 hr   (D) 6 hr

(E) 6.75 hr

3. A tank can be filled by one inlet pipe in 15 minutes. It takes an outlet pipe 75 minutes to drain the tank. If the outlet pipe is left open by accident, how long would it take to fill the tank?

(A) 15.5 min   (B) 15.9 min

(C) 16.8 min   (D) 18.75 min

(E) 19.3 min

4. MIXTURE

Mixture problems present the combination of different products and ask you to solve for different parts of the mixture.

PROBLEM

A chemist has an 18% solution and a 45% solution of a disinfectant. How many ounces of each should be used to make 12 ounces of a 36% solution?

Solution

Let x = Number of ounces from the 18% solution, and

y = Number of ounces from the 45% solution.

$x + y = 12$

$.18x + .45y = .36(12)$

Note that .18 of the first solution is pure disinfectant and that .45 of the second solution is pure disinfectant. When the proper quantities are drawn from each mixture the result is 12 ounces of mixture that is .36 pure disinfectant.

The second equation cannot be solved with two unknowns. Therefore, write one variable in terms of the other and substitute it into the second equation.

$x = 12 - y$

$.18(12 - y) + .45y = .36(12)$

Simplifying,

$$2.16 - .18y + .45y = 4.32$$
$$.27y = 4.32 - 2.16$$
$$.27y = 2.16$$
$$y = 8$$

Substituting 8 for *y* in the first equation,

$$x + 8 = 12$$
$$x = 4$$

Therefore, 4 ounces of the first and 8 ounces of the second solution should be used.

PROBLEM

Clark pays $2.00 per pound for 3 pounds of peanut butter chocolates and then decides to buy 2 pounds of chocolate-covered raisins at $2.50 per pound. If Clark mixes both together, what is the cost per pound of the mixture?

Solution

The total mixture is 5 pounds and the total value of the chocolates is

$$3(\$2.00) + 2(\$2.50) = \$11.00.$$

The price per pound of the chocolates is

$$\frac{\$11.00}{5 \text{ pounds}} = \$2.20.$$

Drill 4: Mixture

1. How many liters of a 20% alcohol solution must be added to 80 liters of a 50% alcohol solution to form a 45% solution?

   (A) 4   (B) 8

   (C) 16   (D) 20

   (E) 32

2. How many kilograms of water must be evaporated from 50 kg of a 10% salt solution to obtain a 15% salt solution?

(A) 15   (B) 15.75

(C) 16   (D) $16.\overline{66}$

(E) 16.75

3. If 1.5 pounds of coffee A at $3.00 a pound are mixed with 2.5 pounds of coffee B at $4.20 a pound, what is the cost per pound of the mixture?

(A) $2.95   (B) $3.45

(C) $3.60   (D) $3.75

(E) $5.00

5. INTEREST

If the problem calls for computing simple interest, the interest is computed on the principal alone. If the problem involves compounded interest, then the interest on the principal is taken into account in addition to the interest earned before.

PROBLEM

How much interest will Jerry pay on his loan of $400 for 60 days at 6% per year?

Solution

Use the formula:

Interest = Principal × Rate × Time ($I = P \times R \times T$).

$400 × 6%/year × 60 days

$$= \$400 \times .06 \times \frac{60}{365}$$

$$= \$400 \times 0.00986 = \$3.94$$

Jerry will pay $3.94.

PROBLEM

Mr. Smith wishes to find out how much interest he will receive on $300 if the rate is 3% compounded annually for three years.

Solution

Compound interest is interest computed on both the principal and the interest it has previously earned. The interest is added to the principal at the end of every year. The interest on the first year is found by multiplying the rate by the principal. Hence, the interest for the first year is

$$3\% \times \$300 = .03 \times \$300 = \$9.00.$$

The principal for the second year is now $309, the old principal ($300) plus the interest ($9). The interest for the second year is found by multiplying the rate by the new principal. Hence, the interest for the second year is

$$3\% \times \$309 = .03 \times \$309 = \$9.27.$$

The principal now becomes $309 + $9.27 = $318.27.

The interest for the third year is found using this new principal. It is

$$3\% \times \$318.27 = .03 \times \$318.27 = \$9.55.$$

At the end of the third year his principal is $318.27 + 9.55 = $327.82. To find how much interest was earned, we subtract his starting principal ($300) from his ending principal ($327.82) to obtain

$$\$327.82 - \$300.00 = \$27.82.$$

To find the total amount with compound interest:

$$A = P(1 + r)^{nt}$$

where P = the principal

  r = interest rate as a decimal

  t = compounding period

  n = the number of compounding periods

In the example above, to find the amount earned after three years

  $P = \$300$

  $r = .03$

  $t = 1$ year

$$n = 3$$
$$A = \$300(1 + .03)^{3(1)}$$
$$= \$300(1.03)^3$$
$$= \$327.82$$

Drill 5: Interest

1. A man invests \$3,000, part in a 12-month certificate of deposit pay-
    ing 8% and the rest in municipal bonds that pay 7% a year. If the
    yearly return from both investments is \$220, how much was invested
    in bonds?

    (A) \$80   (B) \$140

    (C) \$220   (D) \$1,000

    (E) \$2,000

2. A sum of money was invested at 11% a year. Four times that amount
    was invested at 7.5%. How much was invested at 11% if the total
    annual return was \$1,025?

    (A) \$112.75   (B) \$1,025

    (C) \$2,500   (D) \$3,400

    (E) \$10,000

3. One bank pays 6.5% a year simple interest on a savings account
    while a credit union pays 7.2% a year. If you had \$1,500 to invest for
    three years, how much more would you earn by putting the money in
    the credit union than in the bank?

    (A) \$10.50   (B) \$31.50

    (C) \$97.50   (D) \$108

    (E) \$1,500

6. DISCOUNT

If the discount problem asks to find the final price after the discount, first multiply the original price by the percent of discount. Then subtract this result from the original price.

If the problem asks to find the original price when only the percent of discount and the discounted price are given, simply subtract the percent of discount from 100% and divide this percent into the sale price. This will give you the original price.

PROBLEM

A popular bookstore gives a 10% discount to students. What does a student actually pay for a book costing $24?

Solution

10% of $24 is $2.40 and hence the student pays $24 − $2.40 = $21.60.

PROBLEM

Eugene paid $100 for a business suit. The suit's price included a 25% discount. What was the original price of the suit?

Solution

Let x represent the original price of the suit and take the complement of .25 (discount price) which is .75.

$$.75x = \$100 \text{ or } x = 133.34.$$

So, the original price of the suit was $133.34.

Drill 6: Discount

1. A man bought a coat marked 20% off for $156. How much had the coat cost originally?

   (A) $136   (B) $156

   (C) $175   (D) $195

   (E) $205

2. A woman saved $225 on her new sofa, which was on sale for 30% off. What was the original price of the sofa?

(A) $25   (B) $200

(C) $225   (D) $525

(E) $750

3. At an office supply store, customers are given a discount if they pay in cash. If a customer is given a discount of $9.66 on a total order of $276, what is the percent of discount?

(A) 2%   (B) 3.5%

(C) 4.5%   (D) 9.66%

(E) 276%

7. PROFIT

The formula used for the profit problems is

Profit = Revenue – Cost   or

Profit = Selling Price – Expenses

PROBLEM

Four high school and college friends started a business of remodeling and selling old automobiles during the summer. For this purpose they paid $600 to rent an empty barn for the summer. They obtained the cars from a dealer for $250 each, and it takes an average of $410 in materials to remodel each car. How many automobiles must the students sell at $1,440 each to obtain a gross profit of $7,000?

Solution

Total – Total Cost = Gross Profit

Revenue – [Variable Cost + Fixed Cost] = Gross Profit

Let a = number of cars

Revenue = $1,440a$

Variable Cost = ($250 + 410)a$

Fixed Cost = $600

The desired gross profit is $7,000.

Using the equation for the gross profit,

$$1,440a - [660a + 600] = 7,000$$

$$1,440a - 660a - 600 = 7,000$$

$$780a = 7,000 + 600$$

$$780a = 7,600$$

$$a = 9.74$$

or to the nearest car, $a = 10$.

PROBLEM

A glass vase sells for $25. The net profit is 7%, and the operating expenses are 39%. Find the gross profit on the vase.

Solution

The gross profit is equal to the net profit plus the operating expenses. The net profit is 7% of the selling cost; thus it is equal to

$$7\% \times \$25 = .07 \times \$25 = \$1.75.$$

The operating expenses are 39% of the selling price, thus equal to

$$39\% \times \$25 = .30 \times \$25 = \$9.75.$$

$1.75	net profit
+ $9.75	operating expenses
$11.50	gross profit

Drill 7: Profit

1. An item cost a store owner $50. She marked it up 40% and advertised it at that price. How much profit did she make if she later sold it at 15% off the advertised price?

    (A) $7.50   (B) $9.50

    (C) $10.50   (D) $39.50

    (E) $50

2. An antique dealer made a profit of 115% on the sale of an oak desk. If the desk cost her $200, how much profit did she make on the sale?

(A) $230   (B) $315

(C) $430   (D) $445

(E) $475

3. As a graduation gift, a young man was given 100 shares of stock worth $27.50 apiece. Within a year the price of the stock had risen by 8%. How much more were the stocks worth at the end of the first year than when they were given to the young man?

(A) $110   (B) $220

(C) $1,220   (D) $2,750

(E) $2,970

8. RATIOS AND PROPORTIONS

The ratio of two numbers x and y written $x:y$ is the fraction x/y where $y \neq 0$. A ratio compares x to y by dividing one by the other. Therefore, in order to compare ratios, simply compare the fractions.

A proportion is an equality of two ratios. The laws of proportion are listed below:

If $a/b = c/d$, then

(A) $ad = bc$

(B) $b/a = d/c$

(C) $a/c = b/d$

(D) $(a + b)/b = (c + d)/d$

(E) $(a - b)/b = (c - d)/d$

Given a proportion $a:b = c:d$, then a and d are called extremes, b and c are called the means, and d is called the fourth proportion to a, b, and c.

PROBLEM

Solve the proportion $\dfrac{x+1}{4} = \dfrac{15}{12}$.

Solution

Cross multiply to determine x; that is, multiply the numerator of the first fraction by the denominator of the second, and equate this to the product of the numerator of the second and the denominator of the first.

$$(x + 1)12 = 4 \times 15$$

$$12x + 12 = 60$$

$$x = 4$$

PROBLEM

If a car gets 24 miles per gallon of gasoline, how many gallons of gasoline are needed for a trip of 252 miles?

Solution

Given the car uses 1 gallon:24 miles, let x = number of gallons of gas needed. Set up the proportion

$$\frac{1 \text{ gallon}}{24 \text{ miles}} = \frac{x}{252 \text{ miles}}.$$

Cross multiply to determine x.

$$252 = 24x$$

$$x = 10.5 \text{ gallons}$$

PROBLEM

U is inversely proportional with V. If U is 8 when V is 6, how much will U be if V is 24?

Solution

Given that

$$U = \frac{K}{V}, \quad K = \text{constant}$$

$$8 = \frac{K}{6}$$

$$K = 48$$

To find the value of U put in the values of K and V.

$$U = \frac{48}{24}$$

$$= 2$$

Note: Since U is *inversely proportional* to V, as V increases U decreases.

Drill 8: Ratios and Proportions

1. Four out of every five students at West High take a mathematics course. If the enrollment at West High is 785, how many students take mathematics?

    (A) 628   (B) 157

    (C) 705   (D) 655

    (E) 247

2. A summer league softball team won 28 out of the 32 games they played. What is the ratio of games won to games played?

    (A) 4:5   (B) 3:4

    (C) 7:8   (D) 2:3

    (E) 1:8

3. A class of 24 students contains 16 males. What is the ratio of females to males?

    (A) 1:2   (B) 2:1

    (C) 2:3   (D) 3:1

    (E) 3:2

9. GEOMETRY

PROBLEM

A boy knows that his height is 6 ft. and his shadow is 4 ft. long. At the same time of day, a tree's shadow is 24 ft. long. How high is the tree? (See following figure.)

(a) (b)

Solution

Show that $\triangle ABC \approx \triangle DEF$, and then set up a proportion between the known sides AB and DE, and the sides BC and EF.

First, assume that both the boy and the tree are $\perp$ to the earth. Then, $BC \perp BA$ and $EF \perp E\triangle$. Hence,

$$\angle ABC \cong \angle DEF.$$

Since it is the same time of day, the rays of light from the sun are incident on both the tree and the boy at the same angle, relative to the earth's surface. Therefore,

$$\angle BAC \cong \angle EDF.$$

We have shown, so far, that two pairs of corresponding angles are congruent. Since the sum of the angles of any triangle is 180°, the third pair of corresponding angles is congruent (i.e., $\angle ACB \cong \angle DFE$). By the Angle Angle Angle (A.A.A.) Theorem

$$\angle ABC \approx \angle DEF.$$

By definition of similarity,

$$\frac{FE}{CB} = \frac{ED}{BA}.$$

$CB = 6'$, $ED = 24'$, and $BA = 4'$. Therefore,

$$FE = (6') (24'/4') = 36'.$$

Drill 9: Geometry

1. $\triangle PQR$ is a scalene triangle. The measure of $\angle P$ is 8° more than twice the measure of $\angle R$. The measure of $\angle Q$ is two less than three times the measure of $\angle R$. Determine the measure of $\angle Q$.

    (A) 29°   (B) 53°

    (C) 60°   (D) 85°

    (E) 174°

2. Angle A and angle B are supplementary. The measure of angle B is 50 more than four times the measure of angle A. Find the measure of angle B.

    (A) 35°   (B) 125°

    (C) 140°   (D) 145°

    (E) 155°

3. Triangle RUS is isosceles with base $\overline{SU}$. Each leg is 3 less than 5 times the length of the base. If the perimeter of the triangle is 60 cm, find the length of a leg.

    (A) 6   (B) 12

    (C) 27   (D) 30

    (E) 33

4. A glass is 4 inches in diameter and 6 inches tall. If the glass is $^1/_4$ full, how much more liquid is needed to fill the glass?

    (A) 6π   (B) 12π

    (C) 18π   (D) 20π

    (E) 24π

WORD PROBLEM DRILLS

ANSWER KEY

Drill 1 – Algebraic

1. (D)   2. (A)   3. (B)

Drill 2 – Rate

1. (C)   2. (E)   3. (A)

Drill 3 – Work

1. (B)   2. (D)   3. (D)

Drill 4 – Mixture

1. (C)   2. (D)   3. (D)

Drill 5 – Interest

1. (E)   2. (C)   3. (B)

Drill 6 – Discount

1. (D)   2. (E)   3. (B)

Drill 7 – Profit

1. (B)   2. (A)   3. (B)

Drill 8 – Ratios and Proportions

1. (A)   2. (C)   3. (A)

Drill 9 – Geometry

1. (D)   2. (D)   3. (C)   4. (C)

DETAILED EXPLANATIONS
OF ANSWERS

WORD PROBLEMS REVIEW

Drill 1 – Algebraic

1. **(D)** Let x and y represent the two numbers. Since their sum is 41, one equation is $x + y = 41$.

Then if one of the two numbers, say x, is one less than twice the other, the second equation can be written $x = 2y - 1$.

So the two equations are

$$x + y = 41$$

and $x = 2y - 1.$

Solve the first equation for x:

$$x = 41 - y.$$

Substitute $(41 - y)$ for x in the second equation:

$$41 - y = 2y - 1.$$

Solve for y:

$$41 - y = 2y - 1$$
$$42 - y = 2y$$
$$42 = 3y$$
$$14 = y$$

Then if $y = 14$ and $x + y = 41$, $x = 27$.

Check: $27 + 14 = 41$ $27 = 2(14) - 1$

$41 = 41$ $27 = 28 - 1$

$27 = 27$

2. **(A)** If a represents the smaller integer, then its consecutive integer is represented by $a + 1$. So the first equation becomes

$$a + (a + 1) = 111.$$

Three times the larger integer is $3(a + 1)$ while two times the smaller integer is $2a$. "Less" indicates subtraction, so the second equation becomes

$$3(a + 1) - 2a = 58.$$

Solve this equation for a:

$$3(a + 1) - 2a = 58$$
$$3a + 3 - 2a = 58$$
$$a + 3 = 58$$
$$a = 55$$

Since a represented the smaller integer, we have answered the question.

Check: $\quad 55 + (55 + 1) = 111 \qquad 3(55 + 1) - 2(55) = 58$

$$55 + 56 = 111 \qquad\qquad 168 - 110 = 58$$
$$111 = 111 \qquad\qquad\qquad 58 = 58$$

3. **(B)** Let X and Y represent two integers.

"Difference" indicates subtraction, so the first equation can be written as $X - Y = 12$.

"Sum" indicates addition, so the second equation is $X + Y = 2$.

Solve these two equations simultaneously by adding them together. (The Y's are eliminated.)

$$\begin{array}{r} X - Y = 12 \\ \underline{X + Y = 2} \\ 2X = 14 \end{array}$$

Solve for X by dividing both sides by 2.

$$X = 7$$

Then substitute X into either one of the two original equations to find Y.

$$7 - Y = 12$$

$$-Y = 5$$
$$Y = -5$$

Check: $7 - (-5) = 12$ $7 + (-5) = 2$

$7 + 5 = 12$ $2 = 2$

$12 = 12$

Drill 2 – Rate

1.   **(C)**   For a problem such as this, a diagram, a chart, and the formula $D = RT$ are helpful.

As the diagram indicates, this is an addition problem. The distance covered by the first car must be added to the distance covered by the second car to obtain the distance between the two cities.

The chart uses the three parts of the equation $D = RT$. Since the time is the unknown in this problem, it is represented by t.

Car	Rate	Time	Distance
1	55	t	$55t$
2	65	t	$65t$

Now add together the two distances from the chart and set them equal to the total distance.

$$55t + 65t = 420$$

Solve for t $120t = 420$

$$t = 3.5 \text{ hr}$$

Check: $55(3.5) + 65(3.5) = 420$

$$192.5 + 227.5 = 420$$

$$420 = 420$$

2.   **(E)**   A diagram, a chart, and the formula $D = RT$ are used to solve this problem.

Let x represent the walking rate of the second camper.

The diagram indicates that we need to add the two individual distances to equal the entire distance of 15 miles.

In the chart, we fill in the rate and the time for each camper. The formula $D = RT$ is used to find the value in the last column.

	Rate	Time	Distance
1st	3.5	2	7
2nd	x	2	$2x$

Now add the two individual distances together and set them equal to the total distance:

$$7 + 2x = 15.$$

Solve for x:

$$7 + 2x = 15$$
$$2x = 8$$
$$x = 4 \text{ mph}$$

Check: $7 + 2(4) = 15$
$$7 + 8 = 15$$
$$15 = 15$$

3.   **(A)**   Let r = the initial average rate and let t = the initial time. Then since $D = RT$, $75 = rt$.

If the rate is increased by 5 mph, it would be written $r + 5$. If the time is reduced by $^3/_4$, it becomes $^3/_4t$. Using the same formula, $D = RT$,

$$75 = (r+5)\left(\frac{3}{4}t\right).$$

Use the distributive property in the second equation.

$$75 = (r+5)\left(\frac{3}{4}t\right)$$

$$75 = \frac{3}{4}rt + \frac{15}{4}t$$

Multiply both sides of the equation by 4.

$$300 = 3rt + 15rt$$

Since the first equation is $rt = 75$, substitute 75 for the expression rt.

$$300 = 3(75) + 15t$$

Solve for t.

$$300 = 225 + 15t$$

$$75 = 15t$$

$$5 = t$$

Since the problem asked for the rate, use t to find r.

$$rt = 75$$

$$r(5) = 75$$

$$r = 15 \text{ mph}$$

Check: $15(5) = 75$ $(15+5) \times {}^3/_4\,(5) = 75$

               $75 = 75$ $20 \times 3.75 = 75$

                                           $75 = 75$

Drill 3 – Work

1.   **(B)** To solve this problem, decide on a convenient unit of time—here the hour is the easiest choice. Next, write the amount of work that each person can do in that amount of time (this is the *rate* of work).

In one hour, Marty can do $1/3$ of the job.

In one hour, Pat can do

$$\frac{1}{2\frac{1}{4}} \quad \text{or} \quad \frac{1}{\frac{9}{4}} \quad \text{or} \quad \frac{4}{9}$$

of the job.

The unknown in this problem is the amount of time it will take the two working together—call this unknown x. Then multiply each person's rate of work by the amount of time spent working together to obtain the portion of the total job each person did. Marty did $x/3$ and Pat did $4x/9$ of the work.

Then add each person's part of the work together and set it equal to 1; this represents one completed task. Now the equation looks like this:

$$\frac{x}{3} + \frac{4x}{9} = 1.$$

Find the Least Common Denominator (LCD) and multiply both sides of the equation by the LCD.

$$9\left(\frac{x}{3} + \frac{4x}{9}\right) = (1)(9)$$

$$3x + 4x = 9$$

$$7x = 9$$

$$x = \frac{9}{7} \text{ hr } \text{ or } 1\frac{2}{7} \text{ hr}$$

2. **(D)** Let x represent the time it would take for the brother to mow the lawn alone.

Since Troy does the lawn in 3 hours, he does $1/3$ of the lawn in one hour. Since the brother takes x hours to mow the lawn, in one hour he does $1/x$ of the job. Both rates are multiplied by 2 since they complete the job in 2 hours.

	In One Hour	Time	Part of Job
Troy	$1/3$	2	$2/3$
Brother	$1/x$	2	$2/x$

Now add the part that each person does and set the sum equal to 1. The 1 represents one complete job.

$$2/3 + 2/x = 1$$

Multiply by the LCD of $3x$.

$$(2/3)\,(3x) + (2/x)\,(3x) = 1(3x)$$

$$2x + 6 = 3x$$

Solve for x.

$$6 = x$$

It would take the little brother 6 hours to mow the lawn by himself.

Check: $2/3 + 2/6 = 1$

$\qquad 2/3 + 1/3 = 1$

$\qquad\qquad 1 = 1$

3. **(D)** Let x represent the time to fill the tank.

Since it takes 15 minutes for the inlet pipe to fill the tank, in one minute it can fill $1/15$ of the tank. Since the outlet pipe drains the tank in 75 minutes, in one minute it can drain $1/75$ of the tank. The amount done in one minute is multiplied by the time to get the part of the job done in x minutes.

	In One Minute	**Time**	**Part of Job**
Inlet	$1/15$	x	$x/15$
Outlet	$1/75$	x	$x/75$

In setting up the equation, the part of the job done by the outlet pipe must be *subtracted* from that part done by the inlet pipe. The difference is set equal to one to represent one completed job.

The equation is

$$\frac{x}{15} - \frac{x}{75} = 1.$$

Multiply by the LCD, 75.

$$(75)\frac{x}{15} - (75)\frac{x}{15} = (75)1$$

$$5x - x = 75$$

$$4x = 75$$

$$x = 18\frac{3}{4} \text{ minutes}$$

Check: $\dfrac{18.75}{15} - \dfrac{18.75}{75} = 1$

$$1.25 - 0.25 = 1$$

$$1 = 1$$

Drill 4 – Mixture

1. **(C)** For each solution, fill in the chart with the amount of the solution, the percent of alcohol it contains, and the amount of alcohol it contains.

Solution	Amount of Solution	% of Alcohol	Amount of Alcohol
1st	x	.20	.20x
2nd	80	.50	.50(80)
mix	$(x + 80)$	.45	.45$(x + 80)$

Since we don't know how much of the first solution there is, the amount of the first solution is represented by x.

Add the first two amounts of alcohol together and set the sum equal to the amount of alcohol in the mixture. Solve the equation for x.

$$.20x + .50(80) = .45(x + 80)$$

$$.20x + 40 = .45x + 36$$

$$4 = .25x$$

$$x = 16$$

So 16 liters of the 20% alcohol solution must be added to the 50% solution.

Check: $.20(16) + .50(80) = .45(16 + 80)$

$$3.2 + 40 = .45(96)$$

$$43.2 = 43.2$$

2. **(D)** Fill in the chart with the amount of each solution, the percent of salt each solution is, and the amount of salt contained in each solution. Let x represent the amount of water to be evaporated.

Solution	Amount	%	Amount of Salt
Original	50	0.10	0.10(50)
Water	x	0	0
New Sol.	$(50 - x)$	0.15	$0.15(50 - x)$

The amount of salt in the original solution less the amount of salt in the water evaporated (which is 0) equals the amount of salt in the new solution.

$$0.10(50) - 0 = 0.15(50 - x)$$

Solve for x.

$$5 - 0 = 7.5 - 0.15x$$

$$-2.5 = -0.15x$$

$$16^2/_3 = x$$

$$16.\overline{66} = x$$

Sixteen and two-thirds kilograms of water must be evaporated from the original solution.

Check: $5 = 7.5 - 0.15(16^2/_3)$

$$5 = 7.5 - \frac{15}{100} \times \frac{50}{3}$$

$$5 = 7.5 - 2.5$$

$$5 = 5$$

3. (D) Fill in the chart with the amount of each coffee, the price per pound of each coffee, and the total price.

Since the amount of the mixture is the unknown, call it x.

Coffee	Amount	Price/lb	Total Price
A	1.5	3.00	3(1.5)
B	2.5	4.20	2.5(4.2)
mix	(1.5 + 2.5)	x	$x(1.5 + 2.5)$

Add the total prices of the two coffees together and set the sum equal to the total price of the mixture. Solve for x.

$$3(1.5) + 2.5(4.2) = x(1.5 + 2.5)$$

$$4.5 + 10.50 = 4x$$

$$15 = 4x$$

$$3.75 = x$$

The cost of the mixture is $3.75 per pound.

Check: $3(1.5) + 2.5(4.2) = (2.5 + 1.5)(3.75)$

$$4.5 + 10.50 = 4(3.75)$$

$$15 = 15$$

Drill 5 – Interest

1.   **(E)**   Let x = the amount invested at 8%. Then, since the total amount is $3,000, the remaining part is $(3,000 - x)$.

Multiply the amount invested by the % of interest and add these two amounts together to equal the total interest.

$$0.08x + 0.07(3,000 - x) = 220$$

$$0.08x + 210 - 0.07x = 220$$

$$0.01x = 10$$

$$x = 1,000$$

$$3,000 - x = 2,000$$

The amount invested in bonds is $2,000.

Check: $0.08(1,000) + 0.07(2,000) = 220$

$$80 + 140 = 220$$

$$220 = 220$$

2.   **(C)**   Let x = the amount invested at 11%.

Let $4x$ = the amount invested at 7.5%.

Multiply the amount invested by the interest rate to determine the individual interest. Add these two individual interests together and set the sum equal to the total interest.

$$0.11x + 0.075(4x) = \$1,025$$
$$0.11x + 0.3x = 1,025$$
$$0.41x = 1,025$$
$$x = \$2,500$$

$2,500 was invested at 11%.

Check: $0.11(2,500) + 0.075(4 \times 2,500) = 1,025$
$$275 + 750 = 1,025$$
$$1,025 = 1,025$$

3.   **(B)**   Use the simple interest formula, $I = PRT$, to find the interest earned on each account.

Bank: $I = \$1,500 \times 0.065 \times 3 = \$292.50$

Credit Union: $I = \$1,500 \times 0.072 \times 3 = \$324$

Subtract the amounts of interest to see how much more you would earn by keeping the money in the credit union.

$$\$324 - \$292.50 = \$31.50$$

Drill 6 – Discount

1.   **(D)**   Let x be the original price of the coat.

The original price minus 20% of the original price equals $156.

Or, $x - 0.20(x) = 156.$

Or, $1.0(x) - 0.20(x) = 156.$

Or, $0.80(x) = 156$

so $x = 156/0.80 = 195.$

The coat originally cost $195.

Check: $195 - 0.20(195) = 156$
$$195 - 39 = 156$$
$$156 = 156$$

2. **(E)** If x = the original price of the sofa, then $0.30x$ = the amount saved, which was $225.

So, $0.30x = 225$.

Then $x = 225/0.30 = \$750$.

The original price of the sofa was $750.

Check: $0.30(750) = 225$

$225 = 225$

3. **(B)** A good technique to use in this problem is the formula

$$\frac{\text{Percentage}}{\text{Base}} = \frac{\text{Rate}}{100}.$$

In this problem you are asked for the percent of discount, which is the same as the rate—call it r.

The percentage or discount is $9.66 and the base, or total amount, is $276.

The equation becomes

$$\frac{9.66}{276} = \frac{r}{100}.$$

Use cross multiplication to solve.

$$9.66(100) = 276r \text{ so } r = \frac{966}{276} = 3.5$$

The percent of discount is 3.5%.

Drill 7 – Profit

1. **(B)** The profit is the sale price less the initial cost. The initial cost was $50. The sale price is 15% off the advertised price.

The advertised price is marked up 40% over the initial price—or $50 + 0.40($50). This advertised price is $70.

Then the sale price is the advertised price less 15% of the advertised price, or $70 – 0.15(70), or $59.50.

Finally, the profit is $59.50 – $50 = $9.50.

2. **(A)** The profit is 115% of the initial cost of the desk.

$P = 1.15(\$200) = \$230.$

3. **(B)** The profit on the stocks is the new value less the original value.

Original value = $\$27.50 \times 100 = \$2,750$

New value = $\$2,750 + 0.08(\$2,750) = \$2,970$

Profit = $\$2,970 - \$2,750 = \$220$

Drill 8 – Ratios and Proportions

1. **(A)** Let x be the number of students who take mathematics at West High. We know 4:5 take a mathematics course. Set up a ratio as follows:

$$4:5 = x:785$$
$$\frac{4}{5} = \frac{x}{785}$$
$$x = \frac{4}{5}(785)$$
$$x = 628$$

2. **(C)** It is given that the team won 28 games and played 32 games. Therefore, the ratio of games won to games played is

28:32.

Reduce by dividing by 4.

7:8

3. **(A)** To find the ratio of females to males, find how many females are in the class.

Total students – males = females

24 – 16 = females

8 = females

Set up ratio

females:males

8:16

Reduce by dividing both sides by 8.

1:2

Drill 9: Geometry

1.   **(D)**   Draw a sketch of the triangle and label the angles.

Two of the angles are compared to $\angle R$, so let $x =$ the measure of $\angle R$. Then

$$\angle P = 2x + 8 \text{ and } \angle Q = 3x - 2.$$

The sum of the measures of the angles of a triangle is 180°, so add the measures of all three angles and this will equal 180°.

$$x + (2x + 8) + (3x - 2) = 180°$$

$$6x + 6 = 180°$$

$$6x = 174°$$

$$x = 29°$$

The measure of $\angle R$ is 29° and the measure of $\angle Q$ is $3(29°) - 2°$ or 85°.

Check: $29° + [2(29°) + 8°] + [3(29°) - 2°] = 180°$

$$29° + 66° + 85° = 180°$$

$$180° = 180°$$

2.   **(D)**   Let $A =$ the measure of angle A and let $B =$ the measure of angle B. Since the two angles are supplementary, one equation is

$$A + B = 180°.$$

Since B is 5 more than four times the measure of angle A, either subtract 5 from the measure of angle B or add 5 to four times the measure of angle A. The equation becomes

$$B = 4A + 5.$$

Now substitute the value of B into the first equation to get

$A + (4A + 5) = 180°.$

Solve the equation for A:

$$5A + 5 = 180°$$

$$5A = 175°$$

$$A = 35°$$

Then $B = 4(35°) + 5° = 145°.$

Check: $35° + 145° = 180°$ $145° = 4(35°) + 5°$

        $180° = 180°$ $145° = 145°$

3. **(C)** Draw an isosceles triangle and label each side. Let the length of the base be x. Then each leg is five times the base minus 3, or $5x - 3$.

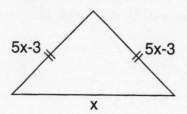

The perimeter is the sum of the sides, so the equation becomes

$x + (5x - 3) + (5x - 3) = 60.$

    Solve for x:

$$11x - 6 = 60$$

$$11x = 66$$

$$x = 6$$

and $5(6) - 3 = 27.$

The length of each leg is 27.

Check: $6 + 27 + 27 = 60$

           $60 = 60$

4.　(C)　To find the volume of a cylinder, use the formula

$$v = \pi r^2 h$$

$r = $ radius

$h = $ height

$$v = \pi(2)^2(6)$$

$$= 24\pi$$

The glass is $^1/_4$ full already. Therefore to fill the glass you need to know what $^3/_4$ of the volume of the glass is,

$$= {}^3/_4 \, (24\pi)$$

$$= 18\pi$$

ELM

Entry Level Mathematics

Test 1

ELM
TEST 1

Time: 90 Minutes
50 Questions (including 5 field test questions)

(Answer sheets appear at the back of the book.)

DIRECTIONS: Solve each problem and select the letter corresponding to the best choice to answer the question.

---

1. What is the area of the shaded portion of the rectangle? The shaded area represents the center of the semicircle.

    (A) $200 - 100\pi$

    (B) $200 - 25\pi$

    (C) $30 - \dfrac{25\pi}{2}$

    (D) $\dfrac{200 - 25\pi}{2}$

    (E) $\dfrac{400 - 25\pi}{2}$

    πr^2
    25π
    $\dfrac{200 - 25\pi}{2}$

2. If the weight of a mass of 10 g stretches a spring 5 cm, how far will a weight of a mass 4 g stretch it?

    (A) 1 cm

    (B) 2 cm

    (C) 4 cm

    (D) 5 cm

    (E) 8 cm

    $10 g$

    $\dfrac{10}{5} = \dfrac{x}{4}$

    40

349

3. $(x + 1)(3x + 4) =$

    [handwritten: $3x^2 + 4x + 3x + 4$ $3x^2 + 7x + 4$]

    (A) $3x^2 + 5$ (B) $3x^2 + 4$

    (C) $3x^2 - 7x - 4$ (D) $3x^2 - 7x + 5$

    (E) $3x^2 + 7x + 4$

4. The box pictured has a square base with side x and a closed top. The surface area of the box is

    (A) $4x + h.$

    (B) $4x + 4h.$

    (C) $hx^2.$

    (D) $x^2 + 4xh.$

    (E) $2x^2 + 4xh.$

[handwritten: $x \cdot h \cdot 6$]

5. $\dfrac{\dfrac{1}{x} - \dfrac{1}{y}}{\dfrac{1}{x^2} - \dfrac{1}{y^2}} =$

    (A) $\dfrac{x^2 y^2}{x^2 + y^2}$ (B) $\dfrac{xy}{x + y}$

    (C) $\dfrac{xy}{(x + y)^2}$ (D) $\dfrac{xy}{y^2 - x^2}$

    (E) $\left(\dfrac{xy}{x + y}\right)^2$

6. What is t equal to if $A = P(1 + rt)$?

    (A) $A - P - Pr$ (B) $(A + P)/Pr$

    (C) $A/P - r$ (D) $(A - P)/Pr$

    (E) None of these

    [handwritten: $A = P1 + Prt$]

7. Fifteen percent of what number is 60?

(A) 9 (B) 51

(C) 69 (D) 200

(E) 400

Use the following graph for Questions 8, 9, and 10.

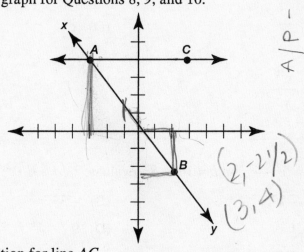

8. Find the equation for line *AC*.

(A) $x = 4$ (B) $y = 4$

(C) $x + y = 4$ (D) $x - y = 4$

(E) Not enough information

9. What is the midpoint of segment *AB*?

(A) $(-1, 2)$ (B) $(0, 0)$

(C) $(-\frac{1}{2}, 1)$ (D) $(-1, \frac{1}{2})$

(E) $(-1, -\frac{1}{2})$

10. What is the slope of line *AB*?

(A) $-\frac{5}{2}$ (B) $-\frac{8}{5}$

(C) $-\frac{6}{5}$ (D) $-\frac{2}{5}$

(E) $\frac{5}{6}$

11. Simplify $\left(\dfrac{x^2}{y}\right)^5$.

(A) $\dfrac{x^2}{y^5}$

(B) $\dfrac{x^7}{y}$

(C) $\dfrac{x^7}{y^5}$

(D) x^8

(E) $\dfrac{x^{10}}{y^5}$

12. If $a = 5^2 - 4^2$ and $b = 10^2 - 8^2$, evaluate $(\sqrt{a} - \sqrt{b})^2$.

(A) -27

(B) -3

(C) 1

(D) 9

(E) 729

13. What number must be added to 28 and 36 to get an average of 29?

(A) 32

(B) 23

(C) 21

(D) 5

(E) 4

14. If the radius of a sphere is increased by a factor of 3, then the volume of the sphere is increased by a factor of

(A) 3.

(B) 6.

(C) 9.

(D) 18.

(E) 27.

15. What is the sum of the roots in the equation $(4x - 3)^2 = 4$?

   (A) $\frac{1}{2}$

   (B) $\frac{6}{5}$

   (C) $1\frac{1}{2}$

   (D) $2\frac{1}{2}$

   (E) 3

16. In the figure shown (not drawn to scale) the line l and m are parallel. Then $x =$

   (A) 140°.

   (B) 120°.

   (C) 70°.

   (D) 50°.

   (E) 40°.

17. $\dfrac{(x^2)^{-4}(x^{-2})^3}{(x^{-3})^{-5}}$

   (A) x^5

   (B) $\dfrac{1}{x^{14}}$

   (C) $\dfrac{1}{x^{29}}$

   (D) x^7

   (E) x^{29}

18. What is the product of $(\sqrt{3} + 6)$ and $(\sqrt{3} - 2)$?

   (A) $9 + 4\sqrt{3}$

   (B) -9

   (C) $-9 + 4\sqrt{3}$

   (D) $-9 + 2\sqrt{3}$

   (E) 9

19. If $x - (4x - 8) + 9 + (6x - 8) = 9 - x + 24$, then $x =$

    (A) 2.

    (B) 4.

    (C) 6.

    (D) 8.

    (E) 10.

20. There are 20 qualified applicants for 3 management positions. How many different groups of applicants can be chosen for these positions?

    (A) 900

    (B) 1,020

    (C) 1,140

    (D) 6,840

    (E) 8,000

21. $\dfrac{1 - \dfrac{1}{1 - x}}{1 - \dfrac{1}{1 - \dfrac{1}{x}}} =$

    (A) x

    (B) $1/x$

    (C) $-1/x$

    (D) $-x$

    (E) 1

22. Which one of the following samples has a mode of 8 and a range of 3?

    (A) 3, 4, 5, 6, 7, 8, 8, 9

    (B) 7, 7, 7, 8, 8, 9, 9, 10

    (C) -1, 2, 5, 8, 11, 14, 17

    (D) 6, 6, 7, 7, 8, 8, 8, 9

    (E) 5, 5, 6, 6, 7, 7, 8

23. Simplify $\dfrac{5 + 3i}{2 - i}$.

    (A) $7 + 11i$

    (B) $\dfrac{7 + 11i}{3}$

(C) $\dfrac{7+11i}{5}$ (D) $\dfrac{13+11i}{3}$

(E) $\dfrac{13+11i}{5}$

24. A teacher earns $25,000 a year and receives a 4% cost of living increase in salary, and a $275 merit increase. His salary increased by

(A) 4.5%. (B) 4.9%.

(C) 5.0%. (D) 5.1%.

(E) 5.2%.

25. A jar contains 10 marbles. Five are red, three are blue, and two are green. Two marbles are randomly selected, one at a time and without replacement. What is the probability that both marbles are red?

(A) $^1/_5$ (B) $^2/_9$

(C) $^1/_2$ (D) $^7/_{10}$

(E) $^{17}/_{18}$

26. The expression $(x + y)^2 + (x - y)^2$ is equivalent to

(A) $2x^2$. (B) $4x^2$.

(C) $2(x^2 + y^2)$. (D) $2x^2 + y^2$.

(E) $x^2 + 2y^2$.

27. Four less than 3 times x is greater than 6. Find all values of x.

(A) $x < {}^{10}/_3$ (B) $x < 5$

(C) $x > {}^2/_3$ (D) $x > {}^{10}/_3$

(E) $x > 8$

28. What is the perimeter of triangle ABC?

(A) $12R$

(B) $16R$

(C) $18R$

(D) $12R^2$

(E) $18R^2$

29. If $\dfrac{7a - 5b}{b} = 7$, then $\dfrac{4a + 6b}{2a} =$

(A) $^{15}/_4$.

(B) 4.

(C) $^{17}/_4$.

(D) 5.

(E) 6.

30. The weight capacity of an elevator is 3,100 pounds. In a group of 10 women and 8 men, the average weight of the women is 138 pounds. What would be the maximum allowable average weight (in pounds) for the men in order for all 18 people to ride the elevator safely?

(A) 225

(B) 215

(C) 205

(D) 195

(E) 185

31. $g(x) = x^2 + 4$, find $g(-3)$.

(A) -5

(B) -3

(C) 3

(D) 4

(E) 13

32. Simplify and express in factored form $6(x - 2) - 4(x + 4)$.

(A) $2(x + 1)$

(B) $2(x + 2)$

(C) $2(x + 7)$

(D) $2(x - 14)$

(E) $2(x - 8)$

33. If $x + 2y > 5$ and $x < 3$, then $y > 1$ is true

(A) never.

(B) only if $x = 0$.

(C) only if $x > 0$.

(D) only if $x < 0$.

(E) always.

34. From a group of 6 women and 5 men, a committee of 6 people is needed. If this committee must consist of 4 women and 2 men, how many different committees are possible?

(A) 150

(B) 128

(C) 120

(D) 96

(E) 48

35. For any integer n, which of the following must be an even integer?

I. $2n + 1$

II. $2n + 2$

III. $2n - 1$

(A) I only

(B) II only

(C) III only

(D) I and II only

(E) II and III only

36. If $\sqrt{x-1} = 2$, then $(x - 1)^2 =$

(A) 4.

(B) 6.

(C) 8.

(D) 10.

(E) 16.

37. Representatives to a student group are being selected to fill vacancies. Two of five freshmen will be selected and three of four sophomores will be selected. In how many different ways can these students be selected?

(A) 480

(B) 120

(C) 40

(D) 22

(E) 9

38. If the hypotenuse of a right triangle is $x + 1$ and one of the legs is x, then the other leg is

(A) $\sqrt{2x+1}$.

(B) $\sqrt{2x}+1$.

(C) $\sqrt{x^2(x-1)^2}$.

(D) 1.

(E) $2x + 1$.

39. If a measurement of 2.25 inches on a map represents 50 miles, what distance does a measurement of 18 inches on the map represent?

(A) 350 miles

(B) 375 miles

(C) 400 miles

(D) 425 miles

(E) 450 miles

40. The fraction $\dfrac{7x-11}{x^2-2x-15}$ was obtained by adding the two fractions

$\dfrac{A}{x-5}+\dfrac{B}{x+3}$. The values of A and B are

(A) $A = 7x, B = 11$.

(B) $A = -11, B = 7x$.

(C) $A = 3, B = 4$.

(D) $A = 5, B = -3$.

(E) $A = -5, B = 3$.

41. The number missing in the series 2, 6, 12, 20, x, 42, 56 is

(A) 24.

(B) 30.

(C) 36.

(D) 38.

(E) 40.

42. If $2^x = \dfrac{16^2 \times 8^3}{2^{19}}$, then $x =$

(A) -3.

(B) -2.

(C) 1.

(D) 2.

(E) 3.

43. The diameter of an automobile tire is 24". How many revolutions does the tire make in traveling a mile? (1 mile = 5,280 feet)

   (A) $\dfrac{220}{\pi}$

   (B) $2,640\pi$

   (C) $\dfrac{2,640}{\pi}$

   (D) $\dfrac{440}{\pi}$

   (E) 440π

44. If $f(x) = x^2 + 3x + 2$, then $[f(x + a) - f(x)]/a =$

   (A) $2x + a + 3.$

   (B) $(x + a)^2 - x^2.$

   (C) $a^2 + 2ax + 3a.$

   (D) $2x + a.$

   (E) $2x + 3.$

45. $m(\angle A) + m(\angle C) =$

   (A) $160°$

   (B) $180°$

   (C) $190°$

   (D) $195°$

   (E) $200°$

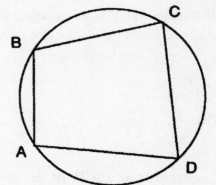

46. George is 4 years older than John, who is 4 years older than Jim, who is 4 years older than Sam, who is $^1/_2$ the age of George. How old is John?

   (A) 8

   (B) 12

   (C) 16

   (D) 20

   (E) 24

47. Sixty percent of 6-year old children participate in the two sports teams offered by the city athletics program. Thirty percent of the children play soccer, and fifty percent play T-ball. What is the probability that a randomly selected child plays both sports?

(A) 0.20   (B) 0.80

(C) 0.25   (D) 1.40

(E) 0.80

48. If in $\triangle ABC$, $AB = BC$ and $\angle A = 46°$, then $\angle B =$

(A) 92°.   (B) 88°.

(C) 56°.   (D) 46°.

(E) 23°.

49. If Richard has 2 pairs of jeans, 6 shirts, and 3 pairs of shoes, how many different outfits does he have?

(A) 11   (B) 24

(C) 32   (D) 36

(E) 44

50. In quadrilateral $ABCD$, BC is parallel to AD and BA is perpendicular to AD. If $BC = 8$, $AD = 12$, and $ABCD$ has area equal to 30, then what is CD?

(A) 3

(B) 4

(C) 5

(D) 6

(E) 25

ELM
TEST 1

ANSWER KEY

1. (E)	18. (C)	35. (B)
2. (B)	19. (C)	36. (E)
3. (E)	20. (C)	37. (C)
4. (E)	21. (D)	38. (A)
5. (B)	22. (D)	39. (C)
6. (D)	23. (C)	40. (C)
7. (E)	24. (D)	41. (B)
8. (B)	25. (B)	42. (B)
9. (C)	26. (C)	43. (C)
10. (C)	27. (C)	44. (A)
11. (E)	28. (C)	45. (B)
12. (D)	29. (A)	46. (D)
13. (B)	30. (B)	47. (A)
14. (E)	31. (E)	48. (B)
15. (C)	32. (D)	49. (D)
16. (A)	33. (E)	50. (C)
17. (C)	34. (A)	

Field test questions were
4, 24, 39, 46, and 49.
Do not count them toward your final score.

DETAILED EXPLANATIONS
OF ANSWERS

TEST 1

1. **(E)**

$$A = lw$$

$$A = 20(10) = 200$$

is the area of the rectangle. The area of the semicircle is half of πr^2 where $r = 5$ or

$$\frac{25\pi}{2}.$$

Therefore, the shaded area is

$$200 - \frac{25\pi}{2} = \frac{400 - 25\pi}{2}$$

2. **(B)**

The length the spring stretches is directly proportional to the weight of the mass on it.

$$\frac{L}{M} = \frac{5 \text{ cm}}{10 \text{ g}} = \frac{l}{4 \text{ g}}$$

$$l = 2 \text{ cm}$$

3. **(E)**

$$(x + 1)(3x + 4) = [x(3x) + 1(3x)] + [x(4) + 1(4)]$$

$$= [3x^2 + 3x] + [4x + 4]$$

$$= 3x^2 + 7x + 4$$

4.   **(E)**

The surface area of the box equals the area of the base, plus the area of the top, plus the sum of the areas of the four faces. Hence, surface area of the box

$$= 2x^2 + 4xh.$$

5.   **(B)**

$$\frac{\dfrac{1}{x} - \dfrac{1}{y}}{\dfrac{1}{x^2} - \dfrac{1}{y^2}} = \frac{\dfrac{y-x}{xy}}{\dfrac{y^2 - x^2}{x^2 y^2}}$$

$$= \frac{y-x}{xy} \times \frac{x^2 y^2}{y^2 - x^2}$$

$$= (y-x) \times \frac{xy}{(y+x)(y-x)}$$

$$= \frac{xy}{x+y}$$

6.   **(D)**

$$A = P(1 + rt)$$

$$A = P + Prt$$

$$A - P = Prt$$

$$t = \frac{A-P}{Pr}$$

7.   **(E)**

If x is the number, then $.15x = 60$. Therefore,

$$x = \frac{60}{.15} = 400.$$

8.   **(B)**
Identify several ordered pairs that are on line A, such as $(0, 4)$, $(1, 4)$, $(2, 4)$, and $(3, 4)$. Notice that the y-term or second term of the ordered pairs is always 4. Therefore, the equation is $y = 4$.

9.   **(C)**
The ordered pairs for points A and B, respectively, are $(-3, 4)$ and $(2, -2)$. The midpoint is calculated by finding the averages of the x and y coordinates. In other words, the midpoint is

$$\left(\frac{-3+2}{2}, \frac{4+(-2)}{2}\right) = \left(-\frac{1}{2}, 1\right).$$

10.   **(C)**
The slope of a line uses the formula

$$m = \frac{y_2 - y_1}{x_2 - x_1}.$$

Assigning point $A(-3, 4)$ as (x_1, y_1) and point $B(2, -2)$ as (x_2, y_2), the formula yields

$$m = \frac{-2 - 4}{2 - (-3)} = \frac{-6}{5} = \frac{-6}{5}.$$

11.   **(E)**
When a fraction is raised to a power, both the numerator and the denominator are raised to that power. So, x^2 taken as a factor 5 times is x^{10}, and y taken as a factor 5 times is y^5.

12. **(D)**

$$a = 25 - 16 = 9$$
$$b = 100 - 64 = 36$$
$$(\sqrt{9} - \sqrt{36})^2 = (3-6)^2$$
$$= (-3)^2$$
$$= 9$$

13. **(B)**

$$\frac{28 + 36 + x}{3} = 29$$
$$64 + x = 3(29)$$
$$x = 23$$

14. **(E)**

If r is the radius of the sphere, then its volume is

$$\frac{4}{3}\pi r^3 .$$

If r is increased by a factor of 3, then the radius becomes $3r$ and the volume is increased to

$$\frac{4}{3}\pi(3r)^3 = \left(\frac{4}{3}\right)27\pi r^3 .$$

Thus, the volume is increased by a factor of 27.

15. **(C)**

Rearrange the equation.

$$(4x - 3)^2 - 4 = 0$$

$$((4x - 3) - 2)\,((4x - 3) + 2) = 0$$

Solve each factor.

$$((4x - 3) - 2) = 0 \qquad\qquad ((4x - 3) + 2) = 0$$

$$4x - 5 = 0 \qquad\qquad 4x - 1 = 0$$
$$4x = 5 \qquad\qquad 4x = 1$$
$$x = {}^5/_4 \qquad\qquad x = {}^1/_4$$

Add the roots.

$${}^5/_4 + {}^1/_4 = {}^6/_4 = 1{}^1/_2$$

16. **(A)**

Since lines *l* and *m* are parallel, the 40° angle and $\angle x$ are supplementary. Hence,

$$40 + x = 180$$
$$x = 140°$$

17. **(C)**

$$\frac{\left(x^2\right)^{-4}\left(x^{-2}\right)^3}{\left(x^{-3}\right)^{-5}} = \frac{\left(x^{-8}\right)\left(x^{-6}\right)}{x^{15}}$$

$$= \frac{1}{x^{15}x^8x^6}$$

$$= \frac{1}{x^{29}}$$

18. **(C)**

Observe that to find the product the following operations should be done.

$$\left(\sqrt{3} + 6\right)\left(\sqrt{3} - 2\right) = \sqrt{3}\left(\sqrt{3} - 2\right) + 6\left(\sqrt{3} - 2\right)$$
$$= 3 - 2\sqrt{3} + 6\sqrt{3} - 12$$
$$= -9 + 4\sqrt{3}$$

19. **(C)**

The most direct way to solve this problem is to perform the indicated operations in the given equation and solve it for *x*. Thus,

$$x - (4x - 8) + 9 + (6x - 8) = 9 - x + 24$$

$$x - 4x + 8 + 9 + 6x - 8 = 9 - x + 24$$

$$(x + 6x - 4x) + (8 - 8 + 9) = (9 + 24) - x$$

$$(7x - 4x) + 9 = 33 - x$$

$$3x + x = 33 - 9$$

$$4x = 24$$

$$x = 6$$

20. **(C)**

The answer is 20^C3, which means the number of combinations of 20 items taken 3 at a time. The formula for the number of combinations of n things taken r at a time (where the order of the selection doesn't matter) is

$$n^c r = \frac{n!}{r!(n - r)!}$$

Therefore,

$$20^C3 = \frac{21!}{(20 - 3)!\, 3!} -$$

$$= 1,140.$$

21. **(D)**

$$\frac{1 - \dfrac{1}{1-x}}{1 - \dfrac{1}{1 - \dfrac{1}{x}}} = \frac{1 - \dfrac{1}{1-x}}{1 - \dfrac{x}{x-1}}$$

$$= \frac{(1-x)\left(1 - \dfrac{1}{1-x}\right)}{(1-x)\left(1 - \dfrac{1}{x-1}\right)}$$

$$= \frac{1 - x - 1}{1 - x + x}$$

$$= -x$$

22. **(D)**

The correct choice is 6, 6, 7, 7, 8, 8, 8, 9. Since the mode is the most common number, only choices (A) and (D) qualify. In choice (D), the range is 9 – 6 = 3, whereas the range of choice (A) is 6.

23. **(C)**

$$\frac{5+3i}{2-i} = \frac{5+3i}{2-i} \times \frac{2+i}{2+i}$$

Multiply by complex conjugate.

$$\frac{5(2+i)+3i(2+i)}{4-i^2} = \frac{10+5i+6i+3i^2}{4-i^2}$$

$$= \frac{10+11i+3i^2}{4-i^2}$$

$$= \frac{10+11i-3i^2}{4+1} = \frac{7+11i}{5}$$

Remember $i^2 = -1$.

24. **(D)**

Cost of living increase on $25,000

$$= 25,000 (.04) = 1,000.$$

Hence, total increase in salary

$$= 1,000 + 275 = 1,275$$

and the percent increase

$$= (1,275/25,000)/100 = 5.1.$$

25. **(B)**

The probability is $(^5/_{10})(^4/_9) = ^2/_9$, since the drawing is done without replacement.

26. **(C)**

$$(x + y)^2 + (x - y)^2 = [x^2 + 2xy + y^2] + [x^2 - 2xy + y^2]$$

$$= 2x^2 + 2y^2$$

$$= 2(x^2 + y^2)$$

27. **(C)**

   Set up the inequality in mathematical symbols and solve.

   $$3x - 4 > 6$$
   $$3x > 6 + 4$$
   $$3x > 10$$
   $$x > {}^{10}/_3$$

28. **(C)**

   Redraw the figure. Given

   $$AC = BC = 5R.$$

Let $x = BD$, then $AB = 2x$. Using the Pythagorean Theorem in triangle BCD

   $$(3R)^2 + x^2 = (5R)^2$$
   $$9R^2 + x^2 = 25R^2$$
   $$x^2 = 16R^2$$
   $$x = 4R$$

and the perimeter of triangle ABC will be

   $$5R + 5R + 2(4R) = 18R.$$

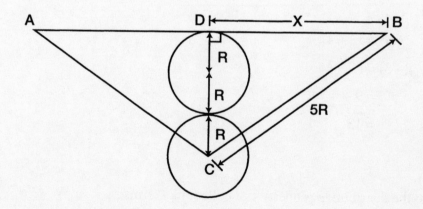

29. **(A)**

$$\frac{7a-5b}{b} = 7$$

$$\frac{7a}{b} - \frac{5b}{b} = 7$$

$$7 \times \frac{a}{b} - 5 = 7$$

$$7\frac{a}{b} = 12$$

$$\frac{a}{b} = \frac{12}{7}$$

$$\frac{b}{a} = \frac{7}{12}$$

$$\frac{4a+6b}{2a} = \frac{4a}{2a} + \frac{6b}{2a}$$

$$= 2 + 3 \times \frac{b}{a}$$

$$= 2 + 3 \times \frac{7}{12}$$

$$= \frac{15}{4}$$

30. **(B)**

The total weight of the ten women is $10 \times 138 = 1,380$ pounds. Therefore,

$$3,100 - 1,380 = 1,720$$

$$\frac{1,720}{8} = 215 \text{ pounds.}$$

31. **(E)**

$$g(x) = x^2 + 4$$

$$g(-3) = (-3)^2 + 4$$

$$= 9 + 4$$

$$= 13$$

32. **(D)**

Use the distributive property and collect like terms:

$$6(x-2) - 4(x+4) = 6x - 12 - 4x - 16$$

$$= 2x - 28$$

$$= 2(x-14)$$

in factored form.

33. **(E)**

If $x + 2y > 5$ and $x < 3$,

then $5 < x + 2y < 3 + 2y$.

Thus, $5 - 3 < 2y$, or $y > 1$.

34. **(A)**

The answer is given by using the combinations formula for both the group of women and the group of men and then multiplying the products.

There are 6 women and 4 will be chosen.

$$6^C4 = \frac{6!}{4!(6-4)!}$$

$$6^C4 = \frac{6 \times 5 \times 4 \times 3 \times 2 \times 1}{(4 \times 3 \times 2 \times 1)(2 \times 1)}$$

$$6^C4 = 15$$

There are 5 men and 2 will be chosen.

$$5^C2 = \frac{5!}{2!(5-2)!}$$

$$5^C2 = \frac{5 \times 4 \times 3 \times 2 \times 1}{(3 \times 2 \times 1)(2 \times 1)}$$

$$5^C2 = 10$$

Since the two events are independent, the values are multiplied ($10 \times 15 = 150$) to determine the number of different ways these students can be selected.

35. **(B)**

For any integer n, $2n + 1$ as well as $2n - 1$ must always be odd integers and

$$2n + 2 = 2(n + 1)$$

must be an even integer.

36. **(E)**
   Since

   $$\sqrt{x-1} = (x-1)^{1/2}$$

and since

   $$\left[(x-1)^{1/2}\right]^4 = (x-1)^2$$

   $$\left(\sqrt{x-1}\right)^4 = 2^4$$

or $$(x-1)^2 = 16.$$

37. **(C)**
   The combinations formula is applied to both the group of freshmen and the group of sophomores.

   $$5^C2 = \frac{5!}{2!(5-2)!}$$

   $$5^C2 = 10$$

   There are 10 different ways to form a committee of freshmen.

   $$4^C3 = \frac{4!}{3!(4-3)!}$$

   $$4^C3 = 4$$

   There are 4 different ways to form a committee of sophomores.

   Since the two events are independent, the values are multiplied ($10 \times 4 = 40$) to determine the number of different ways these students can be selected.

38. **(A)**
   By the Pythagorean Theorem the square of the length of the hypotenuse is equal to the sum of the squares of the lengths of the legs. Therefore, if y is the length of the other leg then

   $$(x + 1)^2 = x^2 + y^2$$

or $$y^2 = (x + 1)^2 - x^2$$

   $$= 2x + 1.$$

Hence,

$$y = \sqrt{2x+1}.$$

39. (C)

Since 2.25 inches on the map represent 50 miles, each one inch on the map represents 50/2.25 miles. Therefore, 18 inches represent

$$\frac{18 \times 59}{2.25} = 400 \text{ miles.}$$

40. (C)

$$\frac{A}{x-5} + \frac{B}{x+3} = \frac{7x-11}{(x-5)(x+3)}$$

On the left side of the equation, add fractions using the LCD in the usual manner, obtaining

$$\frac{Ax+3A+Bx-5B}{(x-5)(x+3)},$$

$$Ax + 3A + Bx - 5B = 7x - 11;$$

equating coefficients of like terms gives the system

$$A + B = 7$$

$$3A - 5B = -11.$$

Solving simultaneously gives $A = 3$ and $B = 4$. Check:

$$\frac{3}{x-5} + \frac{4}{x+3} = \frac{3x+9+4x-20}{(x-5)(x+3)}$$

$$= \frac{7x-11}{(x-5)(x+3)}.$$

41. (B)

The difference between the first two numbers is 4 (6 -- 2); the difference between the second and third numbers is 6 (12 − 6), which is two more than the first difference; the difference between the third and fourth numbers is 8 (20 − 12), which is two more than the second difference; the difference between the fourth and fifth numbers is 10 ($x - 20$). Thus, the value of x is given by

$$x - 20 = 10$$

$$x = 30.$$

42. **(B)**

$$\frac{16^2 \times 8^3}{2^{19}} = \frac{(2^4)^2 \times (2^3)^3}{2^{19}}$$

$$= \frac{2^8 \times 2^9}{2^{19}}$$

$$= \frac{2^{17}}{2^{19}}$$

$$= 2^{-2}.$$

43. **(C)**

One mile = 5,280 ft × 12 in/ft = 63,360 inches.

The circumference of the tire is found by the formula

$$c = \pi d = 2\pi \text{ feet.}$$

Therefore, the number of revolutions is

$$\frac{63,360}{24\pi} = \frac{5,280}{2\pi} = \frac{2,640}{\pi}.$$

44. **(A)**

$$\frac{[f(x+a) - f(x)]}{a} = \frac{\left[\left((x+a)^2 + 3(x+a) + 2\right) - \left(x^2 + 3x + 2\right)\right]}{a}$$

$$= \frac{\left[\left(x^2 \pm 2xa + a^2 + 3x + 3a + 2\right) - \left(x^2 - 3x - 2\right)\right]}{a}$$

$$= \frac{\left[2xa + a^2 + 3a\right]}{a}$$

$$= \frac{a(2x + a + 3)}{a}$$

$$= 2x + a + 3$$

45. (B)

Since $\angle A$ and $\angle C$ are inscribed angles, the measure of each of these angles is half the measure of the intercepted arc. Since the two arcs comprise the entire circle, the sum of the measures of these angles is $\frac{1}{2} \times 360° = 180°$.

46. (D)

The ages of each man may be represented as follows:

$$x = \text{George}$$

$$\frac{1}{2}x = \text{Sam}$$

$$\frac{1}{2}x + 4 = \text{Jim}$$

$$\frac{1}{2}x + 4 + 4 = \text{John or John} = \frac{1}{2}x + 8$$

George is 4 years older than John:

$$x = \frac{1}{2}x + 8 + 4$$

$$x = \frac{1}{2}x + 12$$

Multiplying each term by 2 gives

$$2x = x + 24$$

$$x = 24$$

Therefore, George is 24, John is 20, Jim is 16, and Sam is 12.

47. (A)

The formula to use is $p(A \text{ or } B) = p(A) + p(B) - p(A \text{ and } B)$. 0.60 represents $p(A \text{ and } B)$. 0.30 represents $p(A)$ and 0.50 represents $p(B)$. To find $p(A \text{ and } B)$ substitute the known values into the equation. $0.60 = 0.30 + 0.50 - x$. Solving for x gives 0.20. This is the case since some children played both sports. They were counted twice, so we subtract the quantity out to compensate for the double inclusion.

48. (B)

Since $AB = BC$, $\angle C = 46°$. However, the sum of the measures of the angles of a triangle is $180°$ and

$$180 - (46 + 46) = 88$$

so the measure of $\angle B$ is $88°$.

49. **(D)**

Multiply the number of jeans, shirts, and pairs of shoes to get the total number of possible outfits.

$$3 \times 6 \times 3 = 36$$

50. **(C)**

Since *BC* is parallel to *AD*, the quadrilateral *ABCD* is a trapezoid with

Area = (average of the length of the bases) × height.

Hence,

$$30 = (^1/_2) (8 + 12) \times (\text{height}),$$

giving

$$AB = \text{height} = 3.$$

If *CE* is the perpendicular from *C* to *AD*, then

$$AE = BC = 8, \text{ and } ED = 12 - 8 = 4.$$

By Pythagorean Theorem

$$(CD)^2 = (3)^2 + (4)^2 = 25.$$

Therefore, *CD* = 5.

ELM

Entry Level Mathematics

Test 2

ELM
TEST 2

Time: 90 Minutes
50 Questions (including 5 field test questions)

(Answer sheets appear at the back of the book.)

DIRECTIONS: Solve each problem and select the letter corresponding to the best choice to answer the question.

1. Evaluate $\left(2^{1-\sqrt{3}}\right)^{1+\sqrt{3}}$.

   (A) -4 (B) $\frac{1}{4}$

   (C) $\frac{1}{2}$ (D) 4

   (E) 16

2. A first square has a side of length x while the length of a side of a second square is two units greater than the length of a side of the first square. What is an expression for the sum of the areas of the two squares?

   (A) $2x^2 + 4x + 4$ (B) $x^2 + 2$

   (C) $x^2 + 4$ (D) $2x^2 + 2x + 2$

   (E) $2x^2 + 3x + 4$

3. $\dfrac{3y}{y+1} + \dfrac{2y}{y-1} =$

   (A) $\dfrac{5y}{y^2-1}$ (B) $\dfrac{5y}{y+1}$

(C) $\dfrac{5y^2 - y}{y^2 - 1}$

(D) $\dfrac{5y^2}{y+1}$

(E) $\dfrac{5y}{y^2 + 2y + 1}$

Question 4 refers to the graph below.

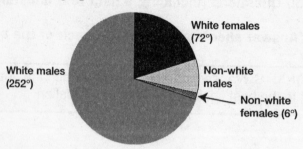

4. What percent of the Ph.D. degrees were awarded in 1986 to males who are non-white?

   (A) 30

   (B) 20

   (C) $8^1/_3$

   (D) $4^1/_6$

   (E) None of these

5. The correct sequence of numbers for a bank's combination lock on its vault consists of four different digits. The first two digits must be odd and the last two digits can be any number, including zero. How many different sequences of numbers are possible?

   (A) 2,500

   (B) 2,025

   (C) 1,675

   (D) 1,120

   (E) 1,000

6. What is the solution of x for the following system?

   $$x - 3y = 9$$
   $$3x + y = 7$$

   (A) -3

   (B) 3

   (C) -2

   (D) No solutions

   (E) Infinite number of solutions

7. A jar contains twelve marbles. Five are white, four are black, and three are yellow. Two marbles are randomly selected, one at a time and with replacement. What is the probability that one of these is white and the other is yellow?

   (A) $5/48$ (B) $5/44$

   (C) $5/24$ (D) $5/22$

   (E) $5/12$

8. One endpoint of a line segment is $(5, -3)$. The midpoint is $(-1, 6)$. What is the other endpoint?

   (A) $(7, 3)$ (B) $(2, 1.5)$

   (C) $(-7, 15)$ (D) $(-2, 1.5)$

   (E) $(-7, 12)$

9. To make lemonade 5 scoops of crystals are needed to make 4 liters. How many scoops are needed to make 10 liters of lemonade?

   (A) $2^1/_2$ (B) 4

   (C) 8   (D) 10

   (E) $12^1/_2$

10. The statement that .3 is between $3/_n$ and $6/_n$ is equivalent to

    (A) $.1 < n < .2$.   (B) $.3 < n < .6$.

    (C) $1 < n < 2$.   (D) $10 < n < 20$.

    (E) $n > 10$.

11. One solution of the equation $2x^2 - 3x - 2 = 0$ is

    (A) -2.   (B) $-3/_2$.

    (C) $1/_2$.   (D) 2.

    (E) no solution.

12. In rolling 3 ordinary dice, what is the probability of getting exactly 3 even numbers?

(A) $^1/_{10}$

(B) $^1/_9$

(C) $^1/_8$

(D) $^1/_6$

(E) $^1/_3$

Question 13 refers to the graph below.

13. By how much was the largest difference between the income earnings of the companies in a given year?

(A) 100

(B) 200

(C) 300

(D) 400

(E) 500

14. $\left(x^2 - x - 2\right) \times \left(\dfrac{x^2 + 3x + 2}{x^2 - 4}\right) =$

(A) $(x - 2)^2$

(B) $(x + 1)(x + 2)$

(C) $(x + 2)^2$

(D) $(x + 1)^2$

(E) $\dfrac{(x+1)^2}{x-2}$

15. If $f(x) = 3x - 2$ and $g(x) = x^2 + x$, what is $(f \circ g)(4)$?

(A) 10

(B) 30

(C) 58

(D) 110

(E) 200

16. I filled $^2/_3$ of my swimming pool with 1,800 ft^3 of water. What is the total capacity of my swimming pool?

    (A) 2,400 ft^3 (B) 2,700 ft^3

    (C) 3,000 ft^3 (D) 3,200 ft^3

    (E) 3,600 ft^3

17. Solve for the value of x: $4x + 7 = 27$.

    (A) – 5   (B) 4

    (C) 5   (D) $^{27}/_4$

    (E) $^{17}/_2$

Questions 18, 19, and 20 refer to the chart below.

18. If the wind speed changes from 5 mph to 20 mph, by what percent does the wind chill temperature drop?

    (A) $16^2/_3\%$ (B) 25%

    (C) $33^1/_3\%$ (D) 42%

    (E) 50%

19. If the wind speed changes from 25 mph to 15 mph, by what percent does the wind chill temperature rise?

    (A) 20%   (B) 16%

    (C) 14%   (D) 10%

    (E) 6%

20. If the wind speeds on 3 different days are 0 mph, 10 mph, and 15 mph, what is the mean of the wind chill temperature?

(A) 36°

(B) 37°

(C) 38°

(D) 40°

(E) 42°

21. $\left[\left(\dfrac{x}{y}\right)^{-1} - \left(\dfrac{y}{x}\right)^{-1}\right]^{-1} =$

(A) xy

(B) $\dfrac{1}{xy}$

(C) $x^2 - y^2$

(D) $y^2 - x^2$

(E) $\dfrac{xy}{\left(y^2 - x^2\right)}$

22. Laura spent $3.89 for milk, $1.29 for bread, and $4.99 for lunch meat. Lana spent $3.45 for milk, $1.39 for bread, and $5.50 for lunch meat. Who spent more and how much more?

(A) Laura spent 27¢ more.

(B) Lana spent 27¢ more.

(C) Laura spent 17¢ more.

(D) Lana spent 17¢ more.

(E) They spent the same amount.

23. Given the population 7, 12, 9, 9, 5, 23, 15, 16, what is the value of the median?

(A) 8

(B) 9

(C) 10.5

(D) 12

(E) 13.5

24. Find the area of the shaded portion in the figure shown.

(A) $\dfrac{ac}{2}$

(B) $\dfrac{ab}{2}$

(C) $\dfrac{bc}{2}$

(D) ac

(E) Cannot be determined

25. Simplify $\dfrac{x^{11}}{x^4}$.

(A) x^{44}

(B) x^7

(C) x^6

(D) $\dfrac{1}{x^4}$

(E) $\dfrac{1}{x^7}$

26. $\dfrac{2x^2 - x - 3}{x^2 - 1} \times \dfrac{x^2 + x - 2}{2x^2 + x - 6} =$

(A) $(x + 1)^2$

(B) 1

(C) $\dfrac{3x^2 - 5}{3x^2 + x - 7}$

(D) $\dfrac{1}{x - 2}$

(E) $\dfrac{(2x - 3)^2}{(x - 1)^2}$

27. $\dfrac{x+2}{x+5} - \dfrac{x-3}{x+7} =$

   (A) $\dfrac{5}{(x+5)(x+7)}$ (B) $\dfrac{7x+29}{(x+5)(x+7)}$

   (C) $\dfrac{2x-1}{(x+5)(x+7)}$ (D) $x^2 - x - 6$

   (E) -2

28. An airplane flying with a tailwind (i.e., blowing in the same direction as the airplane) takes 6 hours to reach its destination. On the return trip, the plane flies with a headwind (i.e., against the wind), and the trip takes 8 hours. The wind speed was 60 km per hour. What was the speed of the airplane in still air?

   (A) 360 km per hr.   (B) 400 km per hr.

   (C) 420 km per hr.   (D) 480 km per hr.

   (E) 500 km per hr.

29. Find the area of a circle with a diameter of 10 inches.

   (A) 5π sq. in.

   (B) 10π sq. in.

   (C) 15π sq. in.

   (D) 25π sq. in.

   (E) 28π sq. in.

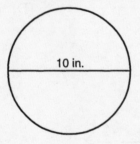

10 in.

30. $5 + 10 + 15 + 20 + \ldots + 100 =$

   (A) 210   (B) 1,050

   (C) 2,100   (D) 5,050

   (E) 25,250

31. Simplify $\dfrac{\frac{1}{3}}{1+\frac{2}{4+5}}$.

    (A) $^3/_{11}$

    (B) $^7/_{24}$

    (C) $^1/_3$

    (D) $^8/_{21}$

    (E) 1

32. $(a+3)^3 =$

    (A) $3a^3 + 9$

    (B) $a^3 + 27$

    (C) $a^3 + 9a^2 + 27a + 27$

    (D) $a^3 + 9a^2 + 9a + 9$

    (E) $a^3 + 27a + 27$

33. If $x = -3$, then $x^x =$

    (A) -27.

    (B) $-^1/_{27}$.

    (C) $^1/_{27}$.

    (D) 9.

    (E) 27.

34. What is the length of side BC?

    (A) 3

    (B) 5

    (C) $\sqrt{34}$

    (D) 7

    (E) None of these

35. Multiply $(x+1)(4x+3)$.

    (A) $4x^2 + 4$

    (B) $4x^2 + 3$

    (C) $4x^2 + 4x + 3$

    (D) $4x^2 + 7x + 3$

    (E) $4x^2 - 7x - 4$

36. Factor completely $x^4 - 81$.

(A) $(x^2 + 9)(x^2 + 9)$

(B) $(x^2 + 3)(x^2 - 3)$

(C) $(x^2 + 9)(x - 3)(x - 3)$

(D) $(x^2 + 9)(x + 3)(x - 3)$

(E) $(x^2 - 9)(x^2 - 9)$

37. Two cars 660 miles apart start traveling toward each other, agreeing to meet midway. One car averages 40 mph, the other 55 mph. How long will the faster car have to wait in order to meet the slower car at the halfway point?

(A) 2 hours

(B) $2^1/_4$ hours

(C) 4 hours

(D) 6 hours

(E) $8^1/_4$ hours

38. $(-a^2 + 2b + 3) - (4a^2 - 2b - 1) =$

(A) $5a^2b$

(B) $3a^2b$

(C) $4a^2 + 4b - 3$

(D) $-5a^2 + 4b + 4$

(E) $3a^2 + 2$

39. Solve for x: $2x^2 + \sqrt{3}x - 4 = 0$.

(A) $\dfrac{-\sqrt{3} \pm \sqrt{35}}{4}$

(B) $\dfrac{\sqrt{3} \pm \sqrt{35}}{2}$

(C) $\dfrac{-\sqrt{3} \pm \sqrt{35}}{2}$

(D) $\dfrac{\sqrt{3} \pm \sqrt{35}}{4}$

(E) No solution

40. In the figure shown, line r is parallel to line l. Find the measure of angle RBC.

    (A) 30°

    (B) 80°

    (C) 90°

    (D) 100°

    (E) 110°

41. What is the distance between $A(3, 4)$ and $B(-1, 1)$?

    (A) $\sqrt{7}$ (B) 5

    (C) $\sqrt{29}$ (D) 6

    (E) $\sqrt{41}$

42. $\dfrac{x+1-\frac{6}{x}}{\frac{1}{x}} =$

    (A) $\dfrac{x^2 + x - 6}{x}$ (B) $\dfrac{x-5}{x^2}$

    (C) $\dfrac{x-5}{x}$ (D) $x^2 + x - 6$

    (E) $x - 5$

43. What is the equation that passes through $(6, 4)$ and has a slope of $^1/_2$?

    (A) $y = 4 + ^1/_2 x$ (B) $6y + ^1/_2 = 4x$

    (C) $4y + 6x = ^1/_2$ (D) $^1/_2 y = 1 + x$

    (E) $y = 1 + ^1/_2 x$

44. Mary wants to cover a small chest with contact paper. The chest is 24" × 12" × 10". How much contact paper is needed?

(A) $1^2/_3$ sq. ft.

(B) 4 sq. ft.

(C) 5 sq. ft.

(D) 9 sq. ft.

(E) 720 sq. ft.

45. Harry bought a sofa priced at $995 and a chair priced at $149. The sales tax is 8%. How much must he pay for the sofa and chair and tax?

(A) $91.52   (B) $1,134.00

(C) $1,144.00   (D) $1,224.72

(E) $1,235.52

46. $15 > 2x - 7 > 9$ is equivalent to

(A) $7.5 > x > 11.5.$ (B) $4 > x > 1.$

(C) $8 > x > 2.$ (D) $22 > x > 16.$

(E) $11 > x > 8.$

47. Robert's fish tank is 48 centimeters long, 35 centimeters wide, and 52 centimeters high. What is the volume of the water in the tank if he leaves 2 centimeters at the top without water?

(A) $1,680 \text{ cm}^3$

(B) $3,360 \text{ cm}^3$

(C) $83,720 \text{ cm}^3$

(D) $84,000 \text{ cm}^3$

(E) $87,360 \text{ cm}^3$

52 cm

48 cm

35 cm

48. Let $f(x) = x^2$, then $f(x + 2) =$

    (A) $x^2 + 4x + 4.$ (B) $x^2 + 2x + 4.$

    (C) $x^2 + 2.$ (D) $x^2 + 4.$

    (E) $x^3 + 2x^2.$

49. Triangles ABC and $A'B'C'$ are similar right triangles. Find the length of side AC.

    (A) 10

    (B) 12

    (C) 13

    (D) 16

    (E) 26

50. $\dfrac{x^2 - y^2}{x^2 + 3y + 2y^2} \times \dfrac{2x + 4y}{x^2 - xy} =$

    (A) $\dfrac{2x^3 - 4y^3}{x}$ (B) $\dfrac{2}{x}$

    (C) 2   (D) $\dfrac{x + y}{x^3 + y^2}$

    (E) $\dfrac{2(x + 2y)}{x}$

ELM
TEST 2

ANSWER KEY

1. (B)	18. (C)	35. (D)
2. (A)	19. (A)	36. (D)
3. (C)	20. (E)	37. (B)
4. (C)	21. (E)	38. (D)
5. (D)	22. (D)	39. (A)
6. (B)	23. (C)	40. (B)
7. (C)	24. (A)	41. (B)
8. (C)	25. (B)	42. (D)
9. (E)	26. (B)	43. (E)
10. (D)	27. (B)	44. (D)
11. (D)	28. (C)	45. (E)
12. (C)	29. (D)	46. (E)
13. (D)	30. (B)	47. (D)
14. (D)	31. (A)	48. (A)
15. (C)	32. (C)	49. (E)
16. (B)	33. (B)	50. (B)
17. (C)	34. (C)	

Field test questions were
9, 23, 36, 46, and 50.
Do not count them toward your final score.

8. **(C)**

$$\text{midpoint} = \left(\frac{x_1 + x_2}{2}, \; \frac{y_1 + y_2}{2} \right)$$

x_2 $\qquad -1 = \dfrac{5 + x_2}{2}$

$\qquad\qquad -2 = 5 + x_2$

$\qquad\qquad x_2 = -7$

y_2 $\qquad 6 = \dfrac{-3 + y_2}{2}$

$\qquad\qquad 12 = -3 + y_2$

$\qquad\qquad y_2 = 15$

9. **(E)**

Let x = the number of scoops needed to make 10 liters. Set up the proportion.

$$\frac{\text{\# of scoops}}{\text{\# of liters}} = \frac{5}{4} = \frac{x}{10}$$

Solve for x.

$\qquad 4x = 50$

$\qquad x = 12\frac{1}{2}$

10. **(D)**

$\qquad ^3/_n < .3 < ^6/_n$

is equivalent to

$\qquad 3 < (.3)n < 6.$

Multiplying the inequality by 10 we get

$\qquad 30 < 3n < 60$, or $10 < n < 20$.

11. **(D)**

$$2x^2 - 3x - 2 = 0$$

Use the quadratic formula to solve.

$$x = \frac{-b \pm \sqrt{b^2 - 4ac}}{2a}$$

$$= \frac{-(-3) \pm \sqrt{(-3)^2 - 4(2)(-2)}}{2(2)}$$

$$= \frac{3 \pm \sqrt{9 + 16}}{4}$$

$$= \frac{3 \pm \sqrt{25}}{4}$$

$$= \frac{3 \pm 5}{4}$$

$$= \frac{-2}{4} \text{ or } \frac{8}{4} = -\frac{1}{2} \text{ or } 2$$

12. **(C)**

Since there are 3 even numbers out of a total of 6 numbers ($^3/_6 = \, ^1/_2$), the probability is $^1/_2 \times \, ^1/_2 \times \, ^1/_2 = \, ^1/_8$.

13. **(D)**

By observation one needs only to find the largest spread between corresponding plotted points on the two lines representing the companies. Thus, the largest difference occurred in 1987 where the difference was 400 million (500 – 100).

14. **(D)**

$$\left(x^2 - x - 2\right) \times \frac{x^2 + 3x + 2}{x^2 - 4}$$

Multiply the fractions.

$$= \frac{\left(x^2 - x - 2\right)\left(x^2 + 3x + 2\right)}{x^2 - 4}$$

Factor each polynomial.

$$= \frac{(x-2)(x+1)(x+1)(x+2)}{(x-2)(x+2)}$$

Divide the common factors and simplify.

$$= (x+1)^2$$

15. **(C)**

$$(f \circ g)(4) = f(g(4))$$

$$g(x) = x^2 + x$$

Substitute the value of x.

$$g(4) = 4^2 + 4$$
$$= 16 + 4$$
$$= 20$$

$$f(x) = 3x - 2$$

Substitute the value of $g(4)$ in $f(x)$.

$$f(20) = 3(20) - 2$$
$$= 60 - 2$$
$$= 58$$

16. **(B)**

Let x be the total capacity of the swimming pool, then

$$\frac{2}{3}x = 1,800$$

$$x = \frac{1,800 \times 3}{2} = 2,700 \text{ ft}^3 .$$

17. **(C)**

$$4x + 7 = 27$$
$$4x = 27 - 7$$
$$4x = 20$$
$$x = {}^{20}/_4$$
$$x = 5$$

18. **(C)**

The temperature drops from 48° to 32°, which is a 16° difference. Then $16° \div 48° = 33^1/_3\%$.

19. **(A)**

The rise in temperature is $36° - 30° = 6°$. Six degrees is 20% of 30° $(6° \div 30° = 20\%)$.

20. **(E)**

$$\frac{50° + 40° + 36°}{3} = \frac{126°}{3} = 42°$$

21. **(E)**

$$\left[\left(\frac{x}{y} \right)^{-1} - \left(\frac{y}{x} \right)^{-1} \right]^{-1} = \left[\left(\frac{y}{x} \right)^{-1} - \left(\frac{x}{y} \right)^{-1} \right]^{-1}$$

$$= \left[\frac{y}{x} - \frac{x}{y} \right]^{-1}$$

$$= \left[\frac{y^2 - x^2}{xy} \right]^{-1}$$

$$= \frac{xy}{y^2 - x^2}$$

22. **(D)**

Laura spent \$10.17 and Lana spent \$10.34, so Lana spent 17¢ more than Laura.

23. **(C)**

Rearrange the data as 5, 7, 9, 9, 12, 15, 16, 20. The median is the average of the fourth and fifth numbers.

$$\frac{9+12}{2} = 10.5$$

24. **(A)**

The shaded portion is a triangle *AEC*, so

$$\text{shaded portion} = \frac{\text{height} \times \text{base}}{2} = \frac{ac}{2}.$$

25. **(B)**

$$\frac{x^{11}}{x^4} = x^{11-4} = x^7$$

26. **(B)**

$$\frac{2x^2 - x - 3}{x^2 - 1} \times \frac{x^2 + x - 2}{2x^2 + x - 6}$$

Multiply the fractions.

$$= \frac{\left(2x^2 - x - 3\right)\left(x^2 + x - 2\right)}{\left(x^2 - 1\right)\left(2x^2 + x - 6\right)}$$

Factor each polynomial.

$$= \frac{(2x-3)(x+1)(x-2)(x-1)}{(x+1)(x-1)(2x-3)(x=2)}$$

$$= 1$$

27. **(B)**

$$\frac{x+2}{x+5} - \frac{x-3}{x+7}$$

Find a common denominator.

$$= \frac{(x+2)(x+7) - (x-3)(x+5)}{(x+5)(x+7)}$$

$$= \frac{(x^2 + 9x + 14) - (x^2 + 2x - 15)}{(x+5)(x+7)}$$

$$= \frac{x^2 + 9x + 14 - x^2 - 2x + 15}{(x+5)(x+7)}$$

$$= \frac{7x + 29}{(x+5)(x+7)}$$

28. **(C)**

The easiest way to solve this is with a chart. The chart below represents the trip going and the trip returning. The distance is the same for both trips. The trip going has the speed of the airplane plus the tail wind. The trip returning has the speed of the airplane minus the tail wind. The times are as stated.

	D =	r	t
going ⇒	D	r + 60	6
returning ⇐	D	r − 60	8

Since the distance equals the rate times the time and the distances are equal, set up an equation of representations of the equal distances and solve:

$$6(r + 60) = 8(r - 60)$$

$$6r + 360 = 8r - 480$$

Then $r = 420$.

29. **(D)**

The formula for the area of a circle is

$$A = \pi r^2.$$

Since the diameter is 10, the radius is 5. Completing the formula:

$$A = \pi \times 25 = 25\pi \text{ sq. in.}$$

30. **(B)**

$$5 + 10 + 15 + 20 + \ldots + 100 =$$

$$5(1 + 2 + 3 + 4 + \ldots + 20)$$

The sum of all of the integers from 1 to n equals

$$\frac{n}{2}(n+1) = 5\left[\frac{20}{2}(20+1)\right]$$

$$= 5(10(21))$$

$$= 1,050.$$

31. **(A)**

$$\frac{\frac{1}{3}}{1+\frac{2}{4+5}} = \frac{\frac{1}{3}}{1+\frac{2}{9}}$$

$$= \frac{\frac{1}{3}}{\frac{11}{9}}$$

$$= \left(\frac{1}{3}\right)\left(\frac{9}{11}\right)$$

$$= \frac{3}{11}$$

32. **(C)**

Using the binomial formula

$$(a+b)^n = \binom{n}{0}a^n + \binom{n}{1}a^{n-1}b + \binom{n}{2}a^{n-2}b^2 + \ldots + \binom{n}{n-1}ab^{n-1} + \binom{n}{n}b^n$$

$$= a^n + na^{-1}b + \binom{n}{2}a^{n-2}b^2 + \dots + nab^{n-1} + b^2$$

$$(a+3)^3 = a^3 + 3a^2(3) + \binom{3}{2}a(3)^2 + 3^3$$

$$= a^3 + 9a^2 + \frac{3(2)}{2(1)}(a9) + 27$$

$$= a^3 + 9a^2 + 27a + 27$$

33. **(B)**

$$-3^{-3} = \frac{1}{(-3)^3}$$

$$= -\frac{1}{27}$$

34. **(C)**

Notice that triangle ABC is a right triangle and that distance $AC = 5 - 2 = 3$ and distance $AB = 6 - 1 = 5$. Use the Pythagorean Theorem to find the length of side BC as follows:

$$(BC)^2 = (AC)^2 + (AB)^2$$

$$(BC)^2 = 3^2 + 5^2$$

$$(BC)^2 = 9 + 25$$

$$BC = \sqrt{34}$$

35. **(D)**

$$(x + 1)(4x + 3) = [(x)(4x) + (1)(4x)] + [(x)(3) + (1)(3)]$$

$$= (4x^2 + 4x) + (3x + 3)$$

$$= 4x^2 + 7x + 3$$

36. **(D)**

We want to find what binomials multiplied together would give $(x^4 - 81)$. $(x^2 + 9)$ and $(x^2 - 9)$ would give the results, but $(x^2 - 9)$ can also be factored into $(x + 3)$ and $(x - 3)$, so $(x^2 + 9) (x + 3) (x - 3)$ are the prime factors.

37. **(B)**

The car traveling 55 mph can get to the halfway point 330 miles away in

$$\frac{330}{55} = 6 \text{ hours.}$$

The 40 mph car covers the same distance in

$$\frac{330}{40} = 8\frac{1}{4} \text{ hours.}$$

The faster car will have to wait

$$8\frac{1}{4} - 6 = 2\frac{1}{4} \text{ hours.}$$

38. **(D)**

$$(- a^2 + 2b + 3) - (4a^2 - 2b - 1)$$

$$= - a^2 + 2b + 3 - 4a^2 + 2b + 1$$

$$= - 5a^2 + 4b + 4$$

39. **(A)**

$$2x^2 + \sqrt{3}x - 4$$

Use the quadratic formula to solve.

$$x = \frac{-b \pm \sqrt{b^2 - 4ac}}{2a}$$

$$a = 2, b = \sqrt{3}, c = -4$$

$$x = \frac{-\sqrt{3} \pm \sqrt{3 - 4(2)(-4)}}{2(2)}$$

$$= \frac{-\sqrt{3} \pm \sqrt{3 + 32}}{4}$$

$$= \frac{-\sqrt{3} \pm \sqrt{35}}{4}$$

40. (B)

Extend *RB* to meet line *l* at point *E*, then angle *ARB* and angle *CER* are alternate interior angles. Since *r* is parallel to *l*, it follows that the measure of angle *ARB* is equal to the measure of angle *CER*. Thus, the measure of angle *CER* = 55°.

Since angle *RBC* is an exterior angle of triangle *BEC*, and the measure of an exterior angle of a triangle is equal to the sum of the measures of the two non-adjacent interior angles of the triangles, it follows that the measure of angle *RBC* is equal to the sum of the measures of angle *BEC* and angle *BCE*. Thus,

$$\text{measure of angle } RBC = 55° + 25°$$

$$= 80°.$$

41. (B)

The distance between *A*(3, 4) and *B*(−1, 1) is found by using the following formula where the subscript 1 refers to coordinates in point *A* and the subscript 2 refers to coordinates in point *B*.

$$\sqrt{(x_2 - x_1)^2 + (y_2 - y_1)^2} = \sqrt{(-1-3)^2 + (1-4)^2}$$

$$= \sqrt{16+9}$$

$$= \sqrt{25}$$

$$= 5$$

42. (D)

$$\frac{x+1-\frac{6}{x}}{\frac{1}{x}} = \frac{\frac{x^2+x-6}{x}}{\frac{1}{x}}$$

$$= \frac{x^2+x-6}{x} \times \frac{x}{1}$$

$$= x^2 + x - 6$$

43. **(E)**

To solve, use the formula to find the slope of the line and put the point in and solve for y.

$$m = \frac{y_2 - y_1}{x_2 - x_1}$$

$$\frac{1}{2} = \frac{4 - y}{6 - x}$$

$$\frac{1}{2}(6 - x) = 4 - y$$

$$y = 1 + \frac{1}{2}x$$

44. **(D)**

The problem is to find the surface area of the rectangular solid. This is done by finding the sum of the areas of every side, including the top and bottom. This problem is complicated by the fact that the measurements in the problem are given in inches, and the answers are given in square feet. We must convert to the same unit of measure. If we convert the inches to feet, the dimensions of the chest are $1 \times 2 \times \frac{5}{6}$. A formula to find the lateral area (area of all the sides, but not the top and bottom) is

$L = ph,$

where p = perimeter of the base and h = the height. The perimeter of the base is

$1 + 2 + 1 + 2$ or 6.

Then

$6 \times \frac{5}{6} = 5$ sq. ft.

for the sides. Now find the area of the top and bottom and add it to the sides. The bottom is a rectangle and the

Area = lw,

where l = length and w = width. So the area is

2×1 or 2 sq. ft.

This is the bottom, but the top is the same. Finally, add the area of the sides and the top and the bottom:

$5 + 2 + 2 = 9$ sq. ft.

45. **(E)**

$$995 + 149 = 1,144$$

and

$$1,144 \times .08 = 91.52 \text{ tax}$$

$$\$1,144 + \$91.52 = \$1,235.52$$

46. **(E)**

$$15 > 2x - 7 > 9$$

$$22 > 2x > 16 \quad \text{Add 7 to all three sides.}$$

$$11 > x > 8 \quad \text{Divide all three sides by 2.}$$

47. **(D)**

The tank is a rectangular solid with length = 48 cm, width = 35 cm, and height = 52 cm. 2 cm at the top will be without water, so the actual height of the water will be only 50 cm. The formula for the volume of a solid is

$$V = \text{Length} \times \text{Width} \times \text{Height}.$$

$$V = 48 \times 35 \times 50$$

$$= 84,000 \text{ cm}^3$$

48. **(A)**

$$f(x) = x^2$$

$$f(x + 2) = (x + 2)^2$$

$$= x^2 + 4x + 4$$

49. **(E)**

The sides of similar triangles are in proportion. Using the Pythagorean Theorem the length of $B'C'$ is:

$$5^2 + (B'C')^2 = 13^2$$

$$25 + (B'C')^2 = 169$$

$$(B'C')^2 = 144$$

$$B'C' = 12.$$

BC and $B'C'$ are corresponding sides of similar triangles in a ratio of 24:12 or 2:1. Similarly, side AC and $A'C'$ have the same ratio; AC must be twice as long as $A'C'$. In other words, $AC = 2(13) = 26$.

50. **(B)**

$$\frac{x^2 - y^2}{x^2 + 3y + 2y^2} \times \frac{2x + 4y}{x^2 - xy}$$

$$= \frac{(x+y)(x-y)}{(x+y)(x+2y)} \times \frac{2(x+2y)}{x(x-y)}$$

$$= \frac{2}{x}$$

ELM

Entry Level Mathematics

Test 3

ELM
TEST 3

Time: **90 Minutes**
50 Questions (including 5 field test questions)

(Answer sheets appear at the back of the book.)

DIRECTIONS: Solve each problem and select the letter corresponding to the best choice to answer the question.

1. Simplify $(m^6n^5q^3)^2$.

    (A) $2m^6n^5q^3$ (B) m^4n^3q

    (C) $m^8n^7q^5$ (D) $m^{12}n^{10}q^6$

    (E) $2m^{12}n^{10}q^6$

2. Jay and his brother Ray own a janitorial service. Jay can do a cleaning job alone in 5 hours and Ray can do the same job in 4 hours. How long will it take them to do the cleaning job together?

    (A) 1 hour   (B) $2^2/_9$ hours

    (C) 4 hours   (D) $4^1/_2$ hours

    (E) 5 hours

3. Find the area of Δxyz.

    (A) 20 cm^2

    (B) 50 cm^2

    (C) $50\sqrt{2} \text{ cm}^2$

    (D) 100 cm^2

    (E) 200 cm^2

4. $\dfrac{15,561}{25} + \dfrac{9,439}{25} =$

   (A) 997
   (B) 1,000
   (C) 1,002
   (D) 1,005
   (E) 1,005.08

Questions 5 and 6 refer to the pie chart below.

5. How many students chose the category "All Other Subjects" for their favorite subject?

   (A) 800
   (B) 900
   (C) 1,000
   (D) 1,100
   (E) 1,200

6. What is the ratio of the combined number of students whose favorite subject is physical education or music to the number of students whose favorite subject is math?

   (A) 3:2
   (B) 5:3
   (C) 2:1
   (D) 5:2
   (E) 3:1

7. If $z > 0$ and $z^2 + z - 2 = 0$, then z is

   (A) -2.
   (B) -1.
   (C) 0.
   (D) 1.
   (E) 2.

8. The surface area of a cube is 54 square feet. What is the volume of the cube in cubic feet?

    (A) 9   (B) 18

    (C) 27   (D) 54

    (E) 216

9. Mary lives 6 miles east of Dave and 8 miles south of Joan. If you could fly from Joan's house to Dave's house, how far would you have to fly?

    (A) 4   (B) 5

    (C) 7   (D) 10

    (E) 12

10. The simplest expression for
    $$\frac{a^2 - 3ab + 2b^2}{2b^2 + ab - a^2}$$

    (A) 1.   (B) $a + b$.

    (C) $\dfrac{2a+b}{b-a}$.   (D) $a - b$.

    (E) $\dfrac{b-a}{b+a}$.

11. The figure shown below is a sketch of $y = f(x)$. What is $f(f(6))$?

    (A) -2

    (B) 1

    (C) 2

    (D) 3

    (E) 0

12. Find the area of parallelogram *MNOP*.

    (A) 19

    (B) 32

    (C) 44

    (D) $32\sqrt{3}$

    (E) $44\sqrt{3}$

13. Simplify $\dfrac{x^{10}y^8}{x^7y^3}$.

    (A) x^2y^5 (B) x^3y^4

    (C) x^3y^5 (D) x^2y^4

    (E) x^5y^3

14. A CD holder has room for ten CDs. If four CDs are placed in this holder, in how many different ways can the CDs be arranged?

    (A) 2,400   (B) 5,040

    (C) 10,000   (D) 400,000

    (E) 1,048,576

15. Two cards are drawn from a standard deck of cards, one at a time without replacement. What is the probability of drawing two queens?

    (A) $1/221$ (B) $1/200$

    (C) $1/169$ (D) $1/156$

    (E) $1/144$

16. Which of the following equations corresponds to the graph below?

    (A) $y = x^2$

    (B) $y = 2x^2$

    (C) $y = 2x^2 + 1$

    (D) $y = 2(x^2 + 1)$

    (E) $y = 2(x^2 - 1)$

17. In a raffle, there are five prizes each worth $1,000, three prizes each worth $5,000, and one prize worth $10,000. A total of 50 tickets are sold. If a person buys one ticket, what is the probability he or she will win a prize of at least $5,000 if it is already known that he or she has already won a prize?

    (A) $^3/_{50}$ (B) $^9/_{50}$

    (C) $^1/_3$ (D) $^4/_9$

    (E) $^3/_4$

18. At a factory, three out of every 1,000 parts produced are defective. In a day, the factory can produce 25,000 parts. How many of these parts would be defective?

    (A) 7   (B) 75

    (C) 750   (D) 7,500

    (E) 75,000

19. $4x + 3y - z - 10y + x =$

    (A) $5x + 3y - 11z$ (B) $-6x + 2y$

    (C) $5x - 7y - z$ (D) $-3xyz$

    (E) $5x - 7y$

20. If one root of $x^2 - ax + 12 = 0$ is 6, then the other root is

    (A) -6.   (B) -4.

    (C) 2.   (D) 8.

    (E) 12.

21. If $f(x) = 3x^2 - x + 5$, then $f(3) =$

    (A) 15.   (B) 17.

    (C) 23.   (D) 27.

    (E) 29.

22. If $x^2 - 3x - 4 < 0$, then the solution set is

(A) $-4 < x < 1$.

(B) $-4 < x < -3$.

(C) $-3 < x < 0$.

(D) $-1 < x < 0$.

(E) $-1 < x < 4$.

23. The fraction

$$\frac{\dfrac{2}{a^2 b^2}}{\dfrac{1}{b^2 - 2b}}$$

may be expressed more compactly as

(A) $\dfrac{2a}{b}$.

(B) $\dfrac{b-4}{b}$.

(C) $\dfrac{ab}{b^2 - a}$.

(D) $\dfrac{b-a}{a}$.

(E) $\dfrac{2b-4}{a^2 b}$.

24. Which of the following alternatives is correct?

(A) $\alpha + \beta + \gamma = 180°$

(B) $\gamma - \alpha + 180° = \beta$

(C) $\alpha = \beta + \gamma$

(D) $\gamma = \alpha + \beta$

(E) $\alpha = 180° - \beta - \alpha$

25. Find a solution to $|2x - 18| = -6$.

(A) -6

(B) -3

(C) 6

(D) 12

(E) No solution

26. Evaluate $10 - 5[2^3 + 27/3 - 2(8 - 10)]$.

    (A) -95 (B) -85

    (C) -55 (D) 65

    (E) 105

27. In the figure, if $BD \parallel AE$, then the following must be true:

    (A) $\angle CBD = \angle CDB$.

    (B) $\angle CAE = \angle CEA$.

    (C) $\dfrac{CB}{CA} = \dfrac{CD}{AE}$.

    (D) $\dfrac{CD}{CE} = \dfrac{BD}{AE}$.

    (E) $\dfrac{CB}{BD} = \dfrac{CD}{CA}$.

28. If $f(x) = x + 1$, $g(x) = 2x - 3$, and an operation $*$ is defined for all real numbers a and b by the equation $a * b = 2a + b - ab$, then $f(3) * g(4) =$

    (A) -9.   (B) -7.

    (C) -1.   (D) 0.

    (E) 5.

29. In the following figure, 0 is the center of the circle. If arc ABC has length 2π, what is the area of the circle?

    (A) 3π

    (B) 6π

    (C) 9π

    (D) 12π

    (E) 15π

30. What is the sixth number in the series:

$$3, 7, 11, \ldots ?$$

(A) 20   (B) 22

(C) 23   (D) 24

(E) 26

31. If $f(x) = -2x + 5$ and $g(x) = 4x - 1$, what is $(g \circ f)(x)$?

(A) $-8x + 7$ (B) $-8x + 19$

(C) $2x + 4$ (D) $8x^2 - 5$

(E) $-6x + 4$

32. If a triangle of base 6 units has the same area as a circle of radius 6 units, what is the altitude of the triangle?

(A) π (B) 3π

(C) 6π (D) 12π

(E) 36π

33. Given the expression

$$\frac{3}{x+4} + \frac{5}{x-4} = \frac{8}{x^2 - 16},$$

solve for x.

(A) 0   (B) 1

(C) 2   (D) 4

(E) 5

34. What is the distance between the points $(3, 4)$ and $(-2, 1)$?

(A) $\frac{1}{3}$ (B) $\sqrt{34}$

(C) $\sqrt{43}$ (D) 7

(E) 17

35. What is the value of x?

    (A) 20°

    (B) 30°

    (C) 40°

    (D) 60°

    (E) 90°

36. The roots of $x^2 + 2x + 5 = 0$ are

    (A) 3, 4.

    (B) $-1 \pm 2i$.

    (C) $3 \pm 4i$.

    (D) 6, 3.

    (E) $2 \pm 3i$.

Question 37 refers to the following table.

ANNUAL INCOME BY SEX OF HEAD OF THE HOUSEHOLD			
Number of heads of households with income			
Sex	Less than $15,000	$15,000– $34,000	$35,000– $49,000	$50,000 and above
Male	12	25	35	8
Female	22	10	6	2

37. What percent of the males earn less than $35,000?

    (A) 31%

    (B) $46^1/_4$%

    (C) $57^1/_2$%

    (D) 60%

    (E) 90%

38. An airplane pilot has to pass four exams. The second exam is weighted twice as much as the first exam. The third and fourth exams are each weighted three times as much as the second exam. The pilot has already earned a score of 74 on the first exam, 88 on the second exam, and 68 on the third. What is the minimum score needed on the

fourth exam in order to achieve a weighted average of all the exams that is 75 or above?

(A) 70.0   (B) 73.6

(C) 75.0   (D) 77.8

(E) 80.3

39. What is the sum of the roots of $x^2 - 2x - 8 = 0$?

(A) 8   (B) 2

(C) 0   (D) -2

(E) -6

40. $\dfrac{m^2 - n^2}{2x^2 + 3x - 2} \div \dfrac{n^2 - m^2}{2x^2 + 5x - 3} =$

(A) $-\dfrac{x+3}{x+2}$ (B) $-\dfrac{x+2}{x+3}$

(C) $\dfrac{x+3}{x+2}$ (D) $\dfrac{x+2}{x+3}$

(E) $-\dfrac{1}{2x+1}$

41. Find the value of y if

$$0 = x - 3y$$
$$y + 3x = 20.$$

(A) -6 (B) -2

(C) 0   (D) 2

(E) 6

42. If $3^x > 1$ then $x =$

(A) $0 < x < 1.$ (B) $x \geq 0.$

(C) $x \geq 1.$ (D) $x > 0.$

(E) $x > 1.$

43. Planes P and Q leave an airport at the same time and travel in oppo-site directions. Plane P travels 50 miles per hour faster than plane Q. How fast is plane Q traveling if they are 1,600 miles apart after two hours?

(A) 350 mph   (B) 375 mph

(C) 425 mph   (D) 475 mph

(E) 500 mph

44. If $abc \neq 0$, then $\dfrac{3a^2bc^3 + 9a^3b^2c}{27ab^2c + 15a^2b^2c^3} =$

(A) $\dfrac{ab(c^2+3)}{c(9+5a)}.$ (B) $\dfrac{a(c^2+3ab)}{b(9+5ac^2)}.$

(C) $\dfrac{a(c^2+3ab)}{c(9+ac^2)}.$ (D) $\dfrac{c^2+3ab}{9+5ac^2}.$

(E) $\dfrac{a}{b(9+5ac^2)}.$

45. If the mean hourly wage for four company employees is \$10, and the first three employees make \$5, \$8, and \$15 per hour, respectively, what does the fourth employee make per hour?

(A) \$9   (B) \$10

(C) \$11   (D) \$12

(E) \$13

46. Given $\angle CBA = 75°$, what is $\angle CAB$ equal to?

(A) $15°$

(B) 25°

(C) 30°

(D) 35°

(E) 45°

47. What percent of 260 is 13?

(A) .05%   (B) .5%

(C) 5%   (D) 20%

(E) 50%

48. What is the range of values for which $|6x - 5| \le 8$ is satisfied?

(A) $-\dfrac{1}{2} \le x \le \dfrac{1}{2}$ (B) $0 \le x \le \dfrac{5}{6}$

(C) $-1 \le x \le \dfrac{1}{2}$ (D) $-\dfrac{1}{2} \le x \le \dfrac{13}{6}$

(E) $-\dfrac{1}{2} \le x \le \dfrac{1}{3}$

49. If $2^{(6x - 8)} = 16$, then $x =$

(A) 1.   (B) 2.

(C) 4.   (D) 6.

(E) 10.

50. What is the sum of the roots of $y^2 + 12y + 27 = 0$?

(A) -12 (B) -6

(C) 6   (D) 12

(E) No unique solution

ELM
TEST 3

ANSWER KEY

1. (D)	18. (B)	35. (B)
2. (B)	19. (C)	36. (B)
3. (B)	20. (C)	37. (B)
4. (B)	21. (E)	38. (D)
5. (A)	22. (E)	39. (B)
6. (E)	23. (E)	40. (A)
7. (D)	24. (B)	41. (D)
8. (C)	25. (E)	42. (D)
9. (D)	26. (A)	43. (B)
10. (E)	27. (D)	44. (B)
11. (A)	28. (B)	45. (D)
12. (E)	29. (C)	46. (A)
13. (C)	30. (C)	47. (C)
14. (B)	31. (B)	48. (D)
15. (A)	32. (D)	49. (B)
16. (B)	33. (A)	50. (A)
17. (D)	34. (B)	

Field test questions were
9, 21, 30, 43, and 50.
Do not count them toward your final score.

DETAILED EXPLANATIONS
OF ANSWERS

TEST 3

1. **(D)**

$$(m^6 n^5 q^3)^2 = m^{(6)(2)} n^{(5)(2)} q^{(3)(2)}$$
$$= m^{12} n^{10} q^6$$

2. **(B)**

The traditional way to solve this problem is to set up and solve an equation. Consider what part of the job could be done in 1 hour by each person. Thus, Jay could do $1/5$ of the job in 1 hour and Ray could do $1/4$ of the job in the same amount of time. What is unknown is the part of the job they could do together in 1 hour, which can be represented by $1/x$. The x represents the amount of time the brothers can do the job together.

The sum of the amount of the job each brother can do in 1 hour equals the amount of the job they can do together in 1 hour. Hence, the equation is given by:

$$\frac{1}{5} + \frac{1}{4} = \frac{1}{x}.$$

Solving for x you calculate as follows:

$$\frac{1}{5} \times \frac{4}{4} + \frac{1}{4} \times \frac{5}{5} = \frac{1}{x}$$

$$\frac{4}{20} + \frac{5}{20} = \frac{1}{x}$$

$$\frac{9}{20} = \frac{1}{x}$$

$$9x = 20$$

$$\frac{9x}{9} = \frac{20}{9}$$

$$x = \frac{20}{9} \text{ or } 2\frac{2}{9} \text{ hours.}$$

3.   **(B)**

Use the Pythagorean Theorem to find the base and the height of the right triangle.

$$b = h$$

since it is a $45°- 45°- 90°$ triangle.

$$b^2 + b^2 = \left(10\sqrt{2}\right)^2$$
$$2b^2 = (100)(2)$$
$$b = 10$$
$$Area = \tfrac{1}{2}bh$$
$$= (\tfrac{1}{2})(10)(10)$$
$$= 50 \text{ cm}^2$$

4.   **(B)**

When $c \neq 0$

$$\frac{a}{c} + \frac{b}{c} = \frac{a+b}{c}.$$

Thus,

$$\frac{15{,}561}{25} + \frac{9{,}439}{25} = \frac{(15{,}561 + 9{,}439)}{25}$$
$$= \frac{25{,}000}{25}$$
$$= 1{,}000.$$

5.   **(A)**

$$100\% - (15\% + 10\% + 20\% + 25\% + 8\% + 6\%) = 16\%$$

$$16\% \times 5{,}000 = 800$$

6.   **(E)**

Forty-five percent of the class prefers either physical education or music. Fifteen percent of students prefer math class. Thus, the ratio of students who prefer either physical education or music class to the students who prefer math is

45%:15% or 3:1.

Therefore, there are three students who prefer either physical education or music to one student who prefers math class.

7. **(D)**
    Solve the quadratic equation by factoring.

    $z^2 + z - 2 = 0$

    $(z + 2)(z - 1) = 0$

Set each factor equal to 0 to find the solution to the equation.

$z + 2 = 0 \quad z - 1 = 0$

$z = -2 \quad\quad z = 1$

$z = -2$ and 1 but the first equation states z must be greater than 0. Therefore the answer is 1.

8. **(C)**
    One needs to first recall that a cube has 6 equal-sized faces. Thus, the area of each face is found by dividing 6 into 54 to obtain 9 square feet. Since each face contains 9 square feet, then one can conclude that each edge of a face is 3 feet long. So, the volume of the cube, given by the formula

    $$V = (\text{length of edge})^3,$$

is found to be

$$V = (3 \text{ feet})^3 = 27 \text{ cubic feet.}$$

9. **(D)**
    Make a diagram from the given information to see that the distance from Joan's house to Dave's house is the hypotenuse of a right triangle.
    Let $d =$ the distance from Joan's house to Dave's house.

$$6^2 + 8^2 = d^2$$

$$36 + 64 = d^2$$

$$100 = d^2$$

$$10 = d$$

Joan

d

8 miles

Dave

6 miles

Mary

10. **(E)**

$$\frac{a^2 - 3ab + 2b^2}{2b^2 + ab - a^2}$$

Factoring the numerator:

$$a^2 - 3ab + 2b^2 = (a - 2b)(a - b).$$

Factoring the denominator:

$$2b^2 + ab - a^2 = (2b - a)(b + a).$$

Rewriting the expression:

$$\frac{(a - 2b)(a - b)}{(2b - a)(b + a)} = \frac{a - 2b}{2b - a} \times \frac{a - b}{b + a}.$$

We note that $a - 2b = -1(2b - a)$. Therefore,

$$\frac{a - 2b}{2b - a} = -1.$$

The expression reduces to

$$-1\left(\frac{a - b}{b + a}\right) = \frac{b - a}{b + a}.$$

11. **(A)**

This is an example of a composite function. First we must evaluate $f(6)$. From the figure, we see that

$$f(6) = 2.$$

Thus,

$$f(f(6)) = f(2).$$

From the figure $f(2) = -2$, so that

$$f(f(6)) = -2.$$

12. **(E)**

To find the height use the Pythagorean Theorem,

$$a^2 + b^2 = c^2.$$

$$4^2 + b^2 = 8^2$$

$$16 + b^2 = 64$$

$$b^2 = 64 - 16$$

$$b^2 = 48$$

Height $$b = 4\sqrt{3}$$

$$A = bh$$

$$A = (11)(4\sqrt{3})$$

$$A = 44\sqrt{3}$$

13. **(C)**

$$\frac{x^{10}y^8}{x^7y^3} = x^{(10-7)}y^{(8-3)}$$

$$= x^3y^5$$

14. **(B)**

The solution is given as 10^P4, which means a permutation of ten items taken four at a time. The formula for the number of permutations of n things taken r at a time (where the order of the selection matters) is

$$n^P r = \frac{n!}{(n-r)!}.$$

$$10^P4 = \frac{10!}{(10-4)!}$$

$$10^P4 = \frac{10!}{6!}$$

$$10^P4 = 5,040$$

15. **(A)**

For the first queen, the probability is $^4/_{52}$. For the second queen, the probability is now $^3/_{51}$, as there is no replacement. Then both probabilities are multiplied.

$$^4/_{52} \times ^3/_{51} = ^1/_{221}$$

16. **(B)**

The general equation of a parabola with a vertex at the origin and symmetrical about the *y*-axis is

$$y = ax^2.$$

Use the point (1, 2) to find *a*:

$$2 = a(1)^2$$

$$a = 2.$$

Therefore, the equation should be $y = 2x^2$.

17. **(D)**

There are a total of nine prizes. Four of them are at least $5,000. Thus, the required probability is 4:9 or $^4/_9$.

18. **(B)**

3:1,000 is the ratio of defective parts to parts produced.
Let x = defective parts.

$$3/1,000 = x/25,000$$

$$1,000x = 3(25,000)$$

$$x = 75,000/1,000$$

$$x = 75$$

19. **(C)**

$$4x + 3y - z - 10y + x = (4x + x) + (3y - 10y) - z$$

$$= 5x - 7y - z$$

20. **(C)**

To find the other root of the quadratic equation, we must first solve for the coefficient a.

Substituting 6 for x we obtain:

$$x^2 - ax + 12 = 0$$

$$6^2 - a(6) + 12 = 0$$

$$36 + 12 = 6a$$

$$48 = 6a$$

$$8 = a.$$

The quadratic equation that we obtain is:

$$x^2 - 8x + 12 = 0.$$

Factoring:

$$(x - 6)(x - 2) = 0,$$

therefore, the roots are 6 and 2.

21. **(E)**

$$f(3) = 3(3)^2 - (3) + 5$$

$$= 27 - 3 + 5$$

$$= 29$$

22. **(E)**

$$x^2 - 3x - 4 < 0$$

$$(x + 1)(x - 4) < 0$$

$$-1 < x < 4$$

23. **(E)**

The fraction is a complex fraction. To simplify, we must multiply both the numerator and the denominator by $b^2 - 2b$:

$$\frac{\frac{2}{a^2b^2}}{\frac{1}{b^2-2b}} \times \frac{b^2 - 2b}{b^2 - 2b} = \frac{2(b^2 - 2b)}{a^2b^2}.$$

Multiplying through in the numerator:

$$\frac{2b^2 - 4b}{a^2b^2}.$$

The numerator is factored and like terms are canceled:

$$\frac{b(2b-4)}{a^2b^2} = \frac{2b-4}{a^2b}.$$

24. **(B)**

Redraw the figure and put the interior angles in the triangle. The sum of the interior angles is 180°.

$$180° - \alpha + 180° - \beta + \gamma = 180°$$

Rearranging and simplifying:

$$180° - \alpha + \gamma = \beta, \text{ or } \gamma - \alpha + 180° = \beta.$$

25. **(E)**

$$|\,2x - 18\,| = -6$$

There is no solution, since an absolute number cannot equal a negative number.

26. **(A)**

Remember the order of operation rules are PEMDAS, meaning parentheses, exponents, multiplication, division, addition, and subtraction. The correct solution is

$$10 - 5[8 + 9 - 2\,(-2)] = 10 - 5(21)$$

$$10 - 105 = -95.$$

27. **(D)**

We are told that segments BD and AE are parallel. This implies that $\angle CBD = \angle CAE$ and $\angle CAE$ and $\angle CDB = \angle CEA$ (corresponding angles formed by parallel lines cut by a transversal are congruent).

$$\angle ACE = \angle BCD \text{ (same angle)}$$

Thus $\triangle BCD$ and $\triangle ACE$ are equiangular and similar. From a theorem, we know that the sides of similar triangles that correspond to each other are proportional. Sides CD and CE and BD and AE are corresponding sides and are thus proportional:

$$\frac{CD}{CE} = \frac{BD}{AE}.$$

28. **(B)**

$$f(3) = 3 + 1$$
$$= 4$$
$$g(4) = 2(4) - 3$$
$$= 5$$
$$f(3) * g(4) = 4 * 5$$
$$= 2(4) + 5 - (4)(5)$$
$$= -7$$

29. **(C)**

$$\frac{2\pi}{120°} = \frac{2\pi r}{360°}$$
$$r = 3$$
$$\text{Area} = \pi r^2 = 9\pi.$$

30. **(C)**

To find the sixth term in an arithmetic progression, find a, the first term, and d, the common difference. The difference between the first two numbers is $7 - 3 = 4$ and $a = 3$.

The nth term of an arithmetic progression equals

$$a + (n - 1)d.$$

Therefore the 6th term

$$= 3 + (6 - 1)4$$

$$= 3 + 5(4)$$

$$= 23.$$

31. **(B)**

$$g(x) = 4x - 1 \qquad f(x) = -2x + 5$$

$$(g \circ f)(x) = g(f(x))$$

$$= 4(-2x + 5) - 1$$

$$= -8x + 20 - 1$$

$$= -8x + 19$$

32. **(D)**

To find the altitude of the triangle one must recall that the area of a triangle is given by

$$A = (^1/_2)bh,$$

where b denotes the base and h denotes the altitude. Also, one must recall that the area of a circle is given by

$$A = \pi r^2,$$

where r denotes the radius of the circle.

Since $b = 6$ units then

$$(^1/_2)(6)h = 3h = A,$$

the area of the triangle. In addition, since $r = 6$ units, then

$$A = \pi r^2 = \pi(6) = 36\pi,$$

the area of the circle. But the area is the same for both figures. Thus,

$$3h = 36\pi$$

$$h = 12\pi$$

is the altitude of the triangle.

33. **(A)**

Given the expression:

$$\frac{3}{x+4} + \frac{5}{x-4} = \frac{8}{x^2-16}$$

Factor the denominator of the right side:

$$\frac{3}{x+4} + \frac{5}{x-4} = \frac{8}{(x+4)(x-4)}$$

Multiply both sides by $(x+4)(x-4)$:

$$3(x-4) + 5(x+4) = 8$$

Simplifying:

$$3x - 12 + 5x + 20 = 8$$

$$8x + 8 = 8$$

$$8x = 0$$

$$x = 0$$

34. **(B)**

$$\text{Distance} = \sqrt{(x_1 - x_2)^2 + (y_1 - y_2)^2}$$
$$= \sqrt{(3-2)^2 + (4-1)^2}$$
$$= \sqrt{25 + 9}$$
$$= \sqrt{34}$$

35. **(B)**

Redraw the figure as below since $l_1 \parallel l_2$.

$$2x + x + 30° + 60° = 180°$$

$$3x + 90° = 180°$$

$$3x = 90°$$

$$x = 30°$$

36. **(B)**

The polynomial is not factorable, so we must use the quadratic formula:

$$x = \frac{-b \pm \sqrt{b^2 - 4ab}}{2a}.$$

In the polynomial $a = 1$, $b = 2$, and $c = 5$. Substituting, we get:

$$x = \frac{-2 \pm \sqrt{2^2 - 4(1)(5)}}{2(1)}.$$

Simplifying:

$$x = \frac{-2 \pm \sqrt{-16}}{2}$$

$$= \frac{-2 \pm 4\sqrt{-1}}{2}$$

$$= -1 \pm 2\sqrt{-1}$$

We know $\sqrt{-1} = i$; so:

$$x = -1 \pm 2i.$$

37. **(B)**

The number of males

$$= 12 + 25 + 35 + 8 = 80.$$

Of these

$$12 + 25 = 37$$

earn less than $35,000. Therefore, the percent of males earning less than $35,000 is

$$\left(\frac{37}{80}\right)100 = 46\frac{1}{4}.$$

38. **(D)**

Let x equal the required score.

$$\frac{74 + (88 \times 2) + (68 \times 6) + 6x}{15} > 75$$

$$\frac{658 + 6x}{15} > 75$$

$$658 + 6x > 1{,}125$$

$$x = 77.8$$

39. **(B)**

First factor.

$$x^2 - 2x - 8 = 0$$
$$(x - 4)(x + 2) = 0$$

Find the roots.

$$x - 4 = 0 \qquad\qquad x + 2 = 0$$

$$x = 4 \qquad\qquad x = -2$$

The sum of the roots $= 4 - 2 = 2$.

40. **(A)**

$$\frac{m^2 - n^2}{2x^2 + 3x - 2} \div \frac{n^2 - m^2}{2x^2 + 5x - 3}$$

Invert divisor and multiply.

$$= \frac{m^2 - n^2}{2x^2 + 3x - 2} \times \frac{2x^2 + 5x - 3}{n^2 - m^2}$$

Factor the polynomials.

$$= \frac{(m-n)(m+n)}{(2x-1)(x+2)} \times \frac{(2x-1)(x+3)}{(n-m)(n+m)} = \frac{(m-n)}{x+2} \times \frac{(x+3)}{-1(m-n)}$$

$$= -\frac{x+3}{x+2}$$

41. **(D)**

$$0 = x - 3y \tag{1}$$

$$y + 3x = 20 \tag{2}$$

Change

$$0 = x - 3y$$

$$3y = x$$

Substitute into equation (2) and solve for y.

$$y + 3(3y) = 20$$

$$y + 9y = 20$$

$$10y = 20$$

$$y = 2$$

42. **(D)**

We need to find the value of x, where $3^x > 1$.

If $x = 0$, then $3^0 = 1$.

If $x = 1$, then $3^1 = 3$.

Given that 3^x must be bigger than 1, $x > 0$.

43. **(B)**

If plane P travels x miles per hour (mph), then Q travels at $(x + 50)$ mph. In two hours P travels $2x$ and Q travels $(2x + 50)$ and since they travel in opposite directions the distance between P and Q is

$$2x + 2(x + 50) = 1,600.$$

Therefore,

$$4x + 100 = 1,600, \text{ or } x = 1,500/4 = 375.$$

44. **(B)**

$$\frac{3a^2bc^3 + 9a^3b^2c}{27ab^2c + 15a^2b^2c^3} = \frac{3a^2bc(c^2 + 3ab)}{3ab^2c(9 + 5ac^2)}$$

$$= \frac{a(c^2 + 3ab)}{b(9 + 5ac^2)}$$

45. **(D)**

Let x equal the fourth employee's wage per hour.

$$\frac{\$5 + \$8 + \$15 + x}{4} = \$10 \text{ per hour}$$

$$\$28 + x = \$40 \text{ per hour}$$

$$x = \$12 \text{ per hour}$$

46. **(A)**

Since $\angle ACB$ is an inscribed angle intercepting a semicircle, it is $90°$. Know that

$$\angle CAB + \angle ACB + \angle CBA = 180°$$

since the angles of a triangle equal $180°$.

$$\angle CAB + 75° + 90° = 180°$$

$$\angle CAB = 180° - 165°$$

$$\angle CAB = 15°$$

47. **(C)**

In order to find what percent of 260 is 13 one needs only to form the following equation:

$$x\%(260) = 13$$

$$\frac{x(260)}{100} = 13$$

$$260x = 13(100)$$

$$x = \frac{1{,}300}{260}$$

$$= 5\%.$$

48. **(D)**

When given an inequality with an absolute value, recall the definition of absolute value:

$$|x| = \begin{cases} x \text{ if } x \geq 0 \\ -x \text{ if } x < 0 \end{cases}$$

$6x - 5 \leq 8$ if $6x - 5 \geq 0$

$-6x + 5 \leq 8$ if $6x - 5 < 0$

$-6x + 5 \leq 8$ can be written as $6x - 5 \geq -8$.

We can set up both of these equations as follows:

$$-8 \leq 6x - 5 \leq 8$$

adding 5:

$$-3 \leq 6x \leq 13$$

dividing by 6:

$$-^1/_2 \leq x \leq {}^{13}/_6.$$

49. **(B)**

$$2^{(6x - 8)} = 16,$$

2 raised to the 4th power equals 16. Thus

$$6x - 8 = 4.$$

Add 8 to both sides.

$$6x = 12$$

Divide both sides by 6.

$$x = 2$$

50. **(A)**

First factor the left-hand side of the equation as follows:

$$y^2 + 12y + 27 = (y + 9)(y + 3) = 0$$

$y + 9 = 0 \qquad y + 3 = 0$

$y = -9 \qquad y = -3$

The sum of the roots

$$= -9 + (-3)$$
$$= -12.$$

ELM
Entry Level Mathematics

Answer
Sheets

ELM – Test 1

Answer Sheet

1. Ⓐ Ⓑ Ⓒ Ⓓ Ⓔ	26. Ⓐ Ⓑ Ⓒ Ⓓ Ⓔ
2. Ⓐ Ⓑ Ⓒ Ⓓ Ⓔ	27. Ⓐ Ⓑ Ⓒ Ⓓ Ⓔ
3. Ⓐ Ⓑ Ⓒ Ⓓ Ⓔ	28. Ⓐ Ⓑ Ⓒ Ⓓ Ⓔ
4. Ⓐ Ⓑ Ⓒ Ⓓ Ⓔ	29. Ⓐ Ⓑ Ⓒ Ⓓ Ⓔ
5. Ⓐ Ⓑ Ⓒ Ⓓ Ⓔ	30. Ⓐ Ⓑ Ⓒ Ⓓ Ⓔ
6. Ⓐ Ⓑ Ⓒ Ⓓ Ⓔ	31. Ⓐ Ⓑ Ⓒ Ⓓ Ⓔ
7. Ⓐ Ⓑ Ⓒ Ⓓ Ⓔ	32. Ⓐ Ⓑ Ⓒ Ⓓ Ⓔ
8. Ⓐ Ⓑ Ⓒ Ⓓ Ⓔ	33. Ⓐ Ⓑ Ⓒ Ⓓ Ⓔ
9. Ⓐ Ⓑ Ⓒ Ⓓ Ⓔ	34. Ⓐ Ⓑ Ⓒ Ⓓ Ⓔ
10. Ⓐ Ⓑ Ⓒ Ⓓ Ⓔ	35. Ⓐ Ⓑ Ⓒ Ⓓ Ⓔ
11. Ⓐ Ⓑ Ⓒ Ⓓ Ⓔ	36. Ⓐ Ⓑ Ⓒ Ⓓ Ⓔ
12. Ⓐ Ⓑ Ⓒ Ⓓ Ⓔ	37. Ⓐ Ⓑ Ⓒ Ⓓ Ⓔ
13. Ⓐ Ⓑ Ⓒ Ⓓ Ⓔ	38. Ⓐ Ⓑ Ⓒ Ⓓ Ⓔ
14. Ⓐ Ⓑ Ⓒ Ⓓ Ⓔ	39. Ⓐ Ⓑ Ⓒ Ⓓ Ⓔ
15. Ⓐ Ⓑ Ⓒ Ⓓ Ⓔ	40. Ⓐ Ⓑ Ⓒ Ⓓ Ⓔ
16. Ⓐ Ⓑ Ⓒ Ⓓ Ⓔ	41. Ⓐ Ⓑ Ⓒ Ⓓ Ⓔ
17. Ⓐ Ⓑ Ⓒ Ⓓ Ⓔ	42. Ⓐ Ⓑ Ⓒ Ⓓ Ⓔ
18. Ⓐ Ⓑ Ⓒ Ⓓ Ⓔ	43. Ⓐ Ⓑ Ⓒ Ⓓ Ⓔ
19. Ⓐ Ⓑ Ⓒ Ⓓ Ⓔ	44. Ⓐ Ⓑ Ⓒ Ⓓ Ⓔ
20. Ⓐ Ⓑ Ⓒ Ⓓ Ⓔ	45. Ⓐ Ⓑ Ⓒ Ⓓ Ⓔ
21. Ⓐ Ⓑ Ⓒ Ⓓ Ⓔ	46. Ⓐ Ⓑ Ⓒ Ⓓ Ⓔ
22. Ⓐ Ⓑ Ⓒ Ⓓ Ⓔ	47. Ⓐ Ⓑ Ⓒ Ⓓ Ⓔ
23. Ⓐ Ⓑ Ⓒ Ⓓ Ⓔ	48. Ⓐ Ⓑ Ⓒ Ⓓ Ⓔ
24. Ⓐ Ⓑ Ⓒ Ⓓ Ⓔ	49. Ⓐ Ⓑ Ⓒ Ⓓ Ⓔ
25. Ⓐ Ⓑ Ⓒ Ⓓ Ⓔ	50. Ⓐ Ⓑ Ⓒ Ⓓ Ⓔ

ELM – Test 2

Answer Sheet

1. (A) (B) (C) (D) (E)
2. (A) (B) (C) (D) (E)
3. (A) (B) (C) (D) (E)
4. (A) (B) (C) (D) (E)
5. (A) (B) (C) (D) (E)
6. (A) (B) (C) (D) (E)
7. (A) (B) (C) (D) (E)
8. (A) (B) (C) (D) (E)
9. (A) (B) (C) (D) (E)
10. (A) (B) (C) (D) (E)
11. (A) (B) (C) (D) (E)
12. (A) (B) (C) (D) (E)
13. (A) (B) (C) (D) (E)
14. (A) (B) (C) (D) (E)
15. (A) (B) (C) (D) (E)
16. (A) (B) (C) (D) (E)
17. (A) (B) (C) (D) (E)
18. (A) (B) (C) (D) (E)
19. (A) (B) (C) (D) (E)
20. (A) (B) (C) (D) (E)
21. (A) (B) (C) (D) (E)
22. (A) (B) (C) (D) (E)
23. (A) (B) (C) (D) (E)
24. (A) (B) (C) (D) (E)
25. (A) (B) (C) (D) (E)

26. (A) (B) (C) (D) (E)
27. (A) (B) (C) (D) (E)
28. (A) (B) (C) (D) (E)
29. (A) (B) (C) (D) (E)
30. (A) (B) (C) (D) (E)
31. (A) (B) (C) (D) (E)
32. (A) (B) (C) (D) (E)
33. (A) (B) (C) (D) (E)
34. (A) (B) (C) (D) (E)
35. (A) (B) (C) (D) (E)
36. (A) (B) (C) (D) (E)
37. (A) (B) (C) (D) (E)
38. (A) (B) (C) (D) (E)
39. (A) (B) (C) (D) (E)
40. (A) (B) (C) (D) (E)
41. (A) (B) (C) (D) (E)
42. (A) (B) (C) (D) (E)
43. (A) (B) (C) (D) (E)
44. (A) (B) (C) (D) (E)
45. (A) (B) (C) (D) (E)
46. (A) (B) (C) (D) (E)
47. (A) (B) (C) (D) (E)
48. (A) (B) (C) (D) (E)
49. (A) (B) (C) (D) (E)
50. (A) (B) (C) (D) (E)

ELM – Test 3
Answer Sheet

1. Ⓐ Ⓑ Ⓒ Ⓓ Ⓔ
2. Ⓐ Ⓑ Ⓒ Ⓓ Ⓔ
3. Ⓐ Ⓑ Ⓒ Ⓓ Ⓔ
4. Ⓐ Ⓑ Ⓒ Ⓓ Ⓔ
5. Ⓐ Ⓑ Ⓒ Ⓓ Ⓔ
6. Ⓐ Ⓑ Ⓒ Ⓓ Ⓔ
7. Ⓐ Ⓑ Ⓒ Ⓓ Ⓔ
8. Ⓐ Ⓑ Ⓒ Ⓓ Ⓔ
9. Ⓐ Ⓑ Ⓒ Ⓓ Ⓔ
10. Ⓐ Ⓑ Ⓒ Ⓓ Ⓔ
11. Ⓐ Ⓑ Ⓒ Ⓓ Ⓔ
12. Ⓐ Ⓑ Ⓒ Ⓓ Ⓔ
13. Ⓐ Ⓑ Ⓒ Ⓓ Ⓔ
14. Ⓐ Ⓑ Ⓒ Ⓓ Ⓔ
15. Ⓐ Ⓑ Ⓒ Ⓓ Ⓔ
16. Ⓐ Ⓑ Ⓒ Ⓓ Ⓔ
17. Ⓐ Ⓑ Ⓒ Ⓓ Ⓔ
18. Ⓐ Ⓑ Ⓒ Ⓓ Ⓔ
19. Ⓐ Ⓑ Ⓒ Ⓓ Ⓔ
20. Ⓐ Ⓑ Ⓒ Ⓓ Ⓔ
21. Ⓐ Ⓑ Ⓒ Ⓓ Ⓔ
22. Ⓐ Ⓑ Ⓒ Ⓓ Ⓔ
23. Ⓐ Ⓑ Ⓒ Ⓓ Ⓔ
24. Ⓐ Ⓑ Ⓒ Ⓓ Ⓔ
25. Ⓐ Ⓑ Ⓒ Ⓓ Ⓔ

26. Ⓐ Ⓑ Ⓒ Ⓓ Ⓔ
27. Ⓐ Ⓑ Ⓒ Ⓓ Ⓔ
28. Ⓐ Ⓑ Ⓒ Ⓓ Ⓔ
29. Ⓐ Ⓑ Ⓒ Ⓓ Ⓔ
30. Ⓐ Ⓑ Ⓒ Ⓓ Ⓔ
31. Ⓐ Ⓑ Ⓒ Ⓓ Ⓔ
32. Ⓐ Ⓑ Ⓒ Ⓓ Ⓔ
33. Ⓐ Ⓑ Ⓒ Ⓓ Ⓔ
34. Ⓐ Ⓑ Ⓒ Ⓓ Ⓔ
35. Ⓐ Ⓑ Ⓒ Ⓓ Ⓔ
36. Ⓐ Ⓑ Ⓒ Ⓓ Ⓔ
37. Ⓐ Ⓑ Ⓒ Ⓓ Ⓔ
38. Ⓐ Ⓑ Ⓒ Ⓓ Ⓔ
39. Ⓐ Ⓑ Ⓒ Ⓓ Ⓔ
40. Ⓐ Ⓑ Ⓒ Ⓓ Ⓔ
41. Ⓐ Ⓑ Ⓒ Ⓓ Ⓔ
42. Ⓐ Ⓑ Ⓒ Ⓓ Ⓔ
43. Ⓐ Ⓑ Ⓒ Ⓓ Ⓔ
44. Ⓐ Ⓑ Ⓒ Ⓓ Ⓔ
45. Ⓐ Ⓑ Ⓒ Ⓓ Ⓔ
46. Ⓐ Ⓑ Ⓒ Ⓓ Ⓔ
47. Ⓐ Ⓑ Ⓒ Ⓓ Ⓔ
48. Ⓐ Ⓑ Ⓒ Ⓓ Ⓔ
49. Ⓐ Ⓑ Ⓒ Ⓓ Ⓔ
50. Ⓐ Ⓑ Ⓒ Ⓓ Ⓔ

ELM – Test ___

Additional Answer Sheet

1. Ⓐ Ⓑ Ⓒ Ⓓ Ⓔ		26. Ⓐ Ⓑ Ⓒ Ⓓ Ⓔ
2. Ⓐ Ⓑ Ⓒ Ⓓ Ⓔ		27. Ⓐ Ⓑ Ⓒ Ⓓ Ⓔ
3. Ⓐ Ⓑ Ⓒ Ⓓ Ⓔ		28. Ⓐ Ⓑ Ⓒ Ⓓ Ⓔ
4. Ⓐ Ⓑ Ⓒ Ⓓ Ⓔ		29. Ⓐ Ⓑ Ⓒ Ⓓ Ⓔ
5. Ⓐ Ⓑ Ⓒ Ⓓ Ⓔ		30. Ⓐ Ⓑ Ⓒ Ⓓ Ⓔ
6. Ⓐ Ⓑ Ⓒ Ⓓ Ⓔ		31. Ⓐ Ⓑ Ⓒ Ⓓ Ⓔ
7. Ⓐ Ⓑ Ⓒ Ⓓ Ⓔ		32. Ⓐ Ⓑ Ⓒ Ⓓ Ⓔ
8. Ⓐ Ⓑ Ⓒ Ⓓ Ⓔ		33. Ⓐ Ⓑ Ⓒ Ⓓ Ⓔ
9. Ⓐ Ⓑ Ⓒ Ⓓ Ⓔ		34. Ⓐ Ⓑ Ⓒ Ⓓ Ⓔ
10. Ⓐ Ⓑ Ⓒ Ⓓ Ⓔ		35. Ⓐ Ⓑ Ⓒ Ⓓ Ⓔ
11. Ⓐ Ⓑ Ⓒ Ⓓ Ⓔ		36. Ⓐ Ⓑ Ⓒ Ⓓ Ⓔ
12. Ⓐ Ⓑ Ⓒ Ⓓ Ⓔ		37. Ⓐ Ⓑ Ⓒ Ⓓ Ⓔ
13. Ⓐ Ⓑ Ⓒ Ⓓ Ⓔ		38. Ⓐ Ⓑ Ⓒ Ⓓ Ⓔ
14. Ⓐ Ⓑ Ⓒ Ⓓ Ⓔ		39. Ⓐ Ⓑ Ⓒ Ⓓ Ⓔ
15. Ⓐ Ⓑ Ⓒ Ⓓ Ⓔ		40. Ⓐ Ⓑ Ⓒ Ⓓ Ⓔ
16. Ⓐ Ⓑ Ⓒ Ⓓ Ⓔ		41. Ⓐ Ⓑ Ⓒ Ⓓ Ⓔ
17. Ⓐ Ⓑ Ⓒ Ⓓ Ⓔ		42. Ⓐ Ⓑ Ⓒ Ⓓ Ⓔ
18. Ⓐ Ⓑ Ⓒ Ⓓ Ⓔ		43. Ⓐ Ⓑ Ⓒ Ⓓ Ⓔ
19. Ⓐ Ⓑ Ⓒ Ⓓ Ⓔ		44. Ⓐ Ⓑ Ⓒ Ⓓ Ⓔ
20. Ⓐ Ⓑ Ⓒ Ⓓ Ⓔ		45. Ⓐ Ⓑ Ⓒ Ⓓ Ⓔ
21. Ⓐ Ⓑ Ⓒ Ⓓ Ⓔ		46. Ⓐ Ⓑ Ⓒ Ⓓ Ⓔ
22. Ⓐ Ⓑ Ⓒ Ⓓ Ⓔ		47. Ⓐ Ⓑ Ⓒ Ⓓ Ⓔ
23. Ⓐ Ⓑ Ⓒ Ⓓ Ⓔ		48. Ⓐ Ⓑ Ⓒ Ⓓ Ⓔ
24. Ⓐ Ⓑ Ⓒ Ⓓ Ⓔ		49. Ⓐ Ⓑ Ⓒ Ⓓ Ⓔ
25. Ⓐ Ⓑ Ⓒ Ⓓ Ⓔ		50. Ⓐ Ⓑ Ⓒ Ⓓ Ⓔ